# THE SUPREME COURT IN AMERICAN POLITICS

# THE SUPREME COURT IN AMERICAN POLITICS

*Isaac Unah*

THE SUPREME COURT IN AMERICAN POLITICS
Copyright © Isaac Unah, 2009.

First published in 2009 by
PALGRAVE MACMILLAN®
in the United States—a division of St. Martin's Press LLC,
175 Fifth Avenue, New York, NY 10010.

Where this book is distributed in the UK, Europe and the rest of the world,
this is by Palgrave Macmillan, a division of Macmillan Publishers Limited,
registered in England, company number 785998, of Houndmills,
Basingstoke, Hampshire RG21 6XS.

Palgrave Macmillan is the global academic imprint of the above
companies and has companies and representatives throughout the world.

Palgrave® and Macmillan® are registered trademarks in the United States,
the United Kingdom, Europe and other countries.

ISBN: 978–1–403–97241–5

Library of Congress Cataloging-in-Publication Data

Unah, Isaac.
    The Supreme Court in American politics / Isaac Unah.
       p. cm.
    ISBN 978–1–4039–7240–8 (alk. paper)
    ISBN 978–1–4039–7241–5 (alk. paper)
    1. United States. Supreme Court. 2. United States—Politics and
    government. I. Title.

KF8742.U52 2009
347.73′26—dc22                                        2009021181

A catalogue record of the book is available from the British Library.

Design by Newgen Imaging Systems (P) Ltd., Chennai, India.

First edition: January 2010

10 9 8 7 6 5 4 3 2 1

Transferred to Digital Printing in 2013

*To Annabel, Daniel, and Nathaniel,*
*You are all much cherished.*

# Contents

# Photos, Figures, Tables, and Text Box

## Photos

## Figures

## Tables

## TEXT BOX

# PREFACE

For more than two hundred years, the U.S. Supreme Court has shaped the course of American democracy by rendering decisions on the greatest legal and political controversies of the day. The Court's historical contribution to democratic structure takes place amidst its own epic struggles for power, independence, and influence in American government. Under the legal framework established in the federal Constitution, the Supreme Court operates as an independent and coequal branch of government and performs several significant functions. Foremost among these is that justices of the Court have legitimate authority to patrol the boundaries of the Constitution when important legal questions concerning public policy and individual rights are raised in Court.

Legal theorists agree that "The Supreme Court is the country's greatest symbol of orderly, stable, and righteous government."[1] It serves as the premiere instrument of democracy. Consequently, the Court occupies a central position in the American scheme of representative government, a position that allows justices to shape not only the direction of national policy but how national policy is constituted and how governmental action matters in every citizen's life, liberty, and pursuit of happiness.

Unfortunately, as important as the Supreme Court's functions are, most Americans are acquainted only vaguely with what the Court does, its historical foundations, and how it really works.[2] I believe that this state of affairs must change. Improved public knowledge of the Court will enhance deliberation and civic engagement, and ultimately further strengthen American democracy and improve quality of life. This book is, therefore, by providing an in-depth coverage in every chapter, intended to help readers gain a firm understanding of the U.S. Supreme Court. In the course of a lifetime, most residents of the United States would become entangled in some kind of conflict with government or a private entity. This could be a disagreement over a denial of service or a failure to render adequate service. It could be a perceived governmental infringement on a citizen's fundamental right to religious practice or a conflict over free speech. More commonly, it could be a traffic violation or a more serious entanglement with law enforcement. In these and similar instances, it is important for citizens to understand how the Constitution protects them. After all, as one former teacher of civil liberties explains plainly, the Constitution is "the most important thing in the life of every person living in the United States. Your way of life is built around it, your government is based upon it, and your rights and privileges as a United States citizen are protected by it."[3] But understanding how the Constitution protects individual rights and liberties requires first and foremost a firm grasp of the Supreme Court (the Constitution's expositor) and its role in American life.

The Court routinely delves into the substance of transformative political conflicts that form the essence of government and what it means to be American. How should the Court settle a conflict between itself and the president? How about one between the federal government and the states? How should the Court protect individual liberties? Who can forget the emotionally charged conflicts and protests surrounding race relations and reproductive rights in the United States? What about controversies surrounding environmental protection and animal rights? The Supreme Court has addressed such consequential questions throughout its history. Recently, many citizens watched with anguish and some with jubilation as the Supreme Court placed its imprimatur on the presidential election of 2000 in Bush v. Gore. The nation learned valuable lessons from each and every one of these momentous events, lessons that we can only hope bode well for a better future.

The approach taken in this book is evolutionary in nature. An evolutionary approach brings clarity to the affairs of governing by using the past as a backdrop for understanding developments in governmental institutions today. Such an approach will demonstrate, for example, that the Supreme Court's foray into the terrain of hot-button political conflicts—which we have witnessed in recent years—is not a new phenomenon but one that accelerated and assumed a laser-like focus when the Great Depression era drew to a close and the Court began to brand itself as the true protector of "insular minorities." In particular, the Court's broad enunciation of the preferred freedoms doctrine in 1938 under the leadership of Chief Justice Harlan Fiske Stone in United States v. Caroline Products (footnote 4), shifted the legal landscape in favor of greater individual rights litigation, a trend that has been emulated and transported worldwide in what has been called the rights revolution.[4]

As a matter of course, individual rights litigation went on to flourish during the reign of Chief Justice Earl Warren. The Supreme Court significantly expanded individual freedoms, forced reformation of school segregation and reapportionment laws, reformed the criminal justice system to gain greater recognition of defendant rights, changed how citizens viewed privacy and reproductive rights, restricted the obligation of states to safeguard the physical well-being of children, and made authoritative statements about presidential power and national policies for fighting terrorism. Gaining a clearer understanding of the Court's functioning and its processes would improve national debate and allow citizens to better evaluate for themselves the policies and decisions emanating from the Court, how these decisions were reached, and the potential impact on their lives.

The fundamental objective of this book then is to explain from an evolutionary perspective how the Supreme Court generates its enduring power and impact in American society through its careful interpretation of the Constitution. Supreme Court justices are representatives of the Constitution; they are responsible for patrolling the Constitution's boundaries and bringing meaning to its esoteric language. As the great Chief Justice John Marshall stated in Marbury v. Madison (1803), "it is emphatically the province and duty of the judicial branch to say what the law is." Justices exercise that function with great care, confidence, and passion but are constrained by the knowledge that they must justify their legal pronouncements with a written opinion to educate the masses and gain their support.

## STRUCTURE OF THE BOOK

The book proceeds with one overriding assumption throughout: the Supreme Court is a legal institution occupied by human decision makers driven by political and to some extent legal incentives in their decisions. To appreciate how the modern Court interprets the Constitution, I address from an evolutionary perspective distinct questions about how we got here from the long past, and what the institutional characteristics of the Court mean, and what their role is in the Court's storied genealogy. Specifically, the book addresses the following questions, which form its organizing structure:

- How and why has the nature and power of the U.S. Supreme Court evolved over time?
- How and why are judicial vacancies created, and what motivates justices to step aside?
- How are justices selected and what role do background, ideology, and politics play in the selection of justices to the Supreme Court?
- How does the Supreme Court build its plenary agenda and what factors influence the type of cases selected for consideration each term?
- Do oral arguments make a difference in the Supreme Court? What makes an effective oral argument and how can lawyers make effective oral arguments?
- How does the Court reach final decisions on the merits in cases the Court agrees to hear? Which theories of decision making best explain the Court's decisions?
- How are Supreme Court decisions implemented, and what determines sincere implementation and impact of these decisions?

Each chapter is introduced with a set of questions that comprise the central focus of that chapter. For most chapters, discussion begins with introduction or analysis of a historical event or issue central to the topic of that chapter. This is then used as a springboard for understanding the causal process, behavior, and politics surrounding the modern Supreme Court from an evolutionary perspective.

The premise of an evolutionary approach is that history matters! It matters because it holds the ingredient and the capacity to enlighten citizens about how the present is a reconfiguration of the past. Furthermore, it matters because it guides the future directions of governmental policies. Despite the value of an evolutionary approach, however, most authors writing about the Supreme Court have failed to adopt the approach as a foundation. What sets The Supreme Court in American Politics apart from recent works on the Court is that it not only gives an in-depth knowledge of important aspects of the Court in every chapter, it also adopts an evolutionary approach as a basis for understanding.

# Acknowledgments

In writing this book, I relied on numerous sources for data and information. Three deserve special mention. The Spaeth Database is the largest general empirical dataset on the Supreme Court. It helped me construct many of the tables and figures used in the book. The Supreme Court Compendium (Epstein et al., various editions) was a valuable data source and a ready point of reference. Finally, from 2005 to 2007, I served as Program Director for the Law and Social Sciences Program at the National Science Foundation in Arlington, VA. I took advantage of my proximity to the Library of Congress in Washington DC by visiting the Manuscript Division on many weekends to examine and draw wisdom from the papers of retired Supreme Court Justices Harry Blackmun, Thurgood Marshall, and Chief Justice Warren Burger. Information gleaned from these papers is used at various places in the book.

I received assistance from numerous individuals to whom I am grateful. Several colleagues either read chapters of the book and offered helpful feedback or engaged me in useful conversations about the Court: Jeffrey Segal (Stony Brook University), Robert Howard (Georgia State University), Harold Spaeth (Michigan State University), Artemis Ward (Northern Illinois University), Richard Pacelle (Georgia Southern University), Paul Wahlbeck (George Washington University), Priscilla Regan (George Mason University), R. Mitch Pickerill (Washington State University), and Susan Haire (University of Georgia). I thank the staff of the Manuscript Division of the Library of Congress for their assistance. I am also grateful to my colleagues in the Department of Political Science at UNC-Chapel Hill for adjusting to my absence for two years to serve at the National Science Foundation. The Foundation is neither connected to nor responsible for the contents of this book. I thank Gale Publishing Group for permission to use part of my previously published work on pp. 11–14.

Many of my undergraduate and graduate students read chapters of the manuscript and offered helpful feedback. I am especially grateful to Ph.D. student K. Elizabeth Coggins for reading the entire manuscript and giving her valuable comments. The editorial staff at Palgrave Macmillan provided assistance, which helped make this book a reality. Finally, special thanks to my wife (Ruth) for her love and support and to our young children (Nathaniel, Daniel, and Annabel) for showing interest in this work.

CHAPEL HILL, NC
March 2009

# Nature and Power of the U.S. Supreme Court in American Politics

The U.S. Supreme Court is an institution whose nature and power evolved gradually in well over 200 years of decision making, punctuated by political turmoil and near disasters that engulfed the Court. In this chapter, we examine the nature and evolution of the Court's power in American politics by focusing on four areas of Supreme Court development:

1. Ambivalence and uncertainty over the Court's power and independence;
2. The Judiciary Act of 1789;
3. Foundation of judicial supremacy and the application of judicial review;
4. Constraints on the exercise of judicial power.

## Ambivalence and Uncertainty over Supreme Court Power and Independence

When the founding fathers assembled in Philadelphia in the summer of 1787 to debate the nature of U.S. Constitution and government, they were particularly interested in preserving *judicial independence*, the principle that judges should be allowed total control over their own decisions in the cases they hear.[1] As indicated in Article 3 of the Constitution, the framers preserved judicial independence by granting federal judges permanent tenure "during good behavior" and prohibited any reduction in their compensation to ensure that neither Congress nor the President can exercise control over the judiciary. Despite this constitutional guarantee of independence, the Supreme Court was quite uncertain about its own power and place in the newly formed government. For the Supreme Court, the road to greatness will be gradual, difficult, and downright contentious.

The first session of the Court opened on February 2, 1790 in the Merchant's Exchange Building in New York City, then the nation's temporary capital.[2] The first justices appointed to the Court by the nation's first president, George Washington, were all statesmen of great honor and accomplishment. Nearly all of them were present at the constitutional convention and had signed both the Declaration of Independence and the Constitution. John Jay of New York was the chief justice. With him on the original Court

**Photo 1.1**  The Opening Session of the Supreme Court, February 2, 1790 Showing from Left to Right, Associate Justice William Cushing, Chief Justice John Jay, Associate Justices John Blair, and James Wilson.

were Associate Justices John Blair of Virginia, William Cushing of Massachusetts, James Iredell of North Carolina, John Rutledge of South Carolina, and James Wilson of Pennsylvania. Washington's selection of these statesmen was designed in part to foster geographic representation and to appease sectional cleavages.

*Low Public Esteem.* That these justices agreed to serve stands as a testament to their commitment to the new Constitution. But that commitment will be severely tested soon because during these formative years, the Supreme Court enjoyed very low public esteem. Commenting on the nature of Supreme Court role in society during that time, Justice Sandra Day O'Connor noted that "the Supreme Court possessed neither public trust nor a particularly prominent national role."[3] The early justices themselves recognized the weak position of the Court. For instance, in 1801 when the nation's second President John Adams asked John Jay to resume as chief justice, Jay declined the offer because he had no faith that the Court could obtain enough "energy, weight and dignity . . . nor acquire the public confidence and respect" necessary to play an important part in the national government.[4] Indeed, Jay had resigned from the Court on June 29, 1795 following his diplomatic mission to England without a hint of regret.

One reason for the Court's low public image was a statutory requirement for justices to engage in circuit riding, essentially turning up twice a year to attend circuit sessions in four or five district courts located in different parts of the country. Circuit riding was a practice Congress instituted to keep the justices abreast of local opinion and state law. There was concern that if justices are allowed to adjudicate cases in a single location, say New York City, their decisions would assume a peculiar localized character and would not reflect diverse views from across the country.

For justices, however, circuit riding was a physically and emotionally demanding experience. It entailed expending a great deal of energy on transportation through the wilderness and over swollen rivers, through pestilential swamps, in rain and snow, hailstorm and sunshine.[5] Transportation under these deplorable conditions was carried out via one-seated gigs such as stagecoaches and horse-drawn carriages. Circuit riding would come to test the commitment of the justices to the Constitution because it sapped their physical and emotional strength. Typically, justices had little energy left to devote to the important affairs of judging after having spent many hours on the road. In this sense, circuit riding was especially hard for justices who covered the Southern circuit because of the scotching heat and extremely poor roads. Thomas Johnson (1791–1793) and James Iredell are two examples of justices who did not last for very long on the Court because of the physical demands of riding the Southern circuit. Johnson lasted only 14 months before resigning on February 1, 1793. Iredell lasted about a decade.

Did justices complain to Congress about the hardship of circuit riding? Indeed, they did. Justices protested and grumbled for years about the burdensome nature of circuit riding, about being taken away from their families half the year, and about lacking the opportunity to consult books. Yet Congress failed to act to improve the situation. Justice James Iredell compared his life to that of a traveling "Post Boy" and seriously considered foregoing $500 of his $3500 annual salary if Congress would eliminate circuit duties.[6]

Giving the hardship associated with circuit riding, it is not surprising that several important statesmen refused appointment to the Court, including Edmund Pendleton of Virginia and Charles Cotesworth Pinckney of South Carolina. Others including Oliver Ellsworth, John Jay, and John Rutledge resigned their appointments in favor of more noteworthy pursuits after a short tenure on the Court. For instance, Jay resigned to become governor of New York State after being elected in absentia.[7] Rutledge resigned to become chief justice of the South Carolina Court of Common Pleas (the state's highest court) because he considered it more prestigious than being the associate justice of the U.S. Supreme Court).[8]

The Court worked hard in the face of tremendous setbacks to improve its public image. A measure of how far the Supreme Court has come in public esteem is to recognize that between 1789 and 2009, 151 individuals were nominated to a seat on the Court. The actual number of nominations is higher since some individuals were nominated multiple times.[9] Of these, 37 (25 percent) held official state government positions as governor, legislator, judge, and so on when they were appointed.[10] Despite the intense scrutiny that attends nominees to the High Court especially during the second half of the 20th century many nominees left their state employment to serve with distinction on the U.S. Supreme Court. Such a change in esteem demonstrates the growing power and influence of the Court in national politics.

## SCATTERED ATTACKS ON THE EARLY SUPREME COURT

In his commentary in the *Federalist Papers* # 78 concerning the judicial function, Alexander Hamilton carefully explained the founding fathers' thinking on the federal judiciary. Specifically, he said that "It will always be the least dangerous" of the three branches of government. With the benefit of hindsight, this perception of harmlessness foreshadowed the vulnerability and the kind of scattered attacks the Supreme Court (and indeed its justices) would endure. The attacks were both direct and indirect and had the cumulative effect of diminishing the power and stature of the Court and its justices in the short run. In a larger sense, these attacks are a part of the evolutionary process that gives the Court its democratic character.

*Slow Action to End Circuit Riding.* It is striking that Congress stubbornly refused to act quickly to eliminate circuit riding despite numerous complaints lodged by the justices. Chief Justice Warren Burger who served from 1969 to 1986 attributes the slowness of reform to "a mix of Congressional indifference and animosity toward the Judiciary [and] the failure of lawmakers to understand the requirements of sound judicial administration…"[11] Such indifference and animosity amount to a silent attack on the integrity of the Court and an attempt to reign in the judiciary. It was mostly in response to rising caseload in the Court about 100 years after circuit riding started that Congress finally enacted the Circuit Court of Appeals Act of 1891 (the Evarts Act), establishing nine circuit courts of appeals staffed with permanent judges and effectively eliminating circuit riding duties.[12]

*Thomas Jefferson's Campaign of Impeachment.* Another major instance of hostility toward the Court came after anti-Federalist Thomas Jefferson (a Virginia Republican) assumed the presidency in 1801. Jefferson believed strongly in states' rights and a truly decentralized governmental structure. It was this constitutional ideology that shaped his vision of the nation's future. Because Presidents George Washington and John Adams (both Federalists) had packed the Court with ideologically like-minded Federalists, Jefferson considered the Supreme Court a stronghold of Federalist troublemakers who should be contained.

Like the struggles of modern political parties, loyalists of the Federalist and Republican parties, during this nascent period of our Republic, continually battled each other for influence over national policy, what the Constitution means, and who should interpret it. A microcosm of this continual battle was the relationship between Thomas Jefferson and his cousin John Marshall.[13] Jefferson was Marshall's principal antagonist throughout his adult life, but especially during Marshall's 35-year-reign as chief justice of the Supreme Court. Jefferson viewed with great disfavor the fact that several justices in the Marshall Court participated vigorously in partisan political activities such as lobbying members of Congress.

As president, Jefferson was fortunate though ultimately unsuccessful in his effort to reign-in the Supreme Court. He received significant assistance and encouragement from Congress, which was controlled by his fellow Republicans. Indeed, Jefferson was urged by Republicans especially his fellow Virginian, Senator William Branch Giles, "to remove all [federal judges of the opposing political party] indiscriminately."[14] The method provided in the Constitution for removing judges is "Impeachment for, and Conviction of, Treason, Bribery, or other high Crimes and Misdemeanors" (Article 2, Section 4). But Jefferson and other Republican leaders believed in a different theory of impeachment, one summarized by Senator Giles as "Impeachment is nothing more than the enquiry, by the two Houses of Congress, whether the office of any public man might not be better filled by another...A trial and removal of a judge need not imply any criminality or corruption by him."[15] In essence, the Republicans who dominated the two political branches of government were willing to remove judges who merely disagreed with them ideologically and to ignore the technical limits set by the Constitution.[16] They wanted to use impeachment of judges to bend the judiciary to their ideological will.

Heeding the request to remove judges "indiscriminately," Jefferson initiated in 1804 the impeachment of Supreme Court Justice Samuel Chase by the House of Representatives, informally placing the Supreme Court under siege. Chase was a bright and accomplished Federalist in the Marshall Court. One of the signers of the Declaration of Independence, Chase had some personality flaws. He was irascible, caustic, and altogether unpleasant to be with.[17] Having these qualities is hardly a high crime worthy of impeachment and removal from office. The Chase impeachment was politically motivated as are most impeachments. He was charged with several crimes arising from his activities on the bench. First, he was accused of actively lobbying for the passage of the Alien and Sedition Act of 1798. Second, he was charged with misconduct when, during one of his circuit riding episodes, he presided over the sedition trial of James Callender in 1800 where he allegedly permitted a biased juror to be seated, barred the testimony of certain witnesses and harangued defense attorneys during their oral presentation. Finally, Chase was alleged to have made up his mind about a point of law during another trial (this time, John Fries, a tax rebellion leader) without giving the defense lawyer a chance to argue the issue first.[18] Reasonable people would conclude that these are hardly "high crimes" that should lead to impeachment. But clearly they did in 1805.

The Sedition Act, which Chase was accused of actively supporting, was the most restrictive piece of legislation ever enacted by Congress regarding freedom of speech and press. The act severely punishes, "by a fine not exceeding $2000 and by imprisonment not exceeding two years," any person who writes, speaks, or publishes words determined to be "false, scandalous and malicious" against the U.S. government, Congress, or the President. The

Act was enacted after the Revolutionary War by a Federalist Congress bent on protecting itself against rising Jeffersonian opposition.[19]

To Jefferson and other Republicans, the sedition act and its subsequent application abridged the freedom of speech and press guaranteed by the First Amendment to the U.S. Constitution. It symbolized for them a perfect example of an unacceptable expansion of federal power and a purely calculated attempt by Federalists to stifle political dissent.

Samuel Chase remains the first and only Supreme Court justice ever impeached, though not convicted.[20] Followed passionately by Washingtonians and citizens across the country, the trial was presided over by Vice President Aaron Burr, who was himself facing felony charges in New York State for the murder of Alexander Hamilton in a duel.[21] Although Republicans dominated the Senate in 1805 during the Chase trial, he was acquitted of all the charges. These Republican senators saw past the political desires of the moment and pushed aside their wish to castigate a political opponent, after all Chase was a member of John Marshall's Court. The Jeffersonians in the Senate agreed with the argument of the defense that "Our property, our liberty, our lives, can only be protected by [independent] judges."[22] Many thought that had Chase been found guilty, Marshall would have been the next target.

The Chase impeachment saga has significant implications for judicial independence. According to Justice Sandra Day O'Connor, "the legacy of the Chase impeachment has been the independent judiciary we know today."[23] Had the campaign of impeachment and removal of federal judges succeeded, it would have permanently and significantly altered the nature of judicial independence and the capacity for the Court to act as a check on other governmental powers.

Indeed, clearly disturbed by the scattered attacks on the Court and fearing an outcome short of full judicial independence for the Supreme Court, Chief Justice John Marshall privately suggested to Justice Chase in 1804 that Congress could be given appellate jurisdiction over Supreme Court decisions, in exchange for ending the campaign of impeachment.[24] To John Marshall, it became preferable to have legal opinions deemed unsound by the legislature reconsidered and possibly reversed by the legislature than to have judges harassed with the threat of impeachment and removal for transgressions that may have been cooked up by their political opponents. Judging from Marshall's track record on the Court, such a suggestion is remarkably unfortunate considering his strong inclination toward expansion and centralization of judicial power.

*Jefferson's Opposition to Ending Seriatim Opinions.* As we have discovered, throughout John Marshall's tenure as chief justice of the Supreme Court, he had an antagonistic relationship with Thomas Jefferson. Therefore, it is not surprising that another instance of early attack on the Court came directly from President Jefferson who was enraged that the Supreme Court under John Marshall had decided to end the practice of requiring justices to write *seriatim* opinions set forth by Chief Justice John Jay. In this practice each justice wrote a separate opinion, resulting in several opinions being issued in each case. The advantage of this practice is that it educates citizens about the diversity of judicial opinion on a case and about how each justice arrived at a decision and the rationale behind the decision. Moreover, it encourages civic discourse. If the decisions are viewed favorably by the general public, they can actually generate support for the Court. The main disadvantage of seriatim opinions is that rather than the Court presenting a unified front through one majority opinion, seriatim opinions tended to diffuse the impact of the Court's decisions, making it difficult for the Court to be regarded as a coequal branch of the federal government. This policy-related disadvantage is not all there is, however.

*[handwritten margin note: Pros and cons of seriatim opinion]*

There is a political disadvantage as well. Seriatim opinions serve the interest of the Court's political opponents by giving them multiple ammunitions for attacking the Court, especially with regard to the political activities of individual justices. For Republican Party leaders such as Thomas Jefferson and James Madison who were unfriendly toward the Court, ending the practice of multiple opinions meant closing this profitable window of opportunity to criticize the Court. In the early 1820s, Jefferson wrote to Associate Justice William Johnson, his appointee and the only Republican on the Court at the time, to voice his complaint:

> The practice [of issuing a single opinion] is certainly convenient for the lazy, the modest & incompetent. It saves them the trouble of developing their opinion methodically and even of making up an opinion at all. That of seriatim argument shews whether every judge has taken the trouble of understanding the case, of investigating it minutely, and of forming an opinion for himself, instead of pinning it on another's sleeve.[25]

To insinuate that Supreme Court justices who do not write their own opinion on a case are "lazy" and "incompetent" is to grossly misunderstand the collaboration, collegiality, and interdependence that majority opinion writing entails, even under Chief Justice John Marshall. As we see in chapter 6, the preliminary vote of the justices during conference ends only their official deliberation on a case. Unofficial discussions through interchamber memos usually continue until the opinion is publicly announced.

## Enlightened Timidity

During its first three years in business, the Supreme Court had virtually no cases to decide. During its first 10 years, the justices heard only 100 cases.[26] To be sure, most of these did not pose a significant national question. Therefore, lacking opportunities to make big national decisions, it is somewhat surprising that during this time of general uncertainty, the Supreme Court rejected an opportunity to usher in institutional greatness for itself. But in retrospect, it was indeed a moment of enlightened timidity, a wise decision whereby justices strategically refused to assist the president in his time of need and in doing so asserted the Court's institutional power and independence.

Here is the situation. On April 2, 1793, President George Washington issued the *Proclamation of Neutrality*, which was designed to signal to France and Great Britain that the United States would not be drawn into their geo-political conflict in which France declared war on England two months ear-lier on February 1, 1793. It turned out that the conflict raised several questions of international law, some of which involved existing treaties between the United States and England. The dispute is relevant today because of the request the president made and the Court's response to it.

Before issuing his proclamation, Washington was unsure of the most appropriate course of action. France was a strong ally of the U.S. Yet England was providing much needed financial support for American ship owners in transatlantic commerce. Washington consulted with his cabinet and eventu-ally sought advice from the Supreme Court by sending 29 questions on international law and treaties to the justices. The Court politely refused to assist the president. Justices informed the president that they do not issue advisory opinions because doing so would be inconsistent with the judicial function of deciding real cases and controversies arising under the laws of the United States (Article 3, Section 2). This became an official policy reaf-firmed numerous times throughout history.[27] The Supreme Court and other federal courts do not issue purely advisory opinions. They resolve live cases and controversies, not hypothetical conflicts without a definite claim under the law. By any measure, this is an important self-imposed limitation on the exercise of judicial power by the Supreme Court because nothing could have stopped the Court from issuing an "off-the-record" statement of advice to the president under those special circumstances.

In essence, the Supreme Court was ambivalent and cautiously timid about its own place and role in the government. Issuing the advisory opinion would have presented the Court with an opportunity to extend its influence in gov-ernment. However, doing so might have subjected the Court to future attacks from critics who disagreed with presidential policies informed by the Court's advice. Paradoxically, by refusing to issue advisory opinions the jus-tices actually protected the Court from future political manipulation and ensured the consistency and predictability of the law.[28] The Court's stance might have seemed weak at first but it is a stance predicated upon enlight-ened institutional self-interest. According to political theorist Robert McCloskey, the early justices of the Supreme Court understood the shaky position of the Court.[29] So while they did not actively shy away from great-ness, they felt that greatness must be achieved gradually or otherwise they jeopardize the very existence of the Court.

An important issue that citizens of the various states favored intensely was state sovereignty and, for many, a view of the Constitution that places the states as principals and the federal government as their agent. In order for the Supreme Court to be thrust into a position of greatness (defined loosely as high esteem), the authority of the federal government had to supplant that of the states and the Supreme Court needed to command a significant amount of confidence in its independence. For advocates of the Court, it is comforting that the justices recognized that the primary obstacle to the Court's greatness lies in the relationship between the states and the national government. Overcoming that obstacle would be to enhance the power of the Court itself and that of Congress.

## ESTABLISHING FEDERAL JUDICIAL STRUCTURE: THE JUDICIARY ACT OF 1789

No federal legislation has done more to formalize the structure of the federal judiciary than the Judiciary Act of 1789. When the Constitution was first debated during the constitutional convention in Philadelphia, the founding fathers saw a need for a federal judiciary. But they could not agree on what form it should take and how much independence it should possess.

Many plans were presented and two were carefully considered in detail. The first was proposed by a delegate from Virginia named Edmund Randolph and so it was called the *Virginia Plan*. This plan would set up both a Supreme Court and several "inferior" federal courts.[30] But some delegates were disturbed by the idea of lower federal courts when there were lower courts at the state level to try cases. In their view such duplication of the trial function was entirely unnecessary and so they responded with the *New Jersey Plan* proposed by William Paterson, a New Jersey delegate. Paterson, who later served on the Supreme Court from 1793 to 1806, proposed that in order to protect national rights and establish uniformity in the law across the country, state courts should hear all cases at trial with a right to appeal straight to the U.S. Supreme Court. Neither plan prevailed. Instead, a compromise was reached to proceed with establishing the foundation for a federal judiciary but to leave its specific form for a future date. The final compromise statement can be found in Article 3 of the Constitution:

> The judicial Power of the United States shall be vested in one Supreme Court, and in such inferior Courts as the Congress may from time to time ordain and establish.[31]

Once the Constitution was ratified, Congress acted quickly to formalize the federal judicial structure. When Congress assembled in 1789, legislators considered Senate Bill 1 to shape the federal judiciary. The lawmakers were many of the same individuals present at the constitutional convention. And so the pressing question soon resolved into whether the judiciary should operate with lower federal courts or have all claims heard by a state trial court first. The law that emerged from that debate was the Judiciary Act of 1789, drafted largely by Senator Oliver Ellsworth who later became the third chief justice of the Supreme Court. This legislation created fundamental legal institutions in the United States and provided the blue print for the current form assumed by the federal judicial system. Specifically, the act created a judicial system that composed of

- one Supreme Court consisting of one chief justice and five associate justices;
- three circuit courts (Eastern, Middle, and Southern), each comprising two Supreme Court justices and a single district judge;
- 13 district courts, one for each state of the union and managed by a single district judge.

The decision to create subsidiary federal courts in addition to the Supreme Court has been described by Justice Felix Frankfurter as the act's "transcendental achievement" because that decision was essential to the creation of an independent federal judiciary.[32] Had the New Jersey Plan prevailed, it is likely that much of the lower federal judiciary would have operated under state control. It is also noteworthy that the act created not just the Supreme Court and district courts but circuit courts as well, although these circuit courts were not assigned their own permanent judges initially. This would change 102 years later when Congress enacted the Circuit Courts of Appeals Act of 1891. Circuit courts now play a central role in the dissemination of justice in the United States.[33] The Judiciary Act of 1789 also created the office of the attorney general but that office is housed in the Department of Justice, which is under the control of the president.

## BUILDING THE FOUNDATION FOR JUDICIAL SUPREMACY

The first instance in which the Court attempted to assert the judicial jurisdiction of the federal government over the states came in the case of *Chisolm v. Georgia* (1793). Jurisdiction is simply the area over which a government entity has controlling authority. In *Chisolm*, a South Carolina citizen, who was the executor of the estate of a merchant who had sold goods to Georgia during the revolutionary war, sued Georgia in federal court to recover the debt. The state failed to appear to defend the charges claiming that it possessed sovereign immunity and cannot be sued in a federal court by a citizen of another state without its consent. The Supreme Court rejected that view, ruling against Georgia. By so ruling, the Court mounted a frontal challenge to state sovereignty. This was the first great decision involving federalism.

The *Chisolm* decision so angered the states that the Eleventh Amendment was proposed and quickly ratified, denying citizens of one state the right to sue another state in federal court. This sudden reversal of a Supreme Court decision by a constitutional amendment further eroded the Court's confidence. It was not until the steadfast leadership, beginning in 1801, of Chief Justice John Marshall that the Supreme Court found its footing and began to emerge as a confident coequal branch of federal government.

## Judicial Review of Federal Legislation: *Marbury v. Madison* (1803)

The case of *Marbury v. Madison* is the most important decision in which the Court established the foundations for what some see as judicial supremacy. The case exemplifies the uncertainties of litigation. The uncertainty was such that prompted Supreme Court Justice Oliver Wendell Holmes to declare that the object of the law is prediction of what "judges will do in fact." Furthermore, the case fulfills Alexander Hamilton's wish for Supreme Court justices to supervise other branches of government and hold them accountable to the Constitution's command.[34]

The story of this case started in earnest with the presidential election of 1800 between incumbent President John Adams and challenger Thomas Jefferson. That contest produced no clear winner after all Electoral College votes were counted.[35] In such a situation the Constitution requires the House of Representatives to choose the president and vice president. In February 1801, Thomas Jefferson was selected president and Aaron Burr vice president. Because the Federalists had lost control of Congress and the presidency, the outgoing president John Adams, a forceful Federalist, proposed and Congress approved the Circuit Court Act of 1801, which authorized six new circuit courts and several district courts to accommodate the new states of Kentucky, Tennessee, and Vermont. This bill guaranteed the Federalists temporary control over the judiciary. During his final six months in office, Adams submitted well over 200 nominations to Congress, with 16 judgeships approved by the Senate during his last two weeks in office.[36]

One important development that took place during this period was that Federalist Oliver Ellsworth resigned his position as chief justice of the Supreme Court, giving Adams an opportunity to name a federalist successor. Without hesitation, Adams first offered the position to former Chief Justice John Jay who had resigned to become the governor of New York. Jay refused. Then Adams turned to his Secretary of State John Marshall. Marshall accepted the appointment and was quickly confirmed by the Senate in January 1801 while he was still serving as secretary of state.

In addition to the Circuit Court Act, the Federalist Congress enacted the Organic Act, authorizing the president to appoint 42 justices of the peace in the District of Columbia. Adams's appointments to fill these positions were called "midnight appointees" and virtually all were Federalists. It is noteworthy that this seemingly trivial act would set the stage for the most dramatic event that led to the Court's decision in *Marbury v. Madison*, the case that firmly established the doctrine of *judicial review*, the power to declare laws unconstitutional.

During the last days of John Adams's administration, there was a sudden rush to clean the House and to make way for the new administration. As a result, Secretary of State John Marshall neglected to deliver some of the commissions for Justice of the Peace. A commission is a signed document naming an individual to a governmental post. If Secretary Marshall had not neglected his duty, the ensuing controversy would have been avoided. One of these commissions belonged to William Marbury. When the new administration assumed power, Thomas Jefferson was displeased with the blatant effort to pack the judiciary with Federalist loyalists. Therefore, he ordered his Secretary of State James Madison not to deliver the commissions. Determined, William Marbury and three others went directly to the Supreme Court, invoking the Court's original jurisdiction powers and requested a writ of mandamus that would order the secretary of state to deliver the commissions. The case was placed on the Court's docket for the 1802 term. But while the case was pending, the new Republican majority in Congress decided to eliminate the 1802 Supreme Court term out of anger toward the actions of a lame duck president, and so the decision in *Marbury v. Madison* was postponed until February 24, 1803 the following term.[37]

This case presented John Marshall and the Supreme Court with a daunting predicament. Should the Supreme Court issue the writ of mandamus? What if the writ is issued and President Jefferson refuses to honor? How damaging that would be for the Court! These are important questions requiring careful deliberation. Certainly, the potential institutional consequences for the Supreme Court could be disastrous if the Court makes the wrong choice. The balance of power in the government would be dramatically altered and the Court would suffer further diminished influence in the current and future affairs of government. Worse still, Thomas Jefferson and subsequent presidents could play fast and loose with the Constitution by assuming an inherit authority to act as they please without the watchful eye of the Court.

We can think of this case as a game of strategy.[38] Figure 1.1 shows the three main actors in the dispute and their strategic options (represented in ovals). The boxes indicate the consequences or potential consequences for each respective strategic option available to the actors. William Marbury whose commission was not delivered must move first. He must decide whether or not to file a lawsuit to reclaim his commission. Clearly, litigation has risks but Marbury had little to lose and much to gain; therefore, he decided to file a lawsuit. In the next two decisional stages of the game, both the Supreme Court and President Thomas Jefferson must move sequentially. They each have real choices to make and each choice presents a real consequence. Since the Supreme Court must make a decision after receiving the petition, it gets to make the next move in the game. The Court must decide whether to issue the writ, not issue it, or choose some other option. If the Court chooses to issue the writ, President Jefferson would likely refuse to enforce it, precipitating a constitutional crisis. In this outcome the Court would be severely weakened since it lacks the power to enforce its own decisions. If Jefferson honors the writ, however, that choice would be viewed as an embarrassing defeat for him and his administration. This would enhance the authority of the Court but Jefferson's power to persuade will be damaged. Neither of these two possible scenarios—the Court's choices or the president's—sounds promising.

If, on the other hand, the Court fails to issue the writ, it would be viewed as weak by members of the Federalist Party in Congress and Marshall's reputation within his party will be severely tarnished, especially in the eyes of fellow partisans in Congress. The remaining decisional choice (the most

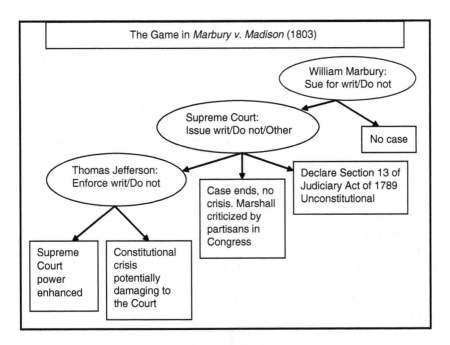

**Figure 1.1**   The Game in *Marbury v. Madison* (1803).

optimal one yet) is for the Court to declare the law authorizing William Marbury's legal request unconstitutional. The Court settled for this "other" option thereby avoiding a constitutional confrontation with President Jefferson. By declaring a federal law null and void for the first time, John Marshall's Court firmly ushered in judicial review and sent a clear message to Congress and the president that the Supreme Court stands ready to assert itself as an independent and coequal branch of the federal government.

Historians of the Marbury affair consider the Court's decision to be something of sheer genius, although by all practical purposes it is plausible that both the Court and the president were merely reacting rationally based upon the information available to them. How did John Marshall and the Court reach that decision? Analysis of the opinion suggests that the Court addressed three interrelated questions raised in the case. First, was William Marbury legally entitled to the commission? The Court answered yes, noting that when a commission has been signed by the president, the appointment is made and it is completed when the secretary of state affixes a seal of the United States. Thus Marbury has suffered a legal injury and as a matter of right is entitled to the commission. Second, does the law afford him a remedy for his claim? Yes. To not deliver the commission would amount to a plain violation of Marbury's right under the Constitution. Finally, is that remedy a mandamus issued by the Supreme Court? No. Even though the law authorizes the Court to issue a writ of mandamus to "persons holding office, under the authority of the United States," the Court lacked the proper jurisdiction to issue a writ of mandamus because Section 13 of the Judiciary of 1789 provides an unconstitutional grant of original powers to the ;eme Court. Article 3 of the Constitution specifies the original jurisdiction powers of the Court. To alter that constitutional grant of power requires a constitutional amendment not a congressional statute.

Judged under today's standard of ethical behavior befitting a government official, it seems that John Marshall should have exempted himself from participating in the case since his own absentmindedness precipitated the conflict in the first place. The law creating the justice of the peace vacancies was later repealed by the anti-Federalist Congress.

The significance of *Marbury v. Madison* is that it declared an Act of Congress unconstitutional, thereby affirming judicial review and independence. Ironically, by rejecting a congressional grant of additional powers, the Court actually gained more power in terms of prestige and political influence. But the idea of judicial review itself was neither new nor born in that case. For instance, in 1795, in the case of *Van Horne's Lessee v. Dorrance*, Justice Paterson explained that in the American form of government

> [A] Constitution is the sun of the political system, around which all Legislative, Executive, and Judicial bodies must revolve. Whatever may be the case in other countries, yet in this there can be no doubt, that every act of the Legislature, repugnant to the Constitution, is absolutely void.[39]

Similarly, James Iredell stated in *Calder v. Bull* (1798) that "If any act of Congress, or of the legislature of a state, violates...constitutional provisions, it is unquestionably void." Iredell further noted that the authority to make such a declaration "is of a delicate nature" only to be exercised in "urgent" situations. Thus, the justices were simply waiting for the appropriate or "urgent" case through which they can firmly establish judicial review. It was this principle expressed by Justice Paterson in *Van Horn's Lesee* and by Justice Iredell in *Calder* that *Marbury v. Madison* confirmed and institutionalized eight years later as the most wide-ranging grant of power to the American judiciary.

## Application of Judicial Review

How did the Court exercise its power of judicial review in the aftermath of *Marbury*? In the years following the Marbury decision, the Supreme Court used its power of judicial review to further establish itself as a coequal governing partner under the Constitution and to firmly declare the superiority of the federal government over the states. Having successfully defined the nature of that power, the Supreme Court of modern times exercises largely a supervisory role in the interaction between citizens and their government.[40]

*Declaring State Laws Unconstitutional:* Fletcher v. Peck *(1810).* After *Marbury*, the Supreme Court issued two decisions in the ensuing years that firmly established the Court's judicial supremacy. The first decision came in the case of *Fletcher v. Peck* (1810), which involved a land-grant scandal. In 1795, Georgia sold at a bargain price a huge track of land comprising most of the modern states of Alabama and Mississippi. It turned out that all but one of the legislators who voted for the sale had been bribed to do so. Citizens were outraged and voted these corrupt politicians out of office. The next legislature, filled with righteous indignation, quickly rescinded the act and took possession of the land. The beneficiary of the sale, Robert Fletcher, sued to recover his purchase price. The question presented to the Court was whether an executed contract in the form of a legislative land grant by the state through its legislature can be rescinded later by the state. The Court said No and invalided the rescinding act. Fletcher became the first clear precedent for the proposition that the Supreme Court is empowered to hold state laws unconstitutional.

The Supreme Court has both a constitutional and statutory foundation to review state laws. The decision in *Fletcher v. Peck* had constitutional foundation because it was based directly on the contract clause of the Constitution, which governs the powers prohibited of states (Article 1, Section 10). The statutory foundation upon which the Court can review state laws is derived from Section 25 of the Judiciary Act of 1789. There Congress granted the Court explicit authority to exercise judicial review over the states in cases appealed from a state's highest court upholding state law against challenges of unconstitutionality or denial of claims based upon the U.S. Constitution. In *Martin v. Hunter's Lessee* (1816) the Court reasserted its authority to hear civil cases tried in state court that presented federal constitutional questions. Then five years later in *Cohen v. Virginia* (1821) the Court exercised its jurisdiction to review criminal cases from state courts raising federal constitutional issues. Importantly, in both cases, the Court exercised its judicial review powers by upholding Section 25 of the Judiciary Act of 1789.

*Establishing Federal Supremacy over the States:* McCulloch v. Maryland *(1819).* Using its implied powers granted under the "necessary and proper" clause of Article 1, Section 8 of the Constitution, Congress established in 1816 the Bank of the United States to act as its financial agent but with the power to perform general banking transactions. A branch of the bank was set up in Maryland and in several other states. Maryland imposed heavily discriminatory taxes on the Bank of the United States and others established within its boundaries "without authority from the state." It was clear that payment of the taxes would drive the Bank of the United States out of business since it would be unable to compete with other banks established with state authority. McCulloch, the cashier of the Baltimore branch of the Bank of the United States, refused to pay the taxes and continued to issue bank notes. Maryland sued to recover the penalties and the Supreme Court of Maryland ruled in favor of the state. McCulloch then appealed to the U.S. Supreme Court. Suggestive of the intricate and important nature of the issues the case raised, oral arguments were held for at least six days in a small room in the basement of the U.S. Senate. The Court occupied this room until 1860.[41]

The case raised two questions for the Court. First, does Congress have the power to form and incorporate a bank? Second, may the State of Maryland impose taxes on a U.S. Bank located in Maryland? The Court answered "yes" to the first question and "no" to the second. Chief Justice John Marshall, writing for a unanimous Court, explained that the Constitution grants Congress the right to make all laws "necessary and proper" to carry out the expressed powers of the Constitution. Setting up a national bank falls well within that right. The Court then turned to the second question, arguing that the Constitution and all laws enacted pursuant to it are supreme and cannot subjugate or be inferior to any state law. If Maryland is allowed to regulate the laws of the United States, then the Constitution itself would be rendered meaningless. And since the power to tax is tantamount to the power to destroy, a tax on the U.S. bank amounts to an illegal attempt to destroy the U.S. government and, therefore, is unconstitutional.

The case of *McCulloch v. Maryland* (1819) is hailed as the most important decision "to the future of America" that the Marshall Court ever handed down.[42] It proclaims the principle of implied congressional powers and of national supremacy over the states. The initial debate over the meaning of the Constitution seems to have been settled. Contrary to the laments of anti-Federalist, such as Thomas Jefferson and James Madison, that the states are the supreme sovereign and principals in the scheme of government debated in Philadelphia, it is the federalists, the advocates of a strong central government, individuals such as Alexander Hamilton and John Marshall, who have prevailed in the great debate over the relationship between the states and the federal government.

The Supreme Court has now exercised the power of judicial review for over 200 years. How often does the Court strike down state or federal laws? Research by political scientist Lawrence Baum indicates that the Court exercises judicial review often, about once in every two years on average, but that the total number of laws struck is a very small proportion of all laws passed by the government. For example, between 1790 and 1996, Congress passed over 60,000 laws and 135 (less than 0.3 percent) were declared unconstitutional. Although the number of overturned laws is small, its significance could be misleading. First, the Court exercises judicial review inconsistently. During the period 1940–1949 only two laws were invalidated whereas during the period 1970–1979, 20 laws were invalidated. This suggests that the extent to which the Court exerts on public policy is highly variable.[43] Second, laws struck down by the Court are not all equally important. Some laws such as the Flag Protection Act (struck down in 1990) are politically important but most are not.[44] Therefore, it does not appear that the Court is abusing its power to review the activities of the legislative and executive branches of government. Rather, the it is restrained and, therefore, regularly shows deference to the authority of these other branches.

## STILL THE LEAST DANGEROUS BRANCH?

### Historical Evidence of Judicial Supremacy

When Alexander Hamilton and the other founding fathers conceived of the judiciary, they considered it the weakest branch of government because "it will be least in a capacity to annoy or injure" the political rights of the Constitution. For judges do not have command over the army and they do not have control over the national budget. The president controls the first and Congress the second. However, today, many are willing to recognize the judiciary as the most powerful branch because as Alexander Hamilton observed in the *Federalist Papers* #78, the judiciary has the power of "judgment," which it now exercises with widespread independence.[45] Furthermore, through the power of judicial review the Court can strike down presidential and legislative enactments and hold recalcitrant officials under contempt of Court. Discussed below are a number of events and decisions, which indicate that the Court has reigned supreme over other political branches.

*Judicial Review.* The Supreme Court avoided confrontation with President Thomas Jefferson in *Marbury v. Madison* (1803). The doctrine of judicial review that was firmly established in that case, allowing courts to declare laws and executive policies unconstitutional, has withstood the test of time in upholding judicial independence and in signaling the supremacy of the Court in the affairs of government.

In our constitutional scheme, the president is bestowed with enormous powers, which are sanctioned by popular elections held every four years. Presidents recognize this power and some have even commented on its elastic nature. For instance, Woodrow Wilson commenting on the president as leader both of his Party and the Nation observed that "If he [the incumbent] rightly interpret the national thought and boldly insist upon it, he is irresistible…His office is anything he has the sagacity and force to make it."[46] Despite its elasticity, presidential power can never be absolute under the Constitution so long as "It is the duty and province of the judge to say what the law is." The nature of judicial review is such that it serves as a reminder that ours is a limited government in which no citizen or government official is above the law and no statute is sacred. Not only can a sitting president be subpoenaed or impeached, a duly enacted congressional statute can be overturned as well through judicial review.

*Thomas Jefferson's Subpoena.* The president is not immune from prosecution or from being served with a judicial subpoena while in office. For a president to be so served at all is clear evidence of judicial power and independence. In many countries of the world, the reach of judicial power never extends that far. But in the United States, it does and the precedent goes as far back as 1807 when the Supreme Court served President Thomas Jefferson with a subpoena requiring him to produce evidence in his possession that was deemed relevant to the criminal prosecution of his former Vice President Aaron Burr. The president responded by producing the letter. Burr was accused of committing the high crime of treason against the United States for plotting to form a new nation out of the area of the lower valley of the Mississippi River.[47]

*Harry Truman's Steel Mills Seizure Case.* Another event that marked judicial supremacy occurred in 1952 during the administration of President

Harry S. Truman. Early in his administration, Truman established the National Wage Stabilization Board. The Board was empowered to find ways to limit wage and price inflation in the economy and to investigate methods for resolving the stalemate in contract talks between the United Steel Workers Union (which demanded higher wages) and major steel manufacturing companies (which argued higher wages could come only from charging higher prices for steel products). The union had to postpone a strike once due to ongoing contract talks and again at the president's request.

With the management-labor dispute coming just one and a half years into the Korean War, there was great concern in the Truman administration that a strike would disrupt weapons shipments to U.S. armed forces in the Korean theater of war. The president could have used the Taft-Hartley Act, which authorizes U.S. presidents to institute an 80-day "cooling off" period when contract talks failed and a strike was threatened. No congressional authorization exists for seizure of an industry during peacetime (the Korean War was actually a self-styled "police action," not a declared war.)

After contract talks failed and a strike was imminent (just two hours away), Truman ordered his Secretary of Commerce Charles Sawyer to seize and operate the steel mills and to call upon the workers to work as federal employees. The secretary implemented the order. The union agreed and workers stayed on the job. But feeling that this seizure was an illegal act, the executives of the steel companies and their lawyers sued Secretary Sawyer in *Youngstown Steel and Tube Company v. Sawyer*, alleging that the seizure order from the president amounted to lawmaking (a legislative function) in violation of the separation of powers and was thus unconstitutional. They requested that the steel mills be returned to the management.

President Truman was politically weak when the case went to Court. The weakness was primarily the result of numerous scandals that engulfed his administration, including his failure to respond swiftly to incidence of corruption by Internal Revenue Service (IRS) officials, and his controversial firing on April 13, 1951 of the popular army commander of allied forces in Korea General Douglas MacArthur.[48] Truman's approval rating sank to the lowest level during his administration in November 1951—23 percent (down from a high 87 percent when he first came to power in 1945) and a percentage point lower than Richard Nixon's a day before he resigned his presidency in 1974. Even though the lawsuit did not mention President Truman by name, it was clear that he was the real target because it was he who ordered the steel seizure. A negative decision from the Court was bound to deal a major setback for his already beleaguered administration.

A district court ruled in favor of the companies and, on appeal, the U.S. Supreme Court affirmed the ruling, severely limiting the president's powers.[49] The Court noted that the president acted without statutory authority from Congress to perform what amounted to a legislative function. As Justice Robert H. Jackson pointed out in his concurring opinion in the case, unchecked presidential power "either has no beginning or it has no end [and] it would plunge us straightway into dictatorship." Although President

Truman considered the Court's decision an affront to his authority, he none-theless acquiesced when he informed the nation from the White House that it was his duty to obey the law as declared by the Supreme Court. The case reminded the nation that even at a time of national emergency such as an ongoing undeclared war, the president could not act outside the limits of his constitutional authority.

*Richard Nixon's Watergate Scandal.* American presidents have always claimed executive privilege whenever their actions become a legal controversy and they are ordered to produce evidence or to testify in a judicial proceeding. In the 1980s, President Ronald Reagan claimed executive privilege when asked by Congress to produce information related to the illegal transfer of federal funds to the Contras in Nicaragua. Bill Clinton claimed executive privilege when asked to testify in a sexual harassment suit brought by Arkansas state employee Paula Jones. George H.W. Bush claimed executive privilege when Democrats in Congress demanded information about energy task force meetings held by his Vice President Dick Chaney, in 2003. We can go on and list many more examples of presidential claims of executive privilege but they would serve only to demonstrate the point that these claims are often exag-gerated and are a tactic to keep out of public view information that could potentially embarrass the president and his administration. More often than not presidents who claim executive privilege lose the fight when it moves into the judicial arena.

President Richard Nixon is a case in point. The Republican president's famous claim of executive privilege came in 1974 in the lead up to the next presidential election; it was a decision that would lead to the disastrous end of his administration. Special Watergate prosecutor Archibald Cox had obtained a lower court order requiring Nixon to release audiotapes of record-ings he had made of White House conversations and plan to break into the Watergate Hotel in Washington DC, the headquarters of the Democratic National Committee. At first, Nixon refused to obey the court order and invoked executive privilege, which is rooted in the constitutional principle of separation of powers. Nixon's defiance was nothing new. As we have seen above, President Thomas Jefferson similarly resisted compliance with a court order when he was subpoenaed in 1807 to produce evidence in his possession for a criminal trial.

In the case of Nixon, things progressed from bad to worse after Archibald Cox appealed to the Supreme Court and the Court ordered the president to release the audiotapes in the case *United States v. Nixon*.[50] In response, Nixon ordered Attorney General Elliot Richardson to dismiss Cox who was commissioned by Congress to investigate the Watergate break-ins. Because Richardson disagreed with Nixon on principle, he refused to dismiss Cox and resigned. The president then asked Deputy Attorney General William Ruckleshaus to dismiss Cox. He too refused to do so and resigned. Then Nixon went to the next in line in the Justice Department, Solicitor General Robert Bork. A strong believer in the Jeffersonian philosophy of limited government, Bork perceived the Court's order as an unconstitutional encroachment on presidential authority and he felt that the order subjugates the president to the will of the Supreme Court. Therefore, he agreed to dismiss the special prosecutor. In a news conference held soon after Cox's dismissal, Archibald Cox issued one single statement: "It is now for the Congress and the people to decide."[51]

The resignation of top Justice Department officials and the firing of Cox over the Watergate affair were met with strong public rebuke. Metropolitan Washington and the entire nation were abuzz over the scandal. The avalanche of criticism that descended upon the White House from citizens, the mass media, and Congress, including members of the president's own Republican Party, was sufficient to force Nixon to tender his resignation. The Watergate scandal gives true meaning to the idea expressed by Chief Justice Marshall in *Marbury v. Madison* that "The government of the United States has been emphatically termed a government of laws, and not of men." An order from the Supreme Court, backed only by public sanction, was sufficient to force a popularly elected president out of office in shame.

*Bill Clinton's Sexual Harassment Scandal.* Democrat Bill Clinton became president of the United States in 1992 after serving as governor of Arkansas. He was a highly popular president during his first term in office, partly because of his skillful stewardship of the economy. He easily won reelection defeating Republican Robert Dole of Kansas in 1996. Halfway into his second term, however, the Clinton administration was embroiled in a scandal owing to Clinton's own personal foibles. Clinton's sexual misconduct with a 24-year-old White House intern Monica Lewinski and a subsequent lie to cover it up resulted in an independent counsel investigation conducted by former Solicitor General Kenneth Starr and ultimately in Clinton's impeachment by the House of Representatives. He was eventually acquitted of all charges by the Senate in 1998.

Before this remarkable political spectacle unfolded, however, Clinton had been stunned by the long arm of Supreme Court justice. In a sexual harassment lawsuit initiated in May 1994 by Paula Jones, a former Arkansas state employee when Clinton was governor, the Supreme Court ruled unanimously in *Clinton v. Jones*[52] that a sitting president can indeed be sued in civil court for activities he had engaged in before he became president. The Court rejected argument advanced by Clinton's lawyers to delay the proceedings until Clinton leaves the White House as a show of respect for the Office, and because allowing the lawsuit to continue would seriously distract the president from discharging the awesome and demanding responsibilities of his Office. But in the Court's view, "The doctrine of Separation of Powers [on which executive privilege rests] does not require federal courts to stay all private actions against the President until he leaves office."[53] The justices were convinced that should the trial become unduly burdensome and distracting to the president, the district court can adjust the pace of the proceeding to accommodate the president. It should be pointed out that on remand, in *Jones v. Clinton*, the district court awarded summary judgment for Clinton.[54]

According to the trial judge, Jones's refusal to submit to unwelcome sexual advances did not result in tangible detriment since her job was upgraded and she received raises consistent with good job evaluation. At the very least, Clinton's eventual "victory" seemed to support the claim of his admirers that the allegations were preposterous and that the case was simply a "Republican political witch hunt," "a vast right-wing conspiracy," and a concerted effort to embarrass the president, especially since Jones failed to bring her complaint until two days before the three-year period of limitation expired.[55]

After fighting Paula Jones's sexual harassment charges for four years, the case was settled out of court on November 13, 1998 for $850,000 ($200,000 went to Paula Jones, the rest to her lawyers). The settlement did not require an apology from the president. In July 1999, the judge handling the Jones trial imposed a $90,000 fine on Clinton for intentionally misleading the court by knowingly giving false testimony when asked under oath whether he had ever sexually harassed other women, notably Monica Lewinski. In April 2001, the Arkansas Supreme Court imposed a $25,000 fine and suspended Clinton's license to practice law in that state until 2006. Clinton's punishment did not end there, however.

Under Rule 8 of the Supreme Court, a lawyer can be disbarred for conduct unbecoming a member of the Supreme Court Bar. Thus on November 13, 2001, rather than face the humiliation of disbarment, Clinton resigned from the Supreme Court Bar and the Court promptly accepted his resignation from the bar; he can no longer practice law in the Supreme Court.[56] It was one of the final acts of humiliation to befall Bill Clinton as a lawyer and politician. But as a testament to his political skill, Bill Clinton left the White House after serving two full terms with a 65 percent approval rating, the highest popularity rating of all modern presidents starting from Harry Truman. He has regained much of his popularity but the Lewinski scandal remains an indelible stain on his otherwise stellar political career.

*Guantanamo Bay Detainees Case:* Rasul v. Bush *(2004).* Following the terrorist attacks of September 11, 2001, which killed nearly 2,800 people in the World Trade Center in New York City, the Pentagon in Washington DC, and a hijacked jetliner that crashed in Pennsylvania, President George W. Bush sought and Congress authorized the use of force against the perpetrators of this senseless violence in the American homeland. Many fingers pointed immediately at Osama bin Laden (a disgruntled Muslim ideologue from a wealthy Saudi Arabian family) and his Al-Qaeda network, a shadowy organization headquartered at the time in Afghanistan and bent on waging a holy war against the West, particularly the United States, for its support of Israel and the government of Saudi Arabia (the site of the holy pilgrimage, the Hajj). In the course of U.S. military hostilities against Al-Qaeda and their Taliban supporters in Afghanistan in 2002, several foreign nationals were arrested by U.S. forces.

Approximately 640 of these foreign nationals were detained indefinitely at the U.S. Naval Base at Guantanamo Bay, Cuba, for questioning. All but three of these detainees were not charged with any wrongdoing but were denied access to legal counsel and to American courts for redress of their grievances. Instead, the Bush administration formed military tribunals to try the detainees. Because such a tribunal lacked transparency, the policy was severely criticized by international human rights organizations and by members of Congress who feared that prisoners would not receive proper due process befitting U.S. democratic ideals.

George W. Bush and his advisors labeled the detainees "enemy combatants" because they are not attached to an organized army of any particular state. Top administration officials and key architects of the war, including Vice President Dick Chaney, Defense Secretary Donald Rumsfeld, and White House Counsel Alberto Gonzalez argued forcefully that as enemy combatants, the detainees were not entitled to protections that international treaties such as the Geneva Convention afforded captured soldiers in wartime. The administration also contended that the civilian court system is out of limits for use by the detainees to seek redress. Plaintiff Shafiq Rasul, a British detainee, and many other foreign nationals, including 2 Australians and 12 Kuwaitis, brought a consolidated suit against President George W. Bush in *Rasul v. Bush*[57] to address the question whether U.S. civilian courts lacked jurisdiction to consider challenges to legality of detainees of foreign nationals captured abroad in connection with hostilities, and incarcerated at the Guantanamo Naval Base in Cuba.

On June 28, 2004, the Supreme Court rejected the administration's claims. The Court held that foreign nationals imprisoned without charge at the Guantanamo Bay interrogation camps were entitled to bring legal action in federal civilian courts to challenge their detention. The decision was a major setback for the administration's terrorism policies. In a broader sense, the decision again makes it clear that government policies that contravene U.S. constitutional tenets are subject to judicial rebuke.

## CONSTRAINTS ON THE EXERCISE OF JUDICIAL POWER

Just as there are limits on the exercise of presidential power as the above examples show, so too are there limits on the exercise of judicial power. Even though the Supreme Court is well recognized as a powerful institution in American politics, its authority is not absolute.

There are a number of institutional weaknesses that limit the Court's ability to exercise its power broadly. The *first* limitation concerns the nature of the judicial function itself: the inability to initiate litigation. In our judicial system, justices cannot initiate litigation on their own to influence public policy. Instead, they must await the opportunity when legal controversies come through the courthouse gate. The essence of this constraint is that a controversy must be justiciable in the eyes of the law. That is, the controversy must be real and resolvable by a court of law. In *Aetna Life*

*Insurance v. Howarth* (1937), the Court explained that a real controversy is

> One that is appropriate for judicial determination. A justiciable controversy is thus distinguished from a difference or dispute of hypothetical or abstract character; from one that is academic or moot... The controversy must be definite and concrete, touching the legal relations of parties having adverse legal interests.[58]

This quotation indicates that the Court cannot review cases that are merely hypothetical, too abstract to be understood by the public, or moot (i.e., the conflict has seized to exist).

A *second* constraint on the exercise of judicial power concerns the legal rights of those who can sue. The Supreme Court cannot decide cases where the parties lack standing to sue. *Standing* simply means that parties to a case have a direct stake in the outcome. There must be an identifiable winner and loser to a conflict before the principle of standing can be invoked. Moot and standing go hand in hand. Take the case of *Roe v. Wade* (1973), for example. When this case was filed at the Supreme Court in 1971, "Jane Roe" had already delivered her baby and had given the baby up for adoption. Technically, she no longer had a stake in the outcome at that point and the case had become moot because the issue of whether or not she should be allowed to have an abortion no longer exists. Under normal circumstances, the Court would have dismissed the case. But *Roe* was filed as a class action lawsuit on behalf of women who were currently pregnant or planning to become pregnant. As a result, the legal controversy in the case remained alive as the case went to Court. "Jane Roe" and the class of women who brought the case thus retained standing.

Third, the Court lacks the capacity to enforce its own decisions. The enforcement of the famous civil rights case, *Brown v. Board of Education* (1954), provides a telling example of this constraint on Supreme Court's ability to exercise its power. When the Court ruled in *Brown* that "in the field of public education, separate but equal has no place," theoretically bringing an end to segregated public schools in the United States, the decision was met with tremendous opposition, particularly from citizens and politicians from Southern states.

According to Professor Gerald Rosenberg of the University of Chicago, the Supreme Court is constrained and, therefore, is unable to produce significant social change in public education or any other field of human endeavor since justices lack the capacity to enforce their own decisions.[59] Rosenberg demonstrated that it was not until the White House and Congress intervened in the implementation of *Brown* that some progress was made in public school integration. First, President Lyndon B. Johnson sent federal troops to Little Rock, Arkansas, to enforce a district court order ending segregation in public education. Second, Congress enacted the Civil Rights Act of 1964, authorizing the Department of Health, Education, and Welfare to withhold federal funding from any school district that fails to integrate its public schools. Only through these extrajudicial measures did integration actually begin in earnest.

Finally, Congress can limit the appellate jurisdiction of the Supreme Court and this is a major constraint on the Court's ability to exercise its power. Although Congress has given the Court almost complete control to decide which cases to hear, the power to determine what kind of cases the Supreme Court can hear under its appellate jurisdiction ultimately rests with Congress. The Constitution authorizes Congress to control the power of the Court to hear appeals. Thus within the Court's appellate jurisdiction, Congress can expand or limit areas where the Court can hear and decide cases. For example, on March 27, 1869, Congress repealed the Habeas Corpus Act of 1867, thereby preventing the Supreme Court from hearing a class of cases involving prisoner rights. That action was prompted by the prosecution of William McCardle, a journalist accused of publishing incendiary and libelous articles urging resistance to civil war reconstruction laws. As the Supreme Court considered McCardle's case (*ExParte McCardle*),[60] reports circulated that the justices were leaning in favor of McCardle. In an action meant to punish the Court, Congress preempted the Court's decision by stripping the Court of its jurisdiction to hear and decide the case and others like it. The Supreme Court was forced to dismiss the case for want of subject-matter jurisdiction.

## CONCLUSION

This chapter forms the basic foundation for understanding the Supreme Court from an evolutionary perspective. We examined several fundamental concepts and developments, including the origins of the Court's power, its struggle to secure judicial independence in the face of repeated attacks from anti-Federalists, and the formation of the federal judicial structure. We examined the question of whether the Supreme Court is still the least dangerous branch as envisioned by the founding fathers. There is significant evidence to suggest that the framers may have grossly underestimated the judiciary's power of judgment when they concluded that the judiciary was the "least dangerous" branch. This is not to suggest that the Court is dangerous but that it has the tools to be dangerous to the political rights of the Constitution.

In its recent history, the Court has faithfully patrolled the boundaries of the Constitution. It has been instrumental in the reformation of civil rights, criminal justice, individual privacy, religious freedom, environmental policy, and many more. Some groups have benefited while have suffered from the Court's decisions, which is inevitable. Finally, we presented historical instances that point to the supremacy of the Supreme Court and discussed ways in which the Court is constrained in its exercise of judicial power.

# SUPREME COURT VACANCIES

*I am old. I'm getting older and coming apart.*

On June 27, 1991, Justice Thurgood Marshall, the first African American ever appointed to the U.S. Supreme Court, sent a short letter to President George H.W. Bush announcing his retirement from the Court. The announcement gave rise to one of the increasingly rare events in modern politics: a vacancy on the Supreme Court.

In his letter, Marshall stated that "The strenuous demands of Court work and its related duties expected of a justice appear at this time to be incompatible with my advancing age and medical condition." He added that he would retire "as soon as a successor is qualified."[1] Retirement announcements are highly infrequent events in the Supreme Court. They are made by justices reluctantly and only after very careful and personal reflection. Marshall's announcement was no exception and it came just four days before his 83rd birthday. Asked by a newspaper reporter why he was retiring and if he could share some medical facts, Marshall responded: "I am old. I'm getting older and coming apart."[2] The announcement signaled the culmination of an illustrious career in which the boisterous defender of the Constitution and former civil rights activist served as leader and chief legal strategist for the Legal Defense Fund of the National Association for the Advancement of Colored People (NAACP), judge on the Court of Appeals for the Second Circuit, solicitor general of the United States, and associate justice of the Supreme Court.

Marshall received rapid professional advancement in two Democratic administrations in the 1960s. In September 1961, President John F. Kennedy appointed him to a seat on the Court of Appeals for the Second Circuit over the objection of his brother Attorney General Robert Kennedy who was concerned about the political cost of getting Marshall confirmed in the Senate.[3] Located in New York City with jurisdiction over New York, Connecticut, and Vermont, the Court decides a large number of highly important business and tax cases, so an appointment there is considered a high honor.

Despite fierce opposition from Southern senators who decried Marshall's activism on civil rights, the Senate confirmed Marshall by a vote of 54 to 16. All 16 nay votes were cast by Southern Democratic senators led by James

**Photo 2.1**  Associate Justice Thurgood Marshall. Collection of the Supreme Court of the United States.

Eastland of Mississippi, who suggested that Marshall was unfit to be a federal judge because he was linked to "radical elements" in society.[4] Four years later in 1965, acting upon the suggestion of his attorney general, Nicholas Katzenbach, President Lyndon B. Johnson convinced Marshall to give up his judgeship, along with the security of lifetime employment, and take a pay cut to serve as solicitor general in his administration. There Marshall would represent the U.S. government in the Supreme Court. "I want folks to walk down the hall at the Justice Department and see a [black man] sitting there," Johnson reportedly said.[5] Marshall was known internationally as "Mr. Civil

Rights";[6] he was widely recognized as "a man who has used [the Constitution] more than any American who ever lived to try to widen the parameters of freedom in America."[7]

The appointment would give Marshall greater exposure to constitutional, statutory, and international law, especially in important national issues other than civil rights. His annual salary would be cut 16 percent, from the $33,000 he earned as a circuit court judge to the $28,500 he would earn as the government's top lawyer, and it carried no employment guarantee. Moreover, only three former solicitors general in history have risen to become Supreme Court justices: William Howard Taft, Stanley Reed, and Robert H. Jackson. Marshall would make only the fourth.

Marshall would later recall that there was no quid pro quo involved in his appointment as solicitor general, no promise of a later elevation to the Supreme Court. Marshall's recollection was later confirmed by President Johnson himself, although Johnson did indeed hold a single-minded focus on Marshall for possible elevation to the Supreme Court.[8] The first president to introduce affirmative action into the American political lexicon, Johnson also obsessed about being the first president to appoint an African American to the Supreme Court. It helps greatly that Marshall's legal experience and qualification were not in doubt in the eyes of neutral observers. He was a first-rate lawyer, and as the grandson of slaves had a unique background among past solicitors general. About two years later in 1967, Johnson made appointment history by naming Marshall to the Supreme Court but only after Marshall overcame even more vociferous opposition from Southern senators. He was confirmed by a comfortable 69–11 margin on August 30, 1967. Clearly among the most influential lawyers in American society during the 20th century, Marshall went on to serve with distinction in the High Court for 24 years.

Outside the Court, Marshall's retirement announcement was a stunning surprise for many like-minded liberals who had hoped, as Marshall himself had always maintained, that he would serve out his term, a life term, and that he would not quit until the ideologically suitable president occupied the White House to name his successor. Thus when Marshall was hospitalized with pneumonia in 1970 at the Navy Medical Center in Bethesda, Maryland, Chief Justice Warren Burger notified President Richard Nixon about Marshall's medical condition. Nixon was apparently so eager to appoint someone to the Court that he called an officer at the Bethesda Naval Hospital for a prognosis. The officer requested permission from Marshall to send the medical information. Sensing that Nixon might have ulterior motives, Marshall gave the officer permission to send Nixon the report, but only after Marshall wrote on the folder the words "not yet!!!" in large black script.[9] The two-word message was clear: Marshall had no intention of vacating his seat during the Nixon administration.

That was not the only instance in which Marshall made known his desire for a like-minded successor. Disheartened by the social policies of the Reagan administration in the 1980s, Marshall reportedly joked to his law clerks that should he die in office during the Reagan years (1981–1988), they should "prop him up" and keep on writing opinions.[10] Marshall's reluctance to retire during a Republican administration underscores the importance of politics and ideology in the Supreme Court and the interplay of politics and ideology in the Court's relationship with Congress and the White House.

Ultimately, one must ask why Marshall, who openly vowed not to retire during a Republican administration, actually retired in 1991 during the reign of conservative President George H.W. Bush. Clearly Marshall's failing health contributed to his decision to retire earlier than he had intended. But poor health is not the sole explanation. According to Columbia law professor Eben Moglen, Marshall's former law clerk, another key reason Marshall retired when he did was the changed ideological center of gravity in the Court. As the only true liberal remaining on the Court in the late 1980s and early 1990s, Marshall realized that he could no longer prevail in privacy, civil rights, and individual liberties cases, which left him isolated and uncomfortable in the Court.[11] In his last opinion delivered from the bench, dissenting in *Payne v. Tennessee* (a case about the admissibility of victim impact statements in capital trials), Marshall lamented that "Power, not reason is the new currency of this Court's decision making." Marshall went on to blast the Rehnquist Court (of which he was a part) for sending "a clear signal that essentially *all* decisions implementing the personal liberties protected by the Bill of Rights and the Fourteenth Amendment are open to reconsideration."[12]

Seen in this context, Marshall's retirement announcement raises a number of interesting questions about the politics of judicial retirement. In this chapter, we discuss the nature of Supreme Court vacancies by addressing the following questions:

1. What is the frequency of vacancies in the Supreme Court overtime?
2. What is the distribution of vacancies across presidential administrations?
3. What are the ways through which vacancies emerge in the Supreme Court?
4. What explains the decision of Supreme Court justices to retire from the bench?

A president can make elaborate plans to appoint the most able jurist, the most admired statesman/woman, or the most active party line ideologue to the Supreme Court. But without a vacancy, there would be no nomination for the president to make, no confirmation hearings to hold in the U.S. Senate, and no legacy for the president to contemplate.

As with many aspects of the Court, the creation of vacancies has undergone significant transformation. While death in office was the most common means of vacancy creation in the 19th century, retirement became the most frequent method of vacancy creation in the 20th century. Keep in mind throughout this discussion that much like any other important event in American government, politics is and always will remain an integral part of the creation of judicial vacancies and the selection of justices to fill those vacancies. After all, the Supreme Court is where ultimate judicial power is exercised by a very small cadre of thoughtful elites who are themselves jousting for influence in constructing the Constitution's meaning and the content of national political discourse.

## THE FREQUENCY OF SUPREME COURT VACANCIES

Until 2006, a total of 124 vacancies emerged in the Supreme Court, about one in every two years.[13] Early on in the Court's history, vacancies occurred more frequently than in later periods because of justices dying in office. For instance, from 1789 to 1900, the Court registered 32 deaths in office, whereas from 1901 to 2006, that number dropped to only 17.[14] A lack of retirement benefits forced justices to linger on the bench well past their productive years. Moreover, medical treatment was rudimentary, making it common for justices to fall ill and die on the bench.

In contrast, vacancies have emerged less frequently during the 20th century. Again, part of the explanation for this infrequency is related to health and longevity. According to the National Center for Health Statistics, the average life expectancy of Americans has increased by 30 years since the turn of the century. A U.S. resident born in 1900 could have expected to live only 47.3 years, whereas one born in 2005 could expect to live 77.8 years.[15] This rise in longevity has obvious implications for the Supreme Court: justices are living longer and serving longer, some to the point of mental decrepitude.[16] Improvements in health benefits have allowed justices to remain on the bench longer and in relatively good health without facing a serious threat of involuntary departure.

In the half-century extending from the start of Dwight Eisenhower's presidency in 1953 to the end of George W. Bush in 2008, the number of vacancies in the Court dropped significantly to only 25 compared to vacancies in administrations spread across all previous 50-year intervals. Overall, this indicates increased stability in Court personnel over time.

In that vein, one of the remarkable developments in modern Supreme Court tenure is the apparent disappearance of short-term justices, those who serve for a term of seven years or less.[17] The development has significant implications for (1) the heated controversy surrounding modern nominations to the Court: increased turnover may reduce the stakes of judicial appointments and, therefore, depoliticize the process; (2) the responsiveness or majoritarian nature of the Court: more frequent appointment will bring to the Court individuals who reflect the majority's will, making the Court more representative; and (3) ameliorate the problem of mental decrepitude: frequent turnover will bring new energy and vigor to the Court along with new constitutional ideas.

We can derive a better sense of the infrequency of vacancies in the Supreme Court by making a comparison to congressional vacancies. Unlike Congress that has 435 elected members and thus a relatively high probability of turnover through electoral defeat, retirement, resignations, or death, the Supreme Court has a maximum of only nine justices. Consequently, the probability of there being a vacancy in any specific year or period is much lower than in Congress. Moreover, members of Congress must obtain voter approval to remain in office (every two years for House members and every six for U.S. senators). In contrast, Supreme Court justices are appointed, and they serve during good behavior (i.e., practically for life) under Article 3 of the Constitution. Both the relatively small membership of the Court and the constitutional guarantee of lifetime employment help make Supreme Court vacancies truly rare events, which often leave some presidents disappointed for being denied an opportunity to appoint a Supreme Court justice.

## DISTRIBUTION OF VACANCIES ACROSS PRESIDENTIAL ADMINISTRATIONS

Historically, Supreme Court vacancies are staggered across presidential administrations. They occur unsystematically without being biased in favor of certain presidents based on party affiliation or geographic region. Most presidents have received at least one opportunity to nominate a Supreme Court justice. The vast majority of these nominees are confirmed. Two notable aspects of Supreme Court vacancies are the number and timing of vacancies. For presidents, there is an element of luck in each.

### Number of Vacancies

Some presidents are more fortunate than others when it comes to the number of Supreme Court vacancies that emerge during their tenure in the White House. President George Washington (Federalist Party), who led the nation through its formative years after independence, received 11 vacancies, the highest for any president. However, his nominee for chief justice, John Rutledge, was rejected by the Senate in 1795. Franklin Delano Roosevelt (Democratic Party, 1933–1945) comes in second, receiving nine Supreme Court vacancies. All his nominees were confirmed. Third was Andrew Jackson (1829–1937), who received seven vacancies and successfully appointed six justices. His nomination of Roger Brook Taney in 1935 was postponed indefinitely. Finally among the leaders, William H. Taft (Republican Party, 1909–1913) received six vacancies and all his nominees were confirmed. From 1789 to 2008, 10 U.S. presidents each received only one vacancy on the Court and 11 presidents were each granted two vacancies.[18]

Figure 2.1 shows the range of vacancy fortunes and the number of presidents who received vacancies within each range. Whereas the two most fortunate presidents in terms of vacancies (Washington and FDR) were endowed with 9–10 vacancies, most presidents received either 1 or 2 vacancies. At the caboose of the Supreme Court vacancy train are four presidents who received zero vacancies. William Henry Harrison (Whig Party) became president in

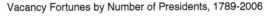

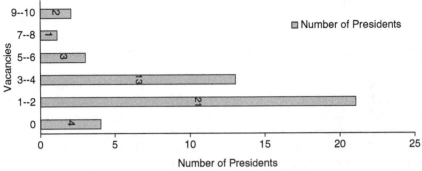

Figure 2.1   Vacancy Fortunes by Number of Presidents, 1789–2006.

February 1841 only to die of pneumonia two months later. Zachary Taylor (Whig Party) served only one year (1849–1850) and died in office of food poisoning after becoming gravely ill from consuming a hasty snack of "iced milk" and "generous quantities of cherries" at the White House after participating in an oppressively hot July Fourth celebration connected with the laying of the foundation of the Washington Monument.[19] Andrew Johnson (Democratic Party) was denied a vacancy by political circumstances. He was unpopular in Congress and his impeachment by the House of Representatives further damaged that relationship. Congress reduced the size of the justices on the Supreme Court from 10 to 7 in 1866 to spite Johnson and prevent him from filling several Supreme Court vacancies. Finally, Jimmy Carter (Democratic Party) was unlucky, a victim of Justice Potter Stewart's strategic retirement. Carter served one full term (1977–1981)[20] but was denied a Supreme Court vacancy. Thus the first notable aspect of Supreme Court vacancies is how many a president receives and this contributes toward establishing presidential legacy on the Court.

## Timing of Vacancies

Another noteworthy aspect of Supreme Court vacancies is the timing of vacancies in a presidential administration. Some presidents were blessed with a Supreme Court vacancy almost as soon as they assumed their office-whereas others waited much longer with hopeful anticipation. One of the immediate actions taken by President George Washington as soon as he came to power was to appoint six members of the original Supreme Court. More recent historical examples of presidents who were rewarded with vacancies soon after they ascended onto the presidency include Dwight Eisenhower who appointed chief justice Earl Warren during his first year as president. President Harry S. Truman is another. He had his first vacancy just three months after assuming the presidency in April 1945; he appointed Senator Harold H. Burton (R-OH). President Ronald Reagan's appointment of Sandra Day O'Connor also came within months after he won the White House in 1980.

Presidents who waited a long time before being presented with an opportunity to appoint a Supreme Court justice include Franklin D. Roosevelt and George W. Bush; they waited their entire first term in office and experienced better luck only thereafter.

The lack of vacancies on the Court during any presidential administration has the effect of lengthening *natural courts* (the interval in years without any membership change in the Court). The Supreme Court experienced its longest 9-member natural court in history (11 years), starting with the appointment by Bill Clinton of Justice Stephen Breyer in 1994 and ending with the appointment by George W. Bush of Chief Justice John G. Roberts in 2005. There was only one natural court in which the justices stayed together longer—for 11 years and 44 days—but that was a 7-member court that existed during the reign of Chief Justice John Marshall from 1812 to 1823.[21]

Supreme Court vacancies represent an opportunity for the nation's political leaders to renew and reinvigorate the intellectual energy and chemistry within the Court and, possibly, to alter the Court's legal traditions and overall direction. Vacancies are sufficiently important to become the subject of extensive research and debate among political scientists, legal scholars, and Court watchers. It is from this research and debate that we now know a great deal about the workings of the U.S. Supreme Court and its place in the political system.

## METHODS FOR CREATING SUPREME COURT VACANCIES

There are several methods through which vacancies emerge in the Supreme Court. Table 2.1 lists these methods along with the number of times in history each method has produced a vacancy on the Court. The methods are grouped here into three categories: (1) voluntary departures from the bench; (2) involuntary departures; and (3) legislation. As we consider these methods, keep in mind that an undercurrent of politics permeates each.

**Table 2.1**  How Supreme Court Vacancies are Created, 1789–2009

| Category | Method | Number of Occurrences |
| --- | --- | --- |
| Voluntary departures | Retirement | 39 |
| | Resignation | 20 |
| | Elevation | 3 |
| Involuntary departures | Death in office | 49 |
| | Chronic Disability | 4 |
| | Senate rejection for chief justice | 1 |
| Legislation | Law creating new vacancies | 11 |

*Source*: Data compiled by author from Warren Burger, *The Supreme Court of the United States: Its Beginnings and its Justices, 1790–1991,* pp. 274–277; *New York Times,* announcing the death in office of Chief Justice William H. Rehnquist, September 4, 2005. Figure for retirement includes Justices White (retired 1993), Blackmun (retired 1994), O'Connor (retired 2006), and Souter (retired 2009).

## Voluntary Departures from the Bench

Voluntary departures from the bench occur when a justice retires, resigns, or is promoted from associate to chief justice. Thus the justice willingly vacates the seat, making it available to a new appointee. During the 20th century, the most frequent mode of departure from the Supreme Court was through voluntary means. But many justices find it difficult to step aside. For example, Justice Blackmun explained his reason to retire this way: "it's not easy to step aside, but I know what the numbers are, and it's time."[22] The "numbers" referred to his age at the time, which was 85 years.

In the late 19th century, justices had to remain on the job for financial reasons; however, this was not the case during the past 50 years. Justices of recent vintage stayed because they enjoyed their work and thought they can still do it effectively. The availability of law clerks and secretaries in a justice's chambers makes this explanation even more plausible. Justices also stayed because of party or ideology. Finally, the increasing prestige of the Supreme Court means that justices have become very influential in American life. As a result, they have been reluctant to leave because doing so would mean a loss of status.

### *Retirement*

Retirements offer an intergenerational explanation for the creation of Supreme Court vacancies whereby older and experienced justices voluntarily depart, having reached the end of their professional careers, and are replaced presumably by younger, more energetic individuals. Among the different modes of voluntary departures identified above, retirement is the most frequent exit method that has been employed by justices during the 20th century. As seen through Justice Marshall's announcement, the constitutional requirement of life tenure gives justices significant control and flexibility to voluntarily step down at a time of their choosing. An extensive line of legal and political science research into judicial retirement suggests multiple explanations for why justices choose to retire when they do. The strongest explanations are based upon political, economic, and personal reasons.

#### Political Influences on the Retirement decision

There is little doubt that political context either within the Court or outside it plays a significant role in the decision of justices to retire from the bench. One example of political context within the Court is ideological compatibility with other justices. As we saw at the beginning of the chapter, Justice Thurgood Marshall is a case in point. Although old age played a substantial role in his retirement decision, Marshall's ideological incompatibility with the Court's conservative majority during the late 1980s and early 1990s contributed significantly to his decision to retire.[23] But the role of internal politics that we observe in Marshall's case is not the whole story.

The influence of politics can also come from outside the Court and take several forms, including external political pressure from the president, impeachment threat, and anticipatory reaction from key political actors such as president, Congress, and organized groups.

Although justices can retire whenever they choose, presidents often wish to influence that retirement decision by applying pressure. If presidents succeed, they would have a vacancy that they can fill with someone who better shares their judicial philosophy. During the early 1960s, President Kennedy successfully persuaded moderate conservative Justice Felix Frankfurter to retire after poor health decreased his effectiveness. Kennedy appointed a more liberal justice, Arthur Goldberg, to replace Frankfurter. In the late 1970s, Justice Thurgood Marshall resisted effort by the Carter administration to pressure him to retire.[24]

Perhaps the most audacious pressure tactic was that of President Lyndon Johnson. In 1967, Johnson persuaded Justice Tom Clark to retire by enticing him with an offer he could not resist. The president promised to appoint Justice Clark's son, William Ramsey Clark, to be attorney general if the elder Clark would retire from the Court. The attorney general heads the Justice Department and occasionally argues cases before the Supreme Court. Since the Justice Department, through the Office of the Solicitor General, is responsible for bringing federal cases before the Court, it would be a direct violation of the cannons of judicial ethics for Justice Clark to rule on cases in which his own son participated. Therefore, Clark agreed to resign paving way for his son to become U.S. attorney general.

While in retirement, Clark continued to serve episodically as a federal judge in the lower courts; he did so under a 1937 law that permits former Supreme Court justices to remain federal judges (if they choose).[25] Clark had a long judicial career in retirement. He sat by designation in various appeals Court panels and contributed to approximately 380 available Court decisions. He wrote majority opinions in 70 of these cases and 24 were appealed to the Supreme Court. The Court granted certiorari in three cases and reversed Justice Clark's opinion in two of these three cases.[26] The two cases were *Hazelwood School District v. United States* appealed from the Eighth Circuit and *Secretary of the Navy v. Avrech* appealed from the DC Circuit. The justices did not mention in either decision that they were reviewing the opinion of a retired colleague.[27]

The examples enumerated above of political pressure to retire are quite tame. Indeed, more vituperative means exists, including the threat of impeachment, a traumatic and politically spellbinding and divisive event. Although only one Supreme Court Justice (Samuel Chase) has been impeached, several attempts have nonetheless been made. Justice William O. Douglas was 78 years old and in poor health in the 1970s when he was tagged for impeachment by the Nixon administration. Yet, he spitefully refused to retire in order to deny President Nixon the opportunity of naming his replacement.

Douglas was no friend of Richard Nixon or his successor Gerald Ford, and for good reason. As part of his grand strategy to remake the U.S. Supreme Court by infusing it with "law and order" justices, Nixon in

**Photo 2.2**  Associate Justice William O. Douglas. Harris & Ewing, Collection of the Supreme Court of the United States.

1970 initiated a campaign to oust liberal justices and replace them with conservatives. In that sense, the Nixon administration marks a significant break with the past. Nixon was the first president at least in the post–World War II era to dramatically raise the role of ideology in judicial selection.[28] Nixon targeted Justice Douglas for removal because of his opposition to Douglas' liberalism. The impeachment effort ultimately failed. But what were the charges? The administration claimed that Douglas wrote articles unbefitting a Supreme Court justice and that Douglas accepted money illegally from the Albert Parvin Foundation in which he was a board member while serving on the Court.[29] In truth, while the board membership may have been unethical, it was neither illegal nor unusual among justices at the time. As Watergate insider John Dean reported, even conservative Chief Justice Warren Burger who served on the Court with Douglas had similar arrangements.[30]

Nixon's attempt to remove Douglass could not have advanced far without significant support from key officials in his administration and in Congress. Nixon relied on his Justice Department, particularly the FBI and its director J. Edgar Hoover, to produce evidence in the form of wiretapped conversations of Douglas.[31] Meanwhile, the drive to impeach Douglas was being directed by Congressman Gerald Ford (R-MI) in the House of Representatives. Ford held a powerful position as the House Minority Whip at the time. He would eventually become president in 1974 after Richard Nixon resigned in disgrace over the Watergate scandal.

Under the Constitution, only the House of Representatives is authorized to draft Articles of Impeachment against high-ranking federal officials. Ford introduced a resolution charging that Douglas had engaged in "fractious behavior" and that he wrote articles that appeared in "a pornographic magazine with a portfolio of obscene photographs on one side of it."[32] A special House committee failed to approve the resolution. The entire episode was designed to influence the composition of the Supreme Court by forcing Douglas into early retirement so that Nixon can appoint his replacement. Overall, Nixon's clandestine activities in the Douglas impeachment drive had the unintended consequences of actually hardening Douglas's resolve to not retire. He felt that should he succumb to the pressure during the Nixon or Ford administration, the president will "appoint some bastard" to replace him and he was unwilling to let that happen.

Thus Douglas stayed on for ideological reasons. He tried to time his retirement to coincide with a Democratic president in the White House. But too sick and too weak to continue in office following a massive stroke in 1974, Douglas eventually took his doctor's advice and retired from the bench in 1975, reluctantly giving Gerald Ford the appointment.

But presidents do not always get what they want in the justices they appoint. Justice John Paul Stevens whom President Ford appointed to replace Douglas is today one of the leading liberals on the Court. In that sense, Douglass should be resting peacefully in his grave, having realized his wish posthumously. Overall, his bitter struggle against impeachment demonstrates how the confluence of politics and ideology can affect a justice's decision to remain on the Court until uncontrollable political or personal circumstances intervene to tip the scale in favor of retirement.

Douglas was certainly not alone in attempting to time his retirement. Political scientists label such ideologically motivated behavior *strategic retirement*. Under strategic retirement, a justice is more likely to retire if the president is of the same political party as the justice. A justice planning on retiring strategically is disappointed if uncontrollable circumstances compel him or her to retire prematurely. After Marshall announced his retirement, he was interviewed by a newspaper reporter on June 29, 1991 and was asked to examine his legal career and name the things he will remember most about serving on the Supreme Court, Justice Marshall responded:

> I don't look back, I look forward...[What] I do know was each job I got was tougher than the one I had before, and *I just retired the wrong direction*, that's all. (emphasis added)[33]

This is clear evidence that Marshall was planning on retiring strategically and was disappointed that he failed.

An important characteristic of strategic retirement is that the retiring justices anticipate the actions of important external actors, especially the president and Congress, and that the justice is satisfied with what that expected reaction would be. Take Justice Sandra Day O'Connor for example. O'Connor was a moderate conservative during the Rehnquist Court and the first woman ever appointed to the Supreme Court. She served for 25 years, from 1981 to 2006. Although her husband, John, was suffering from Alzheimer's disease in the 1990s during her final years on the Court, O'Connor did not retire. Part of the explanation is that a Democrat, Bill Clinton, was in the White House. She anticipated leaving if the next president was Republican. It was not surprising that on election night November 7, 2000, Justice O'Connor became visibly upset and exclaimed "That's terrible" when CBS News anchorman, Dan Rather, announced that the battleground state of Florida had gone to Democrat Al Gore.[34] But to O'Connor's eventual delight, it turned out that Rather's pronouncement was premature.

The Supreme Court, with O'Connor voting with the majority, would later settle the election in favor of Republican George W. Bush. After Bush was reelected in 2004, O'Connor decided it was time to retire, making it possible for Bush to appoint her successor. She tendered her retirement letter in summer 2005 and left the Court in January 2006. The delay was the result of political circumstances. President George W. Bush was unpopular because of the war in Iraq and was being deserted even by his conservative base. His first nominee to replace O'Connor (White House Counsel Harriet Miers) withdrew on October 27, 2005 due to strong opposition from conservatives who considered Miers a crony of George Bush and a constitutional lightweight whose position on cultural issues such as homosexuality, abortion, affirmative action, and the commingling of church and state was either insufficiently conservative or doubtful. But more damaging to Miers' chances for confirmation was her total lack of judicial experience. This is exemplified by the commentary of conservative columnist George F. Will: "there is no evidence that [Miers] is among the leading lights of American jurisprudence, or that she possesses talents commensurate with the Supreme Court's tasks. The president's 'argument' for her amounts to: trust me. There is no reason to."[35] Historically, the lack of judicial experience had not been the death knell of Supreme Court nominees. Indeed, nearly 40 percent of all justices lacked prior judicial experience when nominated, but times have changed. The trend over the past 35 years has been for Supreme Court nominees to work their way up through the federal bench to the Supreme Court. Ultimately, Miers' nomination failed and Judge Samuel Alito of the Third Circuit Court of Appeals was appointed to replace O'Connor in January 2006.

The literature on strategic retirement is in a state of flux. Some researchers have argued forcefully that Supreme Court justices truly engage in strategic retirement and that strategic retirements have become a regular occurrence in modern Supreme Court eras. According to some researchers, 75 percent of justices who left voluntarily between 1937 and 2003 did so strategically.[36] O'Connor's retirement is the most recent demonstration of this trend. Other researchers suggest, however, that strategic retirement is a myth. They instead argue justices retire primarily because of ill health or improvement in retirement benefits.[37] The retirements of liberal justices such as Thurgood Marshall and William O. Douglas during conservative administrations provide good illustrations of departure prompted partly by poor health. These and many other instances suggest that the evidence for strategic retirement in the Supreme Court is inconclusive.

Economic Factors in Retirement Decisions

Another major factor contributing to retirement is *improvement in economic benefits* granted to federal employees such as bureaucrats, judges, members of congress, and their staff. Although political motivations remain a matter of controversy in retirement decisions, there is little disagreement that pocketbook issues featured prominently in the decision of many justices to remain on the bench or retire.

Until 1869, federal judges did not receive retirement benefits such as pension and healthcare from the federal government and social security benefits that today augment the retirement savings of elderly Americans. Consequently, many federal judges and Supreme Court justices remained on the job well past retirement age and well past their prime as judges.

However, the reluctance to leave the bench was not because justices lived in a lap of luxury. Indeed, they were living in a state of glorified poverty, being deprived of the necessities and comforts of life because their salaries were very low compared to salaries they could command in the private sector. At the Court's inception in 1789, the five associate justices received $3500 in annual salary, while the Chief Justice received $4000 split into four quarterly payments.[38] Over the next 30 years, other federal government officials received pay increases while the justices did not. Justice Joseph Story would later remark that justices were "starving in splendid poverty," yet Congress did nothing.[39] Indeed, today Supreme Court salaries remain substantially lower than the average salary of law school deans, lower than the average for associates in large law firms, and significantly lower than the average salary of general counsels in Fortune 500 corporations (excluding annual bonuses!). Interestingly, even Supreme Court law clerks who move into private practice after their one-year clerkship now routinely receive salary offers and signing bonuses that, when combined, provide substantially higher pay than justices for whom they clerked. No doubt, there is high demand for this top talent. In 2005, Supreme Court clerks hired at top Washington DC law firms received a salary of $150,000 plus a signing bonus of around $200,000, enough to make justices jealous.[40]

Because of the lack of pension, finding jurists on the bench who were senile and incoherent was a common feature of the federal judicial landscape. One example was Supreme Court Justice Robert Grier (1848–1870), who at age 75 was so weak and infirm that he required physical assistance to sit in his chair during Court sessions and he admitted being unable to walk or hold a pencil to jot down notes. By his colleagues' account Justice Grier's mind was "getting a little muddy."[41] Because this state of affairs threatened the effective dissemination of justice and public confidence in the Supreme Court, pressure mounted on Congress to act.

After 70 years Congress acquiesced, and research suggests that improvements in retirement benefits for federal judges are among the strongest motivations driving justices into retirement.[42] Relief came after Congress succumbed to pressure from federal judges and included a provision in the Judiciary Act of 1869, giving judges who reached the age of 70 and had served for at least 10 years the right to receive their current salary for life upon retirement. Many justices moved quickly to take advantage of the improved situation. Not surprisingly, only days after the law took effect, Justice Grier tendered his retirement. But Grier was hardly alone in acting quickly. By one estimate, the number of judicial retirements more than tripled after the law took effect.[43]

Retirement benefits were further improved in 1954 and then in 1984, making it possible for federal judges who reach 65 years of age and have accumulated 15 years of service to retire and continue to receive their full salary for life as well as full retirement benefits if the combination of the justice's age and the number of years of service on the bench totaled 80 or more.[44] This *"rule of 80"* led to scores of retirement of lower federal court judges mostly appointed by Democratic presidents over the years and gave then President Ronald Reagan and the Republican-controlled Senate a bonanza of federal judgeships to fill with conservatives.[45]

Personal Factors in Retirement Decisions
The influence of certain personal factors in retirement decisions is incontrovertible. A major personal reason causing justices to retire is infirmities of old age, which accounted for the retirement of many justices, including Oliver Wendell Holmes (1932), Louis Brandies (1939), Charles Evans Hughes (1941), William O. Douglas (1975), William Brennan (1990), and Thurgood Marshall (1991). If a justice is no longer physically able or willing to handle the demands of a burdensome caseload, it is quite fitting for that justice to retire and give others a chance to serve their country.

It is altogether possible that old age might interact with other factors such as a rising caseload to motivate a justice to retire. For example, in 1941 the number of cases filed in the Court was 1302. In 2001, filings jumped to 9174, a 605 percent increase. Even though justices are issuing fewer full opinions than in times past, they still must work hard to keep abreast of this rising case volume. Although a great many older justices are physically active and remain mentally sharp, older justices generally lack the energy and vigor they once possessed to concentrate on a large number of cases during a given Supreme Court term. Thus it is easy to understand why rising workload might figure prominently in an elderly justice's decision to retire.

A second personal reason is family need. Being a justice is a demanding job that typically consumes most of a justice's time and keeps the incumbent away from family members. It is, therefore, logical to expect some justices who have had a long career on the Court to leave for family reasons.

### Resignation

Resignations rank as the second most frequent voluntary means of leaving the High Bench. Before we continue, a clarification is necessary. There is a small but important difference between retirement and resignation. A retirement suggests that the justice has reached the end of a long professional career and, as a matter of personal conviction, either can no longer effectively handle the normal caseload of a justice or desires to spend more time with family and friends. On the other hand, a resignation is a voluntary but premature departure resulting from the intervention of some external force such as an ethics investigation/scandal, political pressure from the president, or a call to serve one's political party in a nonlegal capacity. During the 19th century, resignations were often prompted by the low public esteem of the Court, resulting from poor judicial salaries and circuit riding responsibilities. During the 20th century, justices resigned mostly to serve government in a different capacity.

The normal retirement age in the United States is 65 years but there is no normal resignation age. Justice Benjamin R. Curtis was only 47 years old when he resigned in 1857 because he detested circuit riding duties, the low pay, and his strained social relations on the Court. Justice Arthur Goldberg (1962–1965) was 57 years old and had served only three years when President Lyndon Johnson pressured him to resign and take a United Nations ambassadorship.

Being appointed United Nations representative is an important assignment but one that is notches below a Supreme Court appointment in power and prestige in the United States.[46] But Goldberg, who hoped to be picked as Johnson's running mate in the 1968 presidential campaign, took the job as a show of loyalty to his president and more importantly in hopes of being able to use his new position to pressure the president into withdrawing American troops from the Vietnam War, a war that became increasingly unpopular at home. The president used a carrot-and-stick approach, promising to appoint Goldberg U.S. Ambassador to the United Nations if Goldberg agrees to resign. Had that approach failed the president was intent on relying on his Justice Department to expose Goldberg's potentially inappropriate financial dealings. It was not long before Goldberg resigned and soon thereafter became Ambassador Goldberg.[47]

Goldberg's plans to persuade President Johnson to bring the troops home failed, as did his hope of being selected Johnson's running mate. Seven months before the Johnson administration ended, the president had announced he would not seek reelection, a decision Johnson blamed on Southern disaffection over his appointment of a black man (T. Marshall) to the Court.[48] To make matters worse, American troops remained in Vietnam until well into the Nixon administration in the early 1970s. Upon Goldberg's resignation, Johnson quickly appointed his good friend and legal advisor, Abe Fortas, as replacement. Because Johnson announced that he would forgo a campaign for reelection, he effectively became a lame-duck president.

Despite Johnson's weakened presidency, he ignored possible charges of cronyism and tried to elevate Fortas to the position of chief justice, following the retirement of Earl Warren in 1968. But that effort failed on a tactical Republican filibuster in the Senate.[49] Compounding Justice Fortas's troubles, he would eventually be threatened with impeachment due to ethical malfeasance stemming from his family's financial dealings and money he reportedly received for delivering university lectures while an associate justice. The trauma of the impeachment drive against him along with his rejection for chief justice led Fortas (58 years old) to resign from the Court in 1969 to the elation of Richard Nixon and his Justice Department. As John Dean, former lawyer in the Nixon White House, reported, the Fortas resignation brought jubilation in the attorney general's office that "was capped with a call from the president, congratulating" Justice Department officials "on a job well done."[50]

One cannot say that politics was the main reason Goldberg and Fortas resigned. But politics clearly played a key role. In both instances, President Johnson wanted to reward a political ally, Abe Fortas. He succeeded in driving Goldberg out and making Fortas an associate justice. But he failed to promote him to chief justice. Severely wounded, Fortas, a hero for many liberal causes, became vulnerable to the Nixon impeachment machine and quit.

In the Court's history, we have also witnessed justices who resigned from the Supreme Court to serve their political party in a nonjudicial capacity. The most notable example of this is Charles Evans Hughes, who in 1910 accepted an appointment to the Court from President William Howard Taft. Hughes resigned six years later in response to calls from Republican Party faithful for him to run for president. He campaigned hard against his Democratic opponent, Woodrow Wilson, in 1916 but lost by a mere 13 Electoral College votes. In September 1930, President Hoover appointed Taft Chief Justice of the Supreme Court where he served until his retirement in 1941. Combining his service as both associate and chief justice, Hughes served a total of 30 years in the Supreme Court and is one of only a handful of individuals to serve as both Associate Justice and Chief Justice on the nation's highest Court.

Justices also resign for personal or nonpolitical reasons. The pursuit of "better" professional opportunities outside the Supreme Court is a key personal reason that can motivate a justice to resign. This was common during early American history when the Supreme Court was far less prestigious than it now is. For instance, the pursuit of a more respectable office led John Jay, the nation's first chief justice, to resign in April 1795 to become the governor of New York State. Associate Justice John Rutledge (1789–1791) resigned less than two years after his appointment without taking part in deciding a single case, although he participated in certain Court activities. He resigned to accept the post of chief justice of the Supreme Court of South Carolina.

When Rutledge received word that Jay had resigned following his return from a diplomatic mission to England, Rutledge shamelessly lobbied President Washington for the chief justiceship in a tactless but somewhat effective letter. In the letter, Rutledge suggested that he would have "no objection" to taking Jay's place and that his friends had told him that he had as much "law knowledge" as Jay.[51] Unbelievably, Washington agreed to this lobby and gave Rutledge a recess appointment as chief justice in 1795, ignoring rumors that Rutledge was periodically mentally insane. Rutledge served only four months mostly during the summer of that year before facing Senate confirmation. The Senate refused to confirm him by a vote of 10 to 14, and from the bitter setback, Rutledge tried to drown himself in the Charleston River but was saved by two locals who pulled him out of the water.[52]

### Elevation

Promoting an associate justice to the position of chief justice is rare in Supreme Court selection history but not impossible. Therefore, it represents another way that justices voluntarily leave their seats. Elevations usually allow for a second vacancy to emerge, that of the justice being elevated. Elevations have the tendency to "expose animosities" and provoke "threats of resignation" on the Court.[53] Elevations are also seen as being substantively different from appointment as an associate justice because the chief justice handles administrative and supervisory responsibilities in the Court. Filling the position of chief, therefore, creates greater ideological competition and conflict both in the Court itself and in the Senate than ordinary appointments.[54] This partly explains why historically presidents have been reluctant to elevate from within the Court and why only three vacancies have been created as a result of an associate justice being promoted to chief justice. The three justices were Edward D. White elevated by President William Howard Taft in 1910; Harlan F. Stone elevated by President Franklin D. Roosevelt in 1941; and William H. Rehnquist elevated by President Ronald Reagan in 1986.

## Involuntary Departures

Although uncommon, involuntary departures occur when a Supreme Court justice leaves the Court unwillingly before his or her preferred departure time. Factors contributing to involuntary departures include death while in office, physical disability, and Senate rejection of a justice appointed via recess appointment.

*Death in office.* Throughout the Court's history, death in office has been the single most frequent method by which justices leave the bench. From the installation of the original Jay Court in 1789 to the Roberts Court in 2009 as the Bush administration ended, a total of 49 Supreme Court justices have died while in office (see table 2.2). Justice James Wilson died in office in 1798 becoming the first. In 1869 President Grant nominated Edward M. Stanton to the Court and Stanton was quickly confirmed. However, four days after his confirmation, Justice Stanton died before he could hear a single case. As one can imagine, deaths in office were more common during the Court's first 100 years in business than in the next 100 due to relative advances in health care and greater public health education.

Generally speaking, death was a frequent visitor in the Supreme Court in times past. During the 20th century, 1955 marks an important year. It was the year that began the seeming disappearance of death from the Court. After Justice Robert H. Jackson died of a heart attack in 1954, during consideration of *Brown v. Board of Education,* no deaths occurred on the Court until Chief Justice Rehnquist, who coincidentally clerked for Justice Robert Jackson, died of cancer on August 28, 2005. Justice Jackson's death thus marks an important guidepost signifying the longest period where the Court did not experience a single death among its active-duty members.

*Disability.* Historically, several justices have left the Court because of debilitating disability. The following are four notable examples of vacancies created as a result of justices being physically disabled by a medical condition. These are Associate Justices

1. *Ward Hunt of New York,* who served nine years (1873–1882) and, despite suffering from gout and a stroke that left him permanently paralyzed on one side his body and unable to function as a justice, refused to resign because of the absence of federal pension benefits for retirees. He finally retired in January 1882 at the age of 71 after Congress passed a law giving federal retirees pension benefits.[55]
2. *William H. Moody of Massachusetts,* who served only four years (1906–1910) and terminated his service on November 20, 1910 at the youthful age of 56. He was disabled by acute rheumatism that left him unable to perform his duties as a justice.
3. *Mahlon Pitney of New Jersey,* who served roughly 10 years (1912–1922) and left the Court on December 31, 1922 at the age of 64 after suffering a stroke.
4. *Charles Whittaker of Missouri,* who served 5 years (1957–1962) and left the Court on March 31, 1962 at the age of 61. He hated being a Supreme Court justice because he had great difficulty making tough decisions. Earlier in the month of his stepping down, he experienced a nervous breakdown and collapsed. At the suggestion of Chief Justice Earl Warren, Whittaker retired from the Court in 1962 citing exhaustion from judicial workload.[56]

*Senate rejection of nominee elevated via recess appointment.* When the U.S. Senate is in recess, the president of the United States can use the power granted under Article 2 of the Constitution to temporarily bypass the Senate and appoint someone to a federal government vacancy that normally requires Senate confirmation. This is called *recess appointment*. Federal court judges and members of the most senior executive service in the national government such as ambassadors and cabinet-level officials are examples of high-level jobs for which recess appointments can be made. In the 19th century, presidents used recess appointments to relieve staffing problems when the Senate was away for long periods of time and cannot act on a nomination. In recent years, however, recess appointments have increasingly been used as a tool to circumvent Senate opposition to controversial nominees.[57]

Numerous examples exist throughout American history of presidents making use of the recess appointment provision of the Constitution, the earliest being John Rutledge of South Carolina in 1795 to be chief justice of the Supreme Court. One institutional constraint imposed on presidents in making recess appointments is that such appointments must be confirmed in the Senate within the next session of Congress. If the nominee is rejected, the president can present a new nominee for confirmation. While nothing prevents the president from making another recess appointment, the appointee must work without pay.[58]

In the case of Rutledge, President George Washington presented him to the Federalist-controlled Senate for confirmation after the Senate reconvened. After heated debate, the appointment of Rutledge (a fellow Federalist) was rejected because of his vitriolic attacks on the Jay Treaty, which special U.S. envoy John Jay negotiated with Great Britain to avert a war of commerce and navigation in the high seas between the United States and Great Britain. Most senators at the time supported the treaty. But Rutledge was hardly alone in his opposition. A number of other politicians and ordinary citizens also opposed the Jay Treaty. Indeed, enraged protestors displayed their disapproval by burning an effigy of John Jay. But President Washington pressed for ratification nevertheless and the Jay treaty won ratification in the Senate on June 24, 1795 by a vote of 20 to 10.

Numerous high-profile recess appointments to Courts and executive-branch offices have been made within the past several decades. For example, prompted by staffing need in 1953, following the death of Chief Justice Harlan Fiske Stone, former California governor, Earl Warren, was first placed on the Supreme Court through a recess appointment.[59] In 1997, President Bill Clinton made a recess appointment of former Republican governor of Massachusetts, William Weld, to be U.S. Ambassador to Mexico, a move designed to sidestep opposition from Senate Republicans, especially Foreign Relations Committee Chairman, Jesse Helms (R-NC), who refused to hold hearings on the nomination because Weld was "not conservative enough" on issues of illegal immigration, foreign trade, and illicit drugs.[60] Finally in August 2005, President George W. Bush granted John Bolton a recess appointment to the United Nations due to strong opposition from Senate

Democrats who charged that Bolton was too mean and intemperate to represent the United States at the United Nations.

## Legislation

The Constitution does not specify a fixed number of Supreme Court justices. Instead, the number of justices on the Court is established by Congress and can be modified through legislation. The current number of nine justices was reached after a long stretch of time in which membership fluctuated between five and ten justices, usually in accordance with the fleeting political wishes of legislative majorities.

The most original way for a vacancy to emerge on the Court is for that vacancy to be created by legislation motivated by a need to relieve caseload crunch in the Court. But more often, political expediency is the real motivation. This explains why laws creating new vacancies tend to be very controversial in Washington. The reason is that politically, they benefit the party of the president. How do legislators justify reforms that create new judicial vacancies? Advocates of new judgeships typically base their support on neutral constitutional principles. For example, they would declare that infusing the judicial branch with more judges is necessary to alleviate increased caseload burden on current judges and to improve overall decision making. But the real impetus for creating new judgeships is often to achieve a partisan political agenda. Supporters of new justiceships often wish to reward a president or to pack the Court with party loyalists who will advance partisan values. According to former Chief Justice William H. Rehnquist, nothing in the world should stop a president from packing the Court because "a president who sets out to pack the Court does nothing more than seek to appoint people to the Court who are sympathetic to his political or philosophical principles."[61] Table 2.2 lists statutes that changed the size of the Court and the primary reason for the change.

It affirms that throughout American history, both the legislative and executive branches of government have used the size of the Supreme Court as a partisan weapon to either punish or reward a president or to achieve some other narrow political goal. Fortunately, the effort to achieve a narrow political goal by tinkering with the size of the Court does not always succeed. One example of such failures came in 1937 when President Franklin D. Roosevelt proposed (which Congress rejected) a plan to increase the number of justices to 15 in what is generally known as FDR's *Court-packing plan*. The president argued that the Supreme Court was understaffed and behind in its work. As a result, the president claimed, justices were giving insufficient consideration to cases before them, including cases challenging his New Deal program.

The New Deal was a system of government programs initiated by the FDR administration to boost the sagging U.S. economy and reduce the misery brought on by high unemployment and high inflation that characterized the Great Depression era. It turned out that six of the justices on the Court

**Table 2.2**   Evolution of the Number of Supreme Court Justices since 1789

| Legislation | Justices set at | Time Span | Reason |
| --- | --- | --- | --- |
| Judiciary Act of 1789 | 6 | 1789–1800 | To satisfy geographic/sectional cleavages and unify the nation after independence |
| Judiciary Act of 1801 | 5 | 1801–1802 | Effort by Federalists to deny Thomas Jefferson an appointment to the Court |
| Judiciary Act of 1802 | 6 | 1802–1807 | To undo Federalists' political mischief and therefore restore membership to its original size set in 1789 |
| Judiciary Act of 1807 | 7 | 1807–1839 | To give Thomas Jefferson an appointment to the Court. |
| Judiciary Act of 1837 | 9 | 1837–1863 | To reflect division of the nation into nine geographic circuits |
| Judiciary Act of 1863 | 10 | 1863–1866 | To give Abraham Lincoln an additional appointment |
| Judiciary Act of 1866 | 7 | 1866–1869 | To deny Andrew Johnson the power to fill two vacancies on the Court after Lincoln's assassination |
| Judiciary Act of 1869 | 9 | 1869–present | To give Grant additional appointments, address concern over growing decrepitude of the Bench, and to fix pension for federal judges and justices |

*Source*: Author's compilation from Epstein et al. 2004 and various sources

at the time were over the age of 70 and very conservative. If approved, FDR's plan would bring six new and presumably younger justices to the Court and "make the administration of all federal justice speedier, and, therefore, less costly" for the American people.[62] But the grand objective of the president was to pack the Supreme Court with individuals who are sympathetic to his philosophy and, therefore, would work from the inside to reverse the Supreme Court's hostility toward his New Deal programs.

## Chapter Summary

Supreme Court vacancies furnish the president and the Senate with an opportunity to bring new justices to the Court who would shape the meaning of the Constitution and possibly alter the direction of legal policy in the United States.

Vacancies are created by voluntary departure, involuntary departure, and legislation. Examples of voluntary departure are retirements, resignations, and elevations of associate justices to chief justice. Examples of involuntary departure are death in office and severe disability. There are political, economic (or institutional), and personal reasons why justices may choose to retire from the Court. Political considerations are those that motivate the justice to hold out and retire strategically by leaving when the occupant in the White House can appoint someone who would be ideologically similar to the retiring justice. Economic reasons include improvement in retirement benefits provided by law. Personal reasons are those dealing with old age, workload, and desire to spend time with family and friends.

## CONCLUSION

No president is guaranteed an appointment to the U.S. Supreme Court. There is a strong element of luck involved in the timing of Supreme Court vacancies and in how many vacancies a president will receive. President George Washington knew before he took the job that he would have to appoint at least six justices to the Supreme Court. But his case is unique. No other president has ever assumed the presidency with knowledge of that many vacancies beforehand.

As an institution, the Supreme Court has undergone significant evolution in its size and in the way its justices exited the Court. The number of justices has fluctuated from six original jurists down to five before settling at the current level of nine justices. This number is unlikely to change anytime soon if at all. Any proposal to change the size of the Court is prospective and will be divisive, even traumatic for the nation. We can expect politicians to steer clear of such a proposal unless they can perceive a clear political advantage with minimum risk of a backlash. This would be hard to achieve. Past legislative reforms altering the size of the Court have not occurred by accident. At one level, the reforms are necessitated by caseload increases that reflect the level of litigiousness in the nation. But more realistically, change in the number of justices is often motivated by narrow political objectives of governing majorities in Washington. Because the Court has experienced a long period of stability in the number of its justices, a substantial amount of inertia exists that would likely preserve the number "nine" well into the future.

The manner in which justices leave the Court has changed. Throughout the first half of the Court's history, death was the primary mode of exit from the High Bench. Justices who should have retired refused to do so because they needed the income to maintain themselves and their families in the absence of federal retirement benefits. In the second half of the Court's history, this changed dramatically: voluntary exit through retirement became the primary method.

The power and prestige of the Supreme Court has also evolved throughout history, often in line with constitutional areas the Court chooses to focus its attention and hence its impact in American society. It makes sense to expect the Court's public esteem to have a direct bearing on the decision of justices to retire or remain on the Court. Although some presidents attempt successfully to influence retirement decisions by playing hardball with justices, the decision to voluntarily terminate one's employment in the Supreme Court is ultimately that of the justice alone. In the next chapter, we examine the process of selecting individuals to fill Supreme Court vacancies.

# 3

# Appointment of Justices to the U.S. Supreme Court

The appointment of Supreme Court justices is a major event in American politics. This chapter focuses on the process mandated by the Constitution for selecting individuals to fill federal judicial vacancies and the factors influencing it.

Because the selection of Supreme Court justices generates political controversy that implicates all three branches of government, it is instructive to remind ourselves about the basic powers of each branch of the U.S. government as described in the Constitution. Article 1 describes the powers of Congress, which include enacting laws, raising revenue, and confirming federal judges (via the Senate). Article 2 describes the powers of the president, which include acting as commander-in-chief of the Armed Forces and nominating federal judges. Article 3 describes the powers of the Supreme Court, which include judging cases and controversies arising under the Constitution, the laws of the United States, and treaties signed by the federal government.

When it comes to appointment to the Supreme Court Article 2, Section 2, Clause 2 of the Constitution is crystal clear. The president "shall nominate, and by and with the Advice and Consent of the Senate, shall appoint judges of the Supreme Court." This advice and consent clause is often described as the appointment clause of the Constitution.

As we shall see in this chapter, the meaning and implications of these few words in the Constitution have undergone significant transformation throughout American history. We shall begin the chapter by examining the historical origins of the appointment clause. For it is through an understanding of how this clause originated that we can develop a deeper appreciation for the current politics and process of judicial selection. Specifically, we shall address the following questions:

- What are the historical origins of the appointment clause?
- What is the process involved in filling Supreme Court vacancies?
- What important historical lessons can we draw from the activities of various political actors such as presidents, attorneys general, justices, interest

groups and institutions such as the American Bar Association, mass media and the Senate in the selection of Supreme Court justices?
- How has the role of these actors and institutions evolved and adapted in our political system of judicial selection?
- What conditions lead to confirmation of Supreme Court nominees?

## HISTORICAL ORIGINS OF ADVICE AND CONSENT

Apart from sending soldiers to war, there is no presidential power more important than the appointment of justices to the Supreme Court. The Constitution requires the president to make a regular, permanent appointment to the Supreme Court based solely on the "advice and consent" of the U.S. Senate. Exactly what "advice and consent" means was a matter of intense debate during the drafting of the Constitution and remains so even today. Before engaging that debate, however, it is important to understand the different types of judicial appointments the framers authorize the president to make.

Under Article 2, Section 2 of the Constitution, the president can make a regular appointment or a recess appointment in some cases. There are important differences between these two types of appointment and why the framers thought them necessary.

### Regular and Recess Appointments to the Supreme Court

The president can make a *regular appointment* to a constitutional court. Such appointments are considered permanent once the Senate confirms the nominee. To prevent blind loyalty to those who appointed them, the Constitution protects *judicial independence* by conferring upon Justices job security in the form of service "during good behavior" and a guaranteed no-reduction in salary, irrespective of whatever economic or political strife the nation might face. These constitutional protections free justices from what Thurgood Marshall describes as "the political stresses and strains."[1] The vast majority of appointments to the Supreme Court are regular appointments and we devote our discussion in this chapter to them.

The president can also make a *recess appointment* to a constitutional court. However, such appointment is rare and temporary. A recess appointment is made when the Senate is in recess and, therefore, is unable to formally deliberate and vote on a nomination.

The authority for the president to make recess appointments comes directly from Article 2 of the Constitution: "The President shall have Power to fill up all Vacancies that may happen during the Recess of the Senate, by granting Commissions which shall expire at the End of their next Session." The consent of the Senate is not required for a recess appointment, although the president may find it proper to "sound out" leaders of the Senate before engaging in a recess appointment.

There are no specific guidelines enumerated in the Constitution for making recess appointments, except that the recess appointee must face Senate confirmation when Congress reconvenes. Because recess appointments take effect almost immediately, the appointee would have gained practical experience in the position, which can facilitate confirmation when the Senate reconvenes. Generally speaking, the process and substance of recess appointment are left to the president's discretion. However, recess appointments are not risk-free. Historically, recess appointments have been used as a mechanism to relieve caseload crunch by bringing in new justices when the Senate is away on vacation. But nowadays, many in Congress see recess appointments as a way for the president to circumvent Senate opposition to a controversial nominee. Consequently, a recess appointment can backfire on the president. Senators who oppose the appointment can retaliate by scuttling the president's legislative agenda by voting against legislation proposed by the president or by proposing killer amendments to defeat or delay consideration of bills favored by the president. This explains why recess appointments are made sparingly.

There are three reasons why a president may consider making a recess appointment. First, the president strongly desires to place a particular candidate on the Court. Second, the nominee is controversial and the president is convinced that, in the meantime, there is very little chance of Senate confirmation either for ideological or policy reasons. By making a recess appointment under these circumstances, the president hopes that allowing the candidate an opportunity to actually perform the duties of a justice would improve the chances for confirmation. Third, there is a backlog of cases in the Supreme Court and the need for manpower is urgent to alleviate that backlog. For example, Chief Justice Fred Vinson's death from a heart attack in 1953 prompted President Dwight Eisenhower to make a recess appointment of former California Governor Earl Warren to be chief justice, the first such appointment in over a century. Warren was eventually confirmed when the Senate reconvened.

## Alternative Constitutional Plans Debated by the Founders for Appointing Justices

Having considered the meaning of recess and regular appointment, it is essential to discuss what the origins of advice and consent are. The constitutional requirement of advice and consent is a product of compromise between those Forefathers who favored a strong presidency and those who saw a need for constitutional checks and balances on executive power. The requirement is procedural in nature. It makes no judgment about *who* should be appointed to the Court, only *how* individuals should be qualified or selected.

Several proposals were debated during the constitutional convention, centering on ways to foster judicial independence, but ultimately a compromise prevailed. The *Virginia Plan*, offered by former governor of Virginia,

Edmund J. Randolph (1753–1813), advocated for a judiciary selected by both Houses of Congress. The president and the staff were to have no involvement whatsoever in judicial selection for fear that placing appointment power in the hands of one individual might create the traces of a Monarchy and possibly result in tyranny. But during debate on June 5, 1787, delegates agreed that the proposal was too onerous to work properly. Congress cannot provide an effective check upon itself in the selection of justices without bitter partisan rancor and regionalism eventually getting in the way.

The alternative plan was offered by William Paterson of New Jersey. The *New Jersey Plan* was judicial appointment power to reside solely with the president. But this plan was also problematic, with the most notable concern centering on the addition of imperial presidential powers.

Other delegates such as James Madison suggested that judicial selection should be an exclusive province of a single deliberative body, the U.S. Senate, an institution Madison considers "sufficiently stable and independent" to make careful and intelligent decisions. Madison was apparently only persuasive up to a point. We know now that none of these ideas prevailed outright. After careful consideration, what finally emerged from the constitutional convention was a compromise where the power of judicial appointment will be shared by the president and Senate. The president shall appoint justices based upon the sage counsel and affirmation of the Senate.

This history is relevant to current judicial selection controversies in many ways, not the least of which is that the framers intended "advice and consent" to create real debate and controversy. As it was during the constitutional convention, an important aspect of current selection debates is what the phrase "advice and consent" really means, even among U.S. senators. Former Senate Majority Leader George Mitchell (D-ME) is one of many senators who believe that the phrase calls upon the president and Senate to be coequal partners in judicial selection.[2] Another is Senator Robert P. Griffin (R-MI) who took a clue from the Senate rejection of John Rutledge for the Center Chair in 1795 to remind his colleagues that "[the rejection of Rutledge] in 1795 said to the President then in office and to future Presidents: Don't expect the Senate to be a rubberstamp."[3] Senator Griffin made his statement during Senate debate in 1968 over the nomination of Abe Fortas to be chief justice.

Others see the Senate's responsibility as a subservient one. During the same Fortas confirmation debate in 1968, Senate Majority Leader Mike Mansfield (D-MT) urged the Senate to allow a vote on the president's nominee because "Our responsibility is merely to evaluate the qualification of the nominee and to record our pleasure or displeasure; to give our advice and consent or our advice and dissent."[4]

One can say that the framers' intention to generate conflict has succeeded in light of the storm of controversy surrounding modern judicial selections. Although the power of judicial selection is shared, the Founding Fathers clearly intended the primary role of judicial selection to reside with the president. This explains why the power of appointment is enumerated in Article 2 of the Constitution and not in Article 1.[5] But more importantly, the framers also wanted to prevent the president from appointing only his loyal supporters or even individuals with slim qualifications. This is where the Senate comes in. Under the principle of separation of powers, it is the responsibility of the Senate to curtail the prevailing spirit of favoritism/cronyism in the president when a judicial vacancy emerges.

The Senate serves as a gatekeeper for the Supreme Court. In exercising that role, the Senate has rejected one out of every five Supreme Court nominees in history. A total of 157 nominations were sent to the Senate from 1789 to 2008. Of these, 35 were not confirmed.[6] Through these rejections, the Senate has at various times in history been criticized and accused of being obstructionist. Such criticisms typically come from those who align with the president on policy or ideological grounds and this is especially true when the Senate and the president are from opposing political parties.

Criticism of Senate handling of judicial nominees will never go away. So long as there are vacancies to fill, dissatisfaction with and criticism of whoever is nominated can be expected. More importantly, the issue is not relegated to one political party. Senate Democrats would continue to accuse Senate Republicans of being obstructionist when a Democratic president makes the nomination and vice versa. The musical chorus is well set and the ideological cleavage well entrenched. Each camp is expected to play the role whenever its turn arrives until a fundamental change descends upon Washington.

The squabble over Supreme Court confirmations has always been a part of American politics. But the confirmation process itself has been transformed significantly. Specifically, its intensity has increased dramatically in recent decades as a result of changing national politics, the enhanced power of the Supreme Court in American life, and the transformation of the Senate from a traditionally inner-directed and closed institution to one that is now far more open and democratic.[7] Despite this transformation, debate within the Senate and between senators remains one of the most civil in American society. We shall examine this transformation at various sections throughout the chapter. We begin by considering the source of the intense feeling over Supreme Court appointments: the perceived importance of the Court and its justices in American society.

## WHY SUPREME COURT APPOINTMENTS ARE IMPORTANT

*Direct Effect on Citizens.* The Constitution established a system of government comprised of numerous institutions organized into two levels within one federalist structure. The state system and the federal system operate semiautonomously but share certain responsibilities, for example, fighting crime and educating citizens. The federal government is composed of three institutions (president, Congress, and courts), which also share power. From this perspective, Supreme Court appointments are important primarily because the Court's decisions, for example, allowing death penalty, certain religious practices, and government regulation of business, affect citizens directly. In July 2005, CBS Monthly poll asked citizens nationwide: "How important to you, personally, is the issue of which judges sit on the Supreme Court?" A high proportion, 60.6 percent, of respondents said "extremely important" or "very important."[8] Thus justices must undertake the monumental responsibility of patrolling the boundaries of the Constitution to keep public policy within proper constitutional bounds so that it benefits the people.

*Appointments as National Events.* Modern Supreme Court confirmations have become a national event attracting laser-like media attention, and this constitutes additional evidence of the growing importance of the Court and the selection of its justices. Surely Supreme Court decisions typically reverberate across the nation like a tidal wave and carry significant policy ramifications. Through the help of the mass media, the American public increasingly perceives the Court as being fully integrated into the nation's culture wars and sees the Court's decisions as having a direct impact on their lives, the tone of national discourse, and on which side of the culture wars is up and which is down.

*Issue Salience.* Another explanation for the growing importance of appointments concerns the nature and salience of the issues that have occupied the Court's attention overtime. During the Court's first 100 years in business, the justices mostly dealt with cases raising questions of federalism, states rights, taxation, and commerce, not altogether warm and fuzzy policy areas. But these were the issues the people and hence the Court considered salient at that time. Over the past 100 years, however, the Court attention has shifted toward issues implicating personal freedoms: individual liberties, civil rights, and privacy. Comparatively speaking, these are issue areas that touch human lives intimately and are the subject of deep cultural divisions between social liberals and conservatives. It is no wonder that interest in the selection of justices has risen sharply.

Because of the Court's controversial decisions in the areas of abortion, death penalty, religious freedom, and homosexuality, politicians across the nation and from both sides of the political isle are keenly aware of the power of the Court to shape public policy and to transform debate over national issues. They have become more interested in the importance of Supreme Court appointments because ordinary voters have themselves become more attuned to judicial selection.

Nowadays senators from both sides of the political isle shift into a fevered-pitch of rhetorical flourish whenever a Supreme Court nomination is announced. The media enters into a state of frenzy in anticipation of the confirmation battle. Grassroots organizations mobilize their faithful armies and plot strategies to defend or defeat the nominee in order to "safeguard the Constitution" or rights already won. Finally, a majority of the American public simply watches from a distance with hopeful anticipation that the

Republic would survive. With the enormous attention now being directed at Supreme Court confirmations, one might wonder whether things have always been this way or whether something quite fundamental has changed in American politics.

Although there is now greater appreciation for the direct role that the Supreme Court plays in American life and cumulatively in the course of constitutional governance, the truth is that controversy in judicial confirmations goes back to the period of George Washington. However, the level of scrutiny that nominees face has become more intense, more thorough, and more democratic.

*Uniqueness of the Institution.* An appointment to the Supreme Court is unlike any other in the federal judicial system. All presidents view appointments to the Supreme Court to be critically important to their policy agenda and to their future legacy, especially in light of the Court's ability to change the course of history. Most Americans today have no idea what John Adams did to change American society when he was president from 1795 to 1801. But they do remember through basic civics that Adam's appointment of Chief Justice John Marshall (1800–1835) solidified the doctrine of judicial review, which dramatically changed the relationship between the three branches of government by establishing true equality among them.

Similarly, most Americans would remember that Dwight Eisenhower was a four-star general in the U.S. Army during the Korean War and that his experience and leadership during that war was instrumental in his being elected president. But what policy accomplishments do ordinary Americans remember about the Eisenhower presidency? Most people cannot name one. But most ordinary Americans do know something about how the official policy of racial segregation in American public education came to an end. They know it was the work of the Supreme Court, led by Chief Justice Earl Warren (an Eisenhower appointee) that led to the unanimous decision in *Brown v. Board of Education,* which ended government-sanctioned racial segregation in public education.[9]

## LEVELS OF PRESIDENTIAL INVOLVEMENT IN JUDICIAL SELECTION

Presidents are fairly unified in their view of appointment to the Supreme Court as a potentially transformative event for their administration's agenda and future legacy. According to former Reagan Attorney General Edwin Meese, "No president exercises any power more far-reaching, more likely to influence his legacy, than the selection of federal judges [especially to the Supreme Court]."[10] But presidents are hardly unified about how much direct personal involvement they should have on judicial selection. Personal involvement differs remarkably from one administration to another. Some presidents such as Franklin D. Roosevelt and Richard M. Nixon managed the details of their candidate selection closely and monitor with alacrity every important detail about the nomination and eventual vote in the Senate. Other presidents such as Ronald Reagan and George H. W. Bush delegate the details of judicial selection to their advisors while they themselves focus on establishing the overall strategy to ensure a successful nomination.[11] There is, of course, no set rule for what kind of nomination strategy a president should adopt. Each president simply figures out what strategy will best support the administration's agenda and adapts the strategy to changing political circumstances.

## Presidential Agendas in Judicial Selection

Presidents are motivated by multiple goals when deciding who to place on the nation's highest Court. In a nation of more than 303 million inhabitants and with a multitude of qualified individuals, how does a president select one individual for a Supreme Court vacancy? To understand judicial selection from a historical perspective, we must distinguish between different presidential agendas, that is, the president's motivation for naming a particular individual to the Court. Jerry Goldman, a notable observer of politics of judicial selection in the United States, identifies three presidential agendas that drive judicial selection strategies among American presidents: policy agenda, partisan agenda, and personal agenda.[12]

### Policy Agenda

A president who adopts this type of agenda considers judicial selection to the Supreme Court an important opportunity to advance the substantive policy goals of his administration and sets judicial selection criteria to achieve those goals. Looking historically across different presidential administrations, several examples emerge of presidents who make advancing public policy a centerpiece of their appointment strategy. President George Washington appointed John Jay the first chief justice of the Supreme Court because he believed Jay possessed the capacity to lead his nation-building effort in the Supreme Court. President John Adams appointed John Marshall to help establish the frontiers of judicial supervision in American government, a task that Marshall performed superbly. President Andrew Jackson appointed Roger B. Taney Chief Justice in 1836 to help shape the vexing and divisive holocaust of slavery in the United States. But in what political scientist Robert G. McCloskey described as "one dramatic lapse from judicial self-restraint,"[13] the Taney Court steered the Supreme Court into the center of a political storm when justices decided *Dred Scott v. Sanford* (1857), giving legitimacy to slavery in the United States. President Abraham Lincoln selected his justices with the policy goal of ending the civil war (1862–1865) peacefully and reconstructing Southern economies following the ravages of that war.

Perhaps the most famous example of a president who cultivated a policy agenda through his selection of Supreme Court justices was Franklin Delano Roosevelt. FDR was fortunate to appoint nine justices to the Supreme Court, the second highest for a single president (George Washington appointed 10). Most of FDR's appointments were geared toward enhancing his administration's New Deal objectives. Under the *New Deal*, the federal government established regulations that placed tighter control over the national economy. The goal ultimately was to bring about a national economic recovery following the man-made devastation caused by the Great Depression. Unfortunately for the president, this gallant effort was stymied by a group of 6 conservative justices, all over the age of 70.[14]

FDR won a landslide victory by a margin of over 10 million popular votes in the 1932 presidential election. He earned significant political capital and his policies had strong public support. As a result, he was not amused that the Supreme Court, with its nine unelected justices, slowly derailed his program to fix the economy. FDR fought back aggressively. He accused the justices of being behind in their work due to old age. As a remedy, he proposed to appoint one additional justice for every sitting justice over 70. This would effectively increase the size of the Court from 9 to 15 justices.

A series of interviews with ordinary citizens conducted by the Gallup organization in 1937 showed that the public was slightly opposed to tinkering with the number of Supreme Court justices. On average, 39.84 percent of citizens favored the Court-packing plan while 45.58 percent opposed. In addition, only 20.3 percent of all state bar association members supported the plan.[15] Fearing that the plan, if successful, would give FDR a Democratic Court, Chief Justice Hughes and Associate Justice Owen Roberts made the famous "switch in time that saved nine." The liberals on the Hughes Court were Louis Brandies, Harlan Fiske Stone, and Benjamin Cardozo who supported the New Deal.

*Hugo Black, the New Deal, and the Ku Klux Klan.* Roosevelt's selection of Senator Hugo Lafayette Black of Alabama in August 1937 as his first appointee to the Supreme Court and his elevation of Harlan Fiske Stone to replace retiring Chief Justice Hughes exemplify President Roosevelt's desire to advance his New Deal policies through his Supreme Court appointments. As a senator, Hugo Black worked tirelessly to support the objectives of the New Deal. He also strongly supported the president's Court-packing campaign. But as one can imagine, justices on the Court who opposed the New Deal were unhappy upon hearing the news of Hugo Black's selection. Justice Robert Jackson expressed a sentiment, which was representative of other anti–New Dealers on the Court, when he stated: "The Court will be humiliated by having to accept one its most bitter and unfair critics and one completely alien to the judicial tradition"[16]

Traditionally nominations of current or former U.S. senators in good standing encountered little opposition in the Senate. Because of courtesy and decorum, senators in general have a difficult time scrutinizing the qualification of and eventually voting against one of their own. Indeed, most senators nominated for the Supreme Court were never vigorously evaluated by the Senate Judiciary Committee and many were confirmed shortly after being nominated.[17] But Hugo Black's case was different. For a senator, his nomination was surprisingly very controversial and he faced unusually strong opposition from inside the beltway. This was primarily because his support of New Deal programs and FDR's Court-packing plan made him a lightening rod for criticism among a majority of senators and the organized bar that had opposed the president's effort to increase the size of the Supreme Court.

The opposition gained more strength when it was rumored that as a young lawyer, Black had maintained membership in the Ku Klux Klan in his home state of Alabama. Nevertheless, working closely with the administration, senators supporting the Black nomination rushed it through the Senate, allowing Black to blunt this perfect-storm of charges. When pressed for comments on these charges, FDR denied any knowledge of Black's Klan association during a news conference held on September 14, 1937. Rather he suggested that the news media should apologize to Justice Black for the slur they had caste upon him concerning the KKK story. That the president claimed no knowledge of Black's link to the Klan contradicted Black's own account of his meeting with the president before his nomination was announced. Black recalled discussing the status of his Klan membership with the president before his nomination was announced. Despite all this, Black was confirmed by a vote of 63 to 16.[18]

Not long after Hugo Black was confirmed, the KKK controversy was resurrected when a series of newspaper articles began appearing at the *Pittsburg-Post Gazette* claiming to have uncovered evidence that Justice Black had not only been a member of the Klan but that he was still a member of the Klan in good standing while serving on the Supreme Court. During a national radio address on October 1, 1937, Black admitted to a two-year membership in Robert E. Lee Klan #1 of Birmingham during the 1920s. He denied any continuing membership, saying that the "unsolicited card" given to him after his nomination was not considered by him to be "membership of any kind." Black then pointed to his resignation from the Klan and to his liberal voting record both in the Senate and in the Court as proof that he was indeed a changed man.[19] Black, an absolutist, who believes strongly in what the Constitution actually says, continued his strong support for FDR's economic policies as well as individual liberties until he retired.

*Partisan agenda*

A president pursues a partisan agenda in judicial selection when presidential power of appointment is used to increase support for the president or his political party in the voting booth. Historically, American women have supported the Democratic Party in presidential elections. This is because the Democratic Party is seen as a strong advocate for issues that women care deeply about, including abortion rights, the environment, and support for public schools. In many ways, this lopsided support helped depress the women vote for Republican candidates in national elections before the 1980s. Reagan targeted the women vote as part of his strategy for winning the White House.

Reagan's tactic for achieving this partisan objective was his promise to appoint the first woman to the Supreme Court, which became a cornerstone of his presidential campaign.[20] Soon after Reagan defeated Jimmy Carter in a landslide, Justice Potter Stewart announced his retirement from the Court after serving 23 years. The announcement presented the new president with a golden opportunity to fulfill his campaign promise to American women and establish a legacy for his party. Reagan fulfilled that promise by naming Sandra Day O'Connor, a state appellate judge from Arizona and a former majority leader of Arizona's State Senate, to replace the retiring Justice Stewart.

Many commentators dismissed O'Connor's selection as a symbolic gesture, even though by objective standards, she was well qualified for the position. Conservatives quickly derided O'Connor as inexperienced, questioned her knowledge of the Constitution, and considered her a wasted nomination.[21] Liberals, on the other hand, were pleased that a woman was finally joining this male-dominated institution but questioned her commitment to issues important to women. Nevertheless, O'Connor faced a rather easy confirmation, and the Senate voted unanimously in her favor. O'Connor's appointment has been credited with increasing the number of women who today identify with the Republican Party. Many of these are the so-called Reagan Democrats, voters who previously voted consistently for Democrats but now are willing to cross party lines and vote for a Republican candidate for president. Reagan's calculation paid off, but why?

*Symbolic Representation.* The answer can be derived from empirical research on the politics of symbolic representation. Symbolic representation as a model of judicial selection makes two key assumptions. First, once confirmed for the Court, a symbolic nominee will decide cases in a way that better represents the interest and preferences of the nominee's own demographic group (e.g., Catholic, women, African American, Hispanic). Second, a symbolic nominee will less well represent the attitudes and preferences of outside groups.[22] Reagan's calculation paid off because through O'Connor's selection and her breaking of the proverbial glass ceiling, American women gained a heightened sense of social pride and a strong redemption in their belief that anything is possible in the United States. Equally important, many women shifted their support to the Republican Party and President Reagan was able to close the gender gap temporarily in the next presidential vote in 1984.

Thus there is strong evidence to suggest that symbolic nomination can help fulfill a president's partisan agenda. However, evidence is mixed as to whether symbolic nominees actually do provide the substantive benefits their group members expect after the nomination is confirmed. From the perspective of African Americans, for example, Justice Thurgood Marshall was a symbolic representation success story whereas Justice Clarence Thomas is not. While Marshall is widely seen to have advanced the interest of African Americans during his tenure on the High Bench, Justice Clarence Thomas's tenure thus far is not. Similarly, symbolic nominees don't usually vote alike. Roman Catholic Justices such as William Brennan, Antonin Scalia, Clarence

Thomas, and Anthony Kennedy do not vote alike on issues important to Catholics in American politics such as the separation of church and state.

### Personal Agenda

A president is said to pursue a personal agenda in judicial selection when presidential discretion is used to favor friends, current or former aides, or former associates in judicial selection. The importance of a personal agenda in judicial selection harks back to the presidency of George Washington as most of the original six justices Washington named to the Court were personal friends. President Truman likewise exerted absolute control over the selection process, and tended to favor his closest friends for the job. His appointment of Sherman Minton in 1949, for example, was "the product of simple, unadulterated cronyism."[23] President Kennedy's selection of Byron White in 1962 was to reward a lifelong friendship. The same goes for the appointment of Abe Fortas by Lyndon Johnson, even though Fortas was a renowned lawyer whose qualification for the Court was never in doubt.

Among more contemporary presidents, George W. Bush consistently favored loyal aides for high judicial appointments. In 2005, Bush nominated Harriet Miers to replace the retiring Justice Sandra Day O'Connor. Miers was the president's personal lawyer and close friend during his days as governor of Texas. They remained good friends when Bush became president in 2000. After Bush defeated Massachusetts Senator John Kerry to win his second term in 2004, he asked Miers to join his administration as White House Counsel, a job she performed for only eight months before being nominated to the Supreme Court on October 3, 2005. Miers eventually withdrew her nomination following strong opposition from conservatives who questioned her qualification and commitment to conservative values. Judge Samuel Alito of the Third Circuit Court of Appeals would eventually replace O'Connor in the Supreme Court.

Presidents rarely appoint individuals they do not personally know or individuals their most trusted advisors do not know very well. While most presidents have relied on the advice of trusted advisors in the selection process, some presidents do place a narrow focus on a single candidate of their own choosing. This is true of President Harry Truman's selection of Fred Vinson to the Court. It is also true of Lyndon Johnson's selection of Abe Fortas (his personal friend) and Thurgood Marshall (the first black) to the Court. Under the circumstance where a president becomes fixated on a particular candidate, no matter how many individuals the president considers along the way, the president usually returns to the initial candidate tagged for the vacancy.

## The Process of Appointing Justices to the Supreme Court

When a vacancy occurs on the Court, the White House is usually the first to be notified. The president may decide to sit on the news for a few days or months awaiting an appropriate time to make the announcement. A short delay gives the president lead time to consider possible replacements and avoid the pitfalls that can accompany a hasty decision. However quickly the president decides to act in naming someone, one thing is clear: The selection of a nominee usually involves secret discussions between the president and his top advisors. If the president holds consultation sessions with senators to discuss potential nominees, such sessions are typically conducted behind closed doors.

In this section, we discuss the political actors and institutions that are involved in the decision to appoint Supreme Court justices. Generally speaking, these are the executive branch (including the president, White House office of Legal Policy, and the Justice Department), American Bar Association, U.S. Senate and its judiciary committee, interest groups, the media and the general public. Figure 3.1 is a graphical representation of the process of appointment to the Supreme Court.

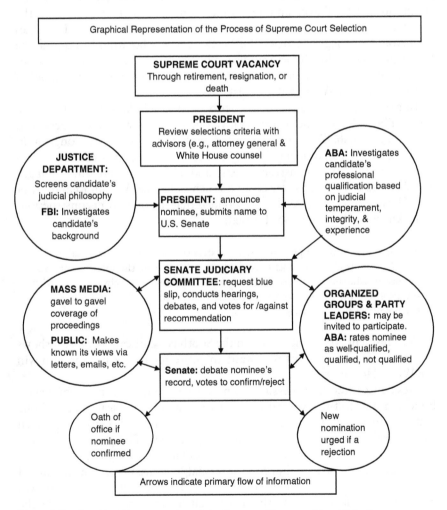

**Figure 3.1** Graphical Representation of the Process of Supreme Court Selection

## The Executive Branch

Upon hearing of an impending vacancy on the Court, the president usually consults his core advisors—especially the vice president, director of the White House Office of Legal Policy, and the attorney general of the United States—regarding suitable individuals for the job. Ordinarily, advisors are permitted wide discretion in the decision-making process but that discretion is constrained by the president's expectations and the selection criteria established by the president beforehand.

During the Nixon administration, the major factors for consideration reflected Nixon's stated goal of restoring law and order to the nation's streets following the upheaval of the 1960s' Vietnam War protests, the civil rights movement, and the women's movement. The president instructed his advisors to seek out individuals who (1) are strict constructionists; (2) are about 50 years of age; and (3) come from a particular region of the country—the South. Nixon understood strict constructionists to be judges who would not legislate from the bench; those who would interpret the Constitution literally. But as a subtext, a justice labeled a strict constructionist is understood in the popular media to be a conservative in the mold of Antonin Scalia or William Rehnquist.

In reality, the term strict constructionist is a nebulous concept because both a liberal justice and a conservative one can be a strict constructionist. In Justice Marshall's papers deposited with the Library of Congress in Washington DC, an unidentified reporter asked: "Mr. Justice Marshall...do you know any strict constructionists, and if so, what are they doing?" Marshall did not point to conservatives such as Justice William Rehnquist or Chief Justice Burger. Instead, he responded that the only strict constructionist he knew on the Court was himself:

> The only one hundred percent strict constructionist that I know is talking to you. And he is also the most reasonable one. [Asked by the interviewer what he meant, Marshall responded] The record will show that I always agree with my brothers on the Court whenever they are right——I always agree with them whenever they are right.[24]

For President Nixon, the focus on the South is significant because it shows a grateful president's effort to reward an entire region for helping him win the White House.

Presidents often face pressure from outside groups that push for a symbolic nominee to fill a woman seat, a black seat, a Jewish seat, or a Catholic seat. For instance, when Sandra Day O'Connor retired, George W. Bush faced pressure to appoint a woman to replace her. The president's father George H.W. Bush faced pressure to nominate a black jurist to preserve "the black seat" after Thurgood Marshall's retirement. He appointed Clarence Thomas, another black. Similarly, President Richard Nixon was pressured by the Roman Catholic Church to appoint a Catholic to the Court. Although Nixon seriously considered several Catholics, he never actually buckled to the pressure. Roman Catholics are now abundantly represented in the Supreme Court, with at least three in Robert's Court: Antonin Scalia, Anthony Kennedy, and Clarence Thomas. Until 1950, presidents also faced pressure to appoint on the basis of geography. But geography does not appear to feature as a viable factor in modern judicial selection.

Before potential nominees are selected for the Supreme Court, they must undergo rigorous background checks, which proceed along two tracks. The first focuses on the legal philosophy of the potential nominee to ensure its consistency with the president's values. The White House Office of Legal Policy and the Justice Department (particularly the attorney general) usually take the lead in conducting and coordinating initial screening of potential candidates. They interview candidates, their colleagues, and associates. They would also examine the judicial writings and speeches of the candidate. During the screening process, candidates are asked broad questions that speak to the candidate's judicial philosophy to ensure that the president's selection criteria are satisfied.

Most presidents disavow any reliance on an ideological litmus test for selecting Supreme Court justices. But we know from extensive empirical evidence that, for the most part, presidents seek candidates whose legal and political philosophies are consistent with their own. After all, with each appointment, the president seeks to leave a lasting judicial legacy. Therefore, from the president's point of view, it makes sense to select individuals who would advance the administration's place in history.

From the information gathered in their investigation, the White House Office of Legal Policy and the attorney general narrow the list of candidates down to two or three individuals who meet the president's selection criteria. These names are then presented to the FBI for further background checks. Thus the FBI is responsible for conducting the second track of the investigation. This investigation looks into the social, financial, and criminal backgrounds of the potential nominee. The personal relationships of the candidates are also examined to determine, for example, whether they have engaged in any extramarital courtship. The FBI also examines the financial dealings of the candidates and work with the Internal Revenue Service and state financial agencies to ensure that the candidates have fulfilled all their federal and state tax obligations. Finally, the FBI works with law enforcement agencies around the country to ensure the candidate has no serious criminal record. The overall purpose of the FBI's investigation is to ensure that there is nothing inappropriate in the candidate's background that can become an embarrassment or a debilitating problem for the president if the candidate were nominated. The information gathered is often confidential, with access granted only to specially designated individuals with security clearances.

After the White House settles on a particular individual, the president announces the nominee and submits the individual's name to the ABA for further investigation and rating and to the Senate for confirmation.

## American Bar Association (ABA)

The ABA is a private professional organization that caters to lawyers and the judicial system. The organization sees as its professional responsibility to pass judgment on the qualification of nominees to the federal courts, especially the nation's highest court, which it has done since the Eisenhower administration (1952–1960). Presidents are not mandated to have their nominees vetted by the ABA. Indeed, some presidents such as Nixon in the 1970s and George H.W. Bush in the 1990s at some point in their tenure decided not to rely on the ABA, believing that the ABA was biased against Republican candidates.

Regardless, the nominees are still vetted by the ABA and the information gathered can be useful to senators and interested publics. Oftentimes, failing to submit a candidate's name to the ABA can be a risky strategy for the president because the ABA's investigation can uncover potentially embarrassing information that the FBI might have missed. First, this could result in a low rating for the nominee. Second, it could potentially derail a nomination. Many nominations to judicial and executive branch posts have failed because the FBI did not conduct a thorough background check on the nominee. For example, Lani Guinier, who was nominated by Bill Clinton in 1995 to be assistant attorney general for civil rights, had employed a live-in nanny to care for her children but she failed to report this information on her income tax returns and failed to pay taxes on this benefit as an employer. The irony was not lost on the public: She was being nominated to a law enforcement post, yet she was accused of violating the law. The resulting political uproar led President Clinton to withdraw her nomination.

The Standing Committee on Federal Judiciary of the ABA is responsible for conducting the evaluation of nominees for the Supreme Court and for all other federal judgeships requiring Senate confirmation. Therefore, the Committee serves as the clearinghouse for the ABA on matters of judicial selection. Its investigation of Supreme Court nominees is the most rigorous because "the significance, range, and complexity of the issues considered by the Supreme Court demand that nominees to the Court be of exceptional ability."[25] The Committee does not recommend candidates to the White House as doing so might compromise its impartiality. The Committee has 17 members and individuals appointed to the Committee must have high professional stature and the highest integrity. Members can serve a maximum of two terms of three years each and are appointed by the president of the ABA.

*ABA Evaluation Criteria.* The Committee evaluates nominees based on professional competence, judicial temperament, and integrity. According to the ABA, professional competence refers to qualities such as intelligence, judgment, knowledge of the law, writing and analytical ability, and judicial experience. Judicial temperament refers to personality traits such as open-mindedness, unbiasedness, decisiveness, compassion, courtesy, and commitment to equality under the law.[26] Integrity refers to the nominee's character, work ethic, and overall reputation in the legal profession. Following its evaluation, the committee would rate nominees as "well qualified," "qualified," or "not qualified." Traditionally, the ABA committee rated the very best candidates as "exceptionally well qualified." However, in 1991, this rating category was dropped in order to simplify matters. Text Box 1 details how the ABA investigates Supreme Court nominees. Overall, there is little variance in the rating assigned to Supreme Court justices. All but one of the justices on the current Robert's Court received the ABA's top rating of "well qualified." Justice Thomas received a rating of "qualified."

Given the saliency of Supreme Court nominations, a rating of not qualified is often sufficient to derail even the most hopeful nomination to the Supreme Court. This was clearly demonstrated during the Nixon administration when President Nixon made the colossal mistake of nominating an

---

**Text Box 1    How the ABA Investigates Supreme Court Nominees**

For more than 50 years, the ABA Standing Committee on Federal Judiciary has evaluated the professional qualifications of nominees to the Supreme Court and to the district and appellate federal courts. The Committee conducts extensive peer reviews of each nominee's integrity, professional competence, and judicial temperament. The use of these criteria to evaluate Supreme Court nominees is especially rigorous because the significance, range, and complexity of the issues considered by the Supreme Court demand that nominees to the Court be of exceptional ability. The Standing Committee takes its role in the process of vetting and screening nominees to the Court very seriously.

Therefore, it conducts the most extensive, nationwide peer review possible on the premise that the highest court in the land requires a person with exceptional professional qualifications. There are several procedural differences between the Committee's investigations of Supreme Court nominees and those of lower courts. For Supreme Court nominees,

- all members of the Committee conduct confidential interviews within their circuit of persons most likely to have information regarding the professional qualifications of the nominee. Typically hundreds of such interviews are conducted.
- teams of law school professors examine the nominee's legal writings (opinions, briefs, articles, etc.) for quality, clarity, knowledge of the law, and analytical ability. Customarily, this is accomplished by dividing the material into areas of law and having it reviewed by professors who are areas of law and having it reviewed by professors who are recognized experts in each area on which the nominee has written, and provide the Committee with comments.

- a national team of leading practicing lawyers with Supreme Court experience—typically former Supreme Court clerks, past members of the Solicitor General's office, and other lawyers with experience arguing before the Supreme Court—also examines the legal writings of the nominee and provides the Committee with comments.

The results of these analyses are reported to the full Committee for evaluation.

The Committee utilizes three rating categories in evaluating a nominee to the Supreme Court: "Well qualified," "Qualified," and "Not qualified." To merit a "Qualified" or "Well qualified" rating, a Supreme Court nominee must be at the top of the legal profession, have outstanding legal ability and exceptional breadth of experience, and meet the highest standards possible. The evaluation of "Well qualified" is reserved for those found to merit the Committee's strongest affirmative endorsement.

*Source*: American Bar Association, the ABA Standing Committee on Federal Judiciary, www.abanet.org/scfedjud/home.html. Visited August 10, 2006

individual of very questionable qualification, Judge G. Harold Carswell of the Fifth Circuit, to the Supreme Court.

G. Harold Carswell had been a circuit judge for only a few months when he was nominated. Although the ABA rated the 50-year-old Carswell as qualified, not many professional lawyers outside the ABA Committee and the Justice Department thought the same. He was viewed in the popular presses as a mediocre judge. Ironically, even Senator Roman Hruska of Nebraska who championed Carswell's nomination in the U.S. Senate admitted obliquely that the candidate lacked qualification. During an interview with a radio reporter, Hruska said: "well even if he were mediocre, there are a lot of mediocre people and judges and lawyers. They are entitled to a little representation, aren't they, and a little chance? We can't have all Brandeises and Frankfurters and Cardozos and stuff like that there."[27] Not surprisingly, Carswell's nomination was defeated in the Senate.[28]

For ideologically controversial nominees, recent experience suggests that even a rating of "qualified" may be insufficient to pass muster in the Senate as was demonstrated in the case of archetypical conservative Robert Bork in 1987. Clarence Thomas who was rated "qualified" also experienced difficulties besides the sexual harassment allegations he faced. He was confirmed by a margin of 52 to 48, the narrowest of all Roberts Court justices.

Overall, the ABA has worked well with most presidents from both parties ever since it started rating judicial nominees. Since the 1970s the relationship between the ABA and U.S. presidents has been shaky, with the ABA coming under criticism for its fluctuating rating of nominees, even within the same presidential administration.

During the 1970s President Jimmy Carter criticized the organization for stifling his effort to appoint women to the federal courts. The ABA was assigning Carter's female nominees poor ratings because most of those nominated lacked the lengthy 15-year judicial experience required by the ABA. This was partly a legacy of the history of gender discrimination and the fact that women did not enter law school in large numbers until the 1960s. The ABA historically is considered a conservative organization. Early on its membership was mostly older corporate lawyers with strong business interests. Consequently, its influence on nominations was strong especially during Republican administrations.[29] But the relationship cooled during the Nixon administration and worsened during the Reagan era due to the failed confirmation of Robert Bork, in which the ABA Committee reported a very split vote, including a not qualified rating by four members of the committee.[30] Nixon's confidence in the ABA evaporated after his two initial nominees for the Supreme Court failed to win Senate confirmation. This was something of an embarrassment for the ABA because both rejected nominees (Carswell and Haynesworth) were indeed evaluated and qualified by the organization.

Following the failed nomination of Carswell to replace Abe Fortas, Nixon was "burning mad" according to his White House counsel John Dean. He expressed a strong desire to nominate someone the Democratic-controlled Senate at the time would have great difficulty rejecting. He wanted to spite the Democrats for rejecting his two nominees and at the same time remove a serious obstacle in the Senate to his policies.[31] Nixon was thinking about nominating Senator Robert Byrd of West Virginia. But why would Byrd fit the president's motivation?

As it turned out, Byrd was a member of the Democratic leadership of the Senate. But there is more. "If Nixon were to nominate Byrd," John Dean points out, "his colleagues would have a problem: they dare not vote against him, for if Byrd was not confirmed they would have to deal with his wrath; yet how could they vote for him when he was totally unqualified?"[32] Byrd had never completed his undergraduate education, although he had gone to American University law school, where he had—over many years—completed his law degree. In addition, Byrd had never passed a bar examination, never been admitted to practice law anywhere, and never practiced a day of law in his life. Nixon was particularly delighted by the fact that Byrd had once been a member of the Ku Klux Klan. Nominating Byrd was equivalent to throwing a stink bomb into the Senate.[33]

But there was one issue working against the president's desire to nominate Byrd. Embarrassed about its shallow vetting of Carswell and Haynesworth, the ABA had vowed to examine subsequent Nixon nominees more carefully. This decision had an impact on Nixon. First, he decided to stop having nominees vetted by the ABA. Second, to avoid further damage to his reputation, he decided against nominating Robert Byrd.

## The Senate

Under Article 2 of the Constitution, the president and Senate share the power of judicial appointment. It is the job of the president to nominate a candidate and the job of the Senate to confirm that nominee. The Senate delegates the responsibility over initial screening of judicial nominees to one of its most important and powerful committees, the Senate Judiciary Committee (SJC). Thus once the president has settled on a particular individual, the name is announced by the president and sent to the SJC.

*The Senate Judiciary Committee (SJC).* The SJC serves as intermediary and watchdog for the Senate in all federal judicial offices requiring confirmation. In that role, the SJC screens candidates for federal judgeship to determine their fit for office before making recommendations to the full Senate. Upon receiving the nominee's name from the White House, the Chairman of the SJC formally convenes confirmation hearings and summons diverse witnesses to testify. Ideally, the president consults Senate leadership for advice on possible candidates. Such consultations engendered confirmations that encountered little controversy. Nowadays, however, the Senate has for the most part been relegated to the role of consenting to the president's choice with little opportunity, if any, granted for advice before the nomination is actually made.

Although the role of the SJC has remained the same over time, the procedural norms developed to make the process work at the committee level and the size of the committee have evolved over time. Until the 1950s, nominees were not required as a matter of policy to appear before the SJC to testify on their own behalf. In 1950, the judiciary committee established a requirement that all federal judicial nominees appear and give testimony for their confirmation. The requirement ushered in the modern age of judicial confirmations. In 1955, John Harlan, the grandson of former Supreme Court Justice John Marshall Harlan became the first nominee to testify on his behalf in front of the SJC after formal institution of this policy. All subsequent Supreme Court appointees have testified before the SJC. For some, the rule requiring candidates to testify before the SJC has "become the ugly centerpiece of the most contested judicial nominations"[34] and has raised concerns that judicial independence may be imperiled.

The size of the SJC has also evolved over the years and currently stands at 19 members selected from both political parties in accordance with each party's proportion in the Senate. In light of this arrangement, when the Senate is controlled by the Republican Party the judiciary committee also would be controlled by Republicans and be chaired by a Republican senator and vice versa. After all hearings have been conducted, committee members vote on whether or not to recommend the nomination to the full Senate. It is common nowadays for the committee to split along party lines when voting on a nominee, especially when the nominee is controversial. When this happens, the majority party would prevail since that party has a majority in the SJC.

Upon receiving the recommendation of the SJC, the full Senate debates the merits of the nomination and the Senate Majority Leader schedules a date and time when each member present would be called upon to render a Yea or Nay vote, assuming a quorum has been reached.

Most nominations are voted on only weeks after SJC sends the nomination to the full Senate. But delays are not uncommon, especially when the president's party does not control the Senate. Empirical research suggests that the longer a nomination lingers in the Senate without a full Senate vote, the greater the chances that the nomination will fail because opponents have ample time to research the nominee and mount a strong challenge.[35]

Delays can be caused by many factors, including a scandal, the president's unwillingness to share information with senators about the nominee, or foot-dragging by senators who oppose the nomination. Delays can also be the result of the ideological distance between the president and the Senate. According to research by Charles R. Shipan and Megan L. Shannon, when ideological distance increases, the length of time it takes to confirm the president's nominees also increase.[36]

A simple majority vote is all that is required for Senate confirmation, which is not always easy to obtain. Despite the possibility of delays and rejection, the vast majority of nominees are indeed confirmed. Since the end of the civil war, the Senate has confirmed 90 percentof the nominees considered for a seat on the Supreme Court.[37]

There exists in the Senate a long-standing norm known as *senatorial courtesy*. This unwritten tradition has been a part of the Senate's way of conducting business since the first session of Congress when senators objected to George Washington's nomination of Benjamin Fishbourn to be a naval officer for the Port of Savannah, Georgia. Senators objected to President Washington's choice not because they disliked Fishbourn but because they liked their fellow senators from Georgia more. In other words, although senators did not have any objection to Fishbourn per se, they were granting courtesy to the two senators from Georgia who, as it turned out, objected to the nomination because they preferred someone else for the position. This innocent action was the birth of the norm of senatorial courtesy, which has become institutionalized in Senate procedure and continues to flourish today.[38]

Under senatorial courtesy, the senator from the president's political party has the capacity to veto the nomination of a judge picked for a lower federal court located in the senator's home state. The home state senator from the president's party is usually asked by the Senate Judiciary Committee to fill out a form known as the *blue slip*, indicating whether the senator supports or opposes the nominee. Should the senator mark on the blue slip "objection" or should the senator refuse to return the slip, the chairman of the SJC is bound by tradition to delay hearings or withhold them altogether. Blue slips are today used only by the SJC.[39]

Senatorial courtesy via blue slips applies mostly to judicial nominations to federal district courts. Thus with senatorial courtesy, the home state senator from the president's party has a virtual veto power over the nomination to a federal district court in his or her state. Sometimes this rule applies to the courts of appeals as well if the vacancy is viewed as belonging to one of the states within a given court of appeals jurisdiction.

## FACTORS CONTRIBUTING TO CONFIRMATION OF SUPREME COURT NOMINEES

From 1789 to 2009, a total of 158 nominations to the Supreme Court were sent to the Senate. Of these, only 35 (or 22 percent) were not confirmed. What explains those unconfirmed nominations? Several explanations exist. Many were withdrawn by the president or the candidate due to strong opposition from a powerful political group. For some, the Senate Judiciary Committee simply failed to act so the nomination died in committee. Finally, others were rejected outright following a vote on the Senate floor.[40]

Supreme Court nominees undergo a variety of confirmation experiences. Some nominees such as Ruth Bader Ginsburg and John G. Roberts were near consensus candidates and so won quick and easy confirmation. Other nominees endure months of waiting as they watch their nomination stall in the Senate under a storm of controversy. Some of these narrowly win confirmation. Still others are defeated after a protracted partisan fight in the Senate. Others simply withdraw their names from consideration as Harriet Myers did in 2005.

In recent years, confirmation of Supreme Court justices has been a vibrant area of research among social scientists and judicial scholars. From this body of research, we understand significantly more about the specific factors that contribute to confirmation of justices. Seven factors consistently found to be important are (1) partisanship; (2) candidate ideology; (3) qualification; (4) presidential term; (5) critical nomination; (6) interest group participation; and (7) ad hoc idiosyncratic factors.

*Partisanship.* Extensive research on judicial selection indicates that the appointment process is dominated by partisanship. Partisanship is the strength of identification or attachment with a particular political party that individuals or groups hold. The primary objective of political parties is, of course, to win elections so as to promote certain values in government and society. And partisanship is the vehicle through which parties win elections and govern effectively. But partisanship is relevant not just to the elected branches of government. It is also important to the appointment of Supreme Court justices. How?

First, partisanship is relevant only when the president's party controls the Senate; in such a situation, a nominee has a stronger chance of winning confirmation than if the Senate is controlled by the other party. Presumably the president and his fellow partisans in the Senate have similar goals of advancing the party and espousing certain core political values, for example, reducing the size of government by cutting taxes or encouraging work and human dignity by increasing the minimum wage. Since defeat of a Supreme Court nominee weakens the president and his party in opinion polling, senators in the president's party have strong incentive to support the president's nominee for the Supreme Court. When they do not, senators can face reprisals at the ballot box because unhappy voters can impose sanctions on senators for voting "incorrectly" on a Supreme Court nominee.

For example, in 1991 Senator Arlen Specter (R-PA), a moderate conservative, who opposed the confirmation of Clarence Thomas to the Court, nearly lost his reelection bid receiving only 49.1 percent of the two-party electoral vote compared to 56.4 in his 1986 reelection bid.[41] Specter's Republican colleagues in the Senate were also unhappy with him over his opposition to Thomas. In 2004 when Specter campaigned for the Senate Judiciary Committee chairmanship, he was opposed by such a large number of fellow Senate Republicans that he nearly lost his bid to lead that powerful committee. In both instances, Specter's poor but ultimately successful showing was partly credited to his moderate stance and strong opposition to a solidly conservative nominee, Clarence Thomas. Similarly, in 1993 Senator Wyche Fowler (D-GA) actually lost his reelection bid because prochoice white Georgian women were dissatisfied with his vote for Clarence Thomas who is widely antiabortion. Thus for individual senators, even those outside the president's party, a vote for or against a Supreme Court nominee must be cast with careful thought and consideration as to effects on one's career.

The second way that partisanship plays a role in Supreme Court appointments is the president's use of appointments to pursue electoral goals with key constituencies. George H.W. Bush's appointment of Clarence Thomas was an attempt to improve the Republican Party's lot with African American voters in the 1992 national election. The gamble failed because Clinton defeated Bush with large African American support. Ronald Reagan's appointment of Sandra Day O'Connor was an effort to help Republicans win more women votes. Richard Nixon's attempted appointment of Clement Haynesworth and Harold Carswell (both from the South) was designed to keep Southern states in the Republican column in presidential voting. Although both nominees were defeated in the Senate, the South acknowledged Nixon's efforts and remained loyal to the Republican Party. Finally, Bill Clinton's appointments of Ruth Bader Ginsburg and Stephen Breyer were instrumental in helping him win the Jewish vote in his successful reelection bid against Republican Bob Dole in 1996.

*Candidate Ideology.* Candidate ideology is a measure of how intensely conservative, liberal, or moderate a nominee to the Supreme Court is perceived to be. For candidate ideology to play a role, it is often viewed in relation to the ideology of the Senate itself. The ideological distance between the nominee and the median senator is decidedly a good predictor of whether the nominee will win confirmation. Empirical research suggests that when a nominee is ideologically similar to the median senator, that nominee is likely to win confirmation.[42] A senator's ideology is typically measured using ADA score, an index calculated by the Americans for Democratic Action based on the votes that the senator has cast in a variety of bills considered in Congress. The score ranges from 0 to 100, with the most conservative senator scoring 0, the most moderate senator scoring 50, and the most liberal senator scoring 100.

In conjunction with the ADA score used to assess the ideology of senators, two political scientists, Jeffrey Segal and Albert Cover, have devised a measure of candidate ideology, which is independent of the Senate and its voting.[43] The measure is based on analysis of newspaper editorials about the nominee from the time the president announces the nomination until the time the Senate votes on it. They examined the editorials for views about the ideology of the nominee. To achieve ideological balance, Segal and Cover relied on four of the nation's leading newspapers, the *New York Times* and the *Washington Post*, which are liberal in orientation and the *Chicago Tribune* and the *Los Angeles Times*, which are conservative in orientation. They read each paragraph to determine whether the paragraph speaks of the nominee as holding a liberal, moderate, or conservative view on a range of issues. Liberal editorial statements are those that, for example, suggest that the nominee supports defendants in criminal justice cases or supports the individual against the government in First Amendment cases. Conservative statements are those that favor the government against the individual. Moderate statements are those that ascribe both liberal and conservative views to the candidate.

To derive candidate's ideological scores, Segal and Cover subtracted the fraction of paragraphs coded conservative from the fraction that is coded liberal and divided by the total number of paragraphs (i.e., the sum of all paragraphs coded liberal, moderate, or conservative). The resulting scale ranges from –1 (unanimously conservative) to 0 (moderate) to 1 (unanimously liberal). In order to compare the nominee ideology score with the senator's ADA scores, both scores must be converted into a percentage.[44] The scores reveal that the most conservative justices include Antonin Scalia, William Rehnquist, and Samuel Alito while the most liberal justices include William Brennan, Thurgood Marshall, and Abe Fortas.

By knowing the ideological score for the median senator and the nominee, it is possible to predict fairly accurately whether the nominee will be confirmed. Thus if the median senator is moderately conservative, say, with an ADA score of –.30, a Supreme Court nominee that is liberal, say someone scoring +.20 on the Segal/Cover ideology measure, will have little chance of being confirmed. To win confirmation, it is advisable for the president to pick a nominee who is ideologically as close as possible to the median senator.

Presidents who fail to heed this advice do so at their own political peril. When President Ronald Reagan nominated conservative DC Circuit Judge Robert Bork (a former law professor and staunch conservative) in 1987 to replace the retiring Justice Lewis Powell (a moderate), the Senate was controlled by Democrats and the median senator was decidedly liberal, in the mold of Senator John Kerry of Massachusetts. Democratic senators warned Reagan publicly what would happen should he nominate an ultra conservative like Judge Bork to the position.

Reagan ignored these warnings and nominated Judge Bork. Bork had a controversial background. In a law review article, Bork argued that the equal protection clause of the Fourteenth Amendment does not apply to women.[45] Because of the wide ideological distance between the median senator at that time and Judge Bork, the nomination quickly ran into serious trouble and Bork was soundly defeated on October 23, 1987 by a vote of 42 to 58. It should be noted that Bork's fight for a seat on the Court was made more difficult because his nomination was to replace a swing justice (Powell). Had Bork's nomination succeeded, it would have shifted the ideological center of gravity in the Court in a decidedly conservative direction.

*Qualification.* As indicated earlier, assessing the qualification of nominees to the Supreme Court is a difficult matter since legislators and other informed observers of the Court disagree over the defining features that make for a qualified candidate. For many in Congress, qualification is defined politically rather than on the basis of pure legal merit. For instance, in the opinion of Senator Orrin Hatch (R-UT), Judge Samuel Alito who was appointed to the Court in early 2006 was well qualified for a seat on the Court. However, in the opinion of Senator Ted Kennedy (D-MA), Alito did not possess the proper temperament suitable for a seat on the nation's highest court. But generally speaking, the most important and concrete measure of qualification that judicial nominees receive is the rating assigned the candidates by the ABA (see text box 1). In the modern era, an ABA rating of "not qualified" is a virtual guarantee that the candidate will not muster enough votes in the Senate to win confirmation. A rating of "qualified" usually implies that the candidate must work harder to convince senators that he or she is worthy of the risk of a permanent appointment to the nation's highest court. Since 1980, most nominees have received the highest rating of "well qualified" and all who received this top rating have been confirmed.

Apart from the ABA, another important way of assessing qualification is public opinion as reflected in citizen participation in the confirmation fight. In our opinionated culture, citizens often voice their opinion about a nominee by making phone calls, sending a fax or e-mail to the offices of their U.S. senators. These communications allow senators to assess public sentiment on the nominee and signal to senators the importance of their impending vote. Research suggests that senators do respond to public pressure in their voting, especially when the senator is facing reelection. For example, political scientists have examined the role of public opinion on Senate voting during the confirmation of Judge Clarence Thomas to the Supreme Court. They found that Southern senators facing reelection were more likely to support Judge Thomas because a majority of local constituents who called the senators' offices supported Thomas, and because of the large black electorate in Southern states.[46]

The nomination of Judge Samuel Alito of the U.S. Court of Appeals for the Third Circuit by George W. Bush in late 2005 provides another example of the importance of public opinion on the confirmation vote and shows that when public sentiment favors a candidate who is perceived to have a reputation for integrity and fairness, confirmation is more likely assuming the judge is also perceived as being qualified.

Judge Alito was rated well qualified by the ABA and most observers thought that by virtue of his long service as an appeals court judge, he was qualified to be a Supreme Court justice. Alito benefited from what political scientists James Gibson and Gregory Caldiera call "positivity bias" in which citizen's long-standing commitment to a given national institution such as the Supreme Court predisposes them to support judicial nominees deemed to possess high integrity.[47] Although Judge Alito was opposed by most Democrats in the Senate, public opinion poll taken during his consideration for the Court shows that a majority of the public thought Judge Alito was a man of high integrity, intellect, and fair-mindedness.[48] Partly because the public supported more than opposed him, Judge Samuel Alito was confirmed by a vote of 58 to 42.

A final way to assess qualification is again provided by the Segal and Cover scores as explained above only that this time the researchers examined newspaper editorials to determine whether the view of the nominee's qualification was negative or positive. In their methods, the final qualification scores range from $-1$ (very unqualified) to 0 (moderately qualified) to 1(very qualified).[49] The most qualified candidates seem to win confirmation more easily regardless of whether they are very liberal or very conservative. Antonin Scalia is a good example. He was one of the most conservative nominees but because he was also highly qualified, the Senate confirmed him unanimously by a vote of 98 to 0.

*Presidential Term.* It matters whether a president is serving a first or second term when a vacancy emerges. Presidents in their first term are generally more successful at having their Supreme Court nominees confirmed than those in their second term. First-term presidents typically enjoy a higher stock of goodwill and political capital from the American people than second-term presidents whose effectiveness at pushing for confirmation of their nominees is often compromised by their lame duck status.

*Critical Nomination.* A critical nomination is one that, if successful, is expected to bring about a complete ideological shift in the balance of power and representation in the Supreme Court either from conservative to liberal or vice versa. It is a transformative nomination to replace *the* swing justice. Political science and legal research indicate that the potential for ideological shift in the Court is one of the strongest reasons why political actors, including senators and interest groups, mobilize for a pitched confirmation battle.[50] Compared to other nominees, a critical nominee is more likely to face a difficult confirmation fight especially when the president is unpopular or in a second term of office. In this sense, presidential term is a conditioning factor in the success or failure of critical nominations.

Justice Lewis Powell was considered a swing vote on the Court and so his retirement announcement on June 26, 1987 raised the stakes for different political and social groups. Ronald Reagan was a lame duck president in the final year of his second term and considered politically weak partly because of on-going congressional investigations into whether his administration illegally shipped military armaments to Central America in violation of federal law. Yet, critics of the administration expected the president to nominate a hardcore conservative who will shift the balance of power in the Court to the right. Reagan confirmed his critics' fears with his nomination of Robert Bork. It is partly because Bork's was a critical nomination that he was easily defeated by the Democratic-controlled Senate. A critical nominee has a better chance for confirmation if he or she is well qualified, perceived as a moderate, and the president is newly elected to a first term of office and thus enjoys significant public support. Overall, in our nation's history, critical nominations have been defeated more often than nominations that are not expected to shift the balance of power in the Supreme Court.[51]

*Interest Group Participation.* An interest group is an organization that serves as an intermediary between citizens and government and sees its task as that of converting the desires and goals of its members into actual policies.[52]

Throughout much of American history, interest groups played little or no role in the confirmation of Supreme Court justices. During the 19th century, the comparatively low status of the Court characterized the politics of choosing justices; there was little public interest and no fireworks in Supreme Court confirmations. Scholars have no evidence of any U.S. senator experiencing reelection difficulty during that time as a result of a stance taken on a Supreme Court nominee. Moreover, the Court featured as an important issue in very few presidential election campaigns.[53]

Indeed, it is likely that even if interest groups had participated in confirmations early on, senators would have cared little since there was no direct election of U.S. senators until 1913 after ratification of the Seventeenth Amendment. Moreover, during the 19th century senators debated and voted on Supreme Court and other federal judicial nominations in executive sessions that were closed to the public so that interest groups lacked a reliable way of monitoring the behavior of individual senators in order to hold them accountable.[54] It is little wonder then that interest group participation in Supreme Court nominations was virtually nonexistent during the 19th century. Supreme Court nominations were incredibly low-keyed events. A nomination would be announced by the president and, following cordial and often brief discussions by senators a day or so later, a confirmation vote would be held and the nomination would be approved without much fanfare or public disputation. Amazingly, several nominations were approved the same day the president forwarded the nominee's name to the Senate.

Confirmations are no longer this modulated. Things began to change during the early part of the 20th century. Direct election of senators became a constitutional requirement. Confirmation voting no longer took place in closed executive sessions; it became public. The American people were invited in and interest groups slowly began to voice their opinions. The nomination of Louis D. Brandies in 1916 marked "the first of the modern episodes in organized conflict" in judicial selection.[55] Opposition to Brandies was strong and well-orchestrated by business interests that opposed his muckraking activities on behalf of consumers when he was Chief Economic Adviser to President Woodrow Wilson.[56] Dubbed the people's lawyer, Brandies overcame the opposition and won confirmation.

Judge John Parker of the Fourth Circuit Court of Appeals was less fortunate in his confirmation ordeal. His nomination by President Hoover in 1930 was defeated due to strong opposition from organized labor and the NAACP. First, he was perceived as antilabor based on his appeals court decision upholding "yellow dog" contracts, those that bar new hires from joining a union.[57] Second, he was tagged as a racist for supporting denying voting rights to African Americans during his campaign for Governor of North Carolina.[58]

The involvement of group activism in Supreme Court selection has increased dramatically. Nowadays Supreme Court nominations are big media events, with all the expense of modern political campaigns. Interest groups now prepare to wage confirmation war long before a vacancy is reported and a nomination is announced. Groups from the right and left now routinely spend millions of dollars to launch Internet, newspaper, television, and radio advertisements as well as direct lobbying and research to support or oppose Supreme Court nominees. According to a Brennan Center study, liberal groups spent $1,365,857 and conservatives spent $1,041,535 for television advertising alone on the Alito nomination from the time Harriet Miers withdrew her nomination on October 27, 2005 to when Judge Alito was confirmed on January 31, 2006.[59]

Indeed, because of the important role the media plays in modern Supreme Court confirmations, there is now a tendency for presidents to nominate individuals who are photogenic and will look good and perform well on television. For their part, interest groups have become quite savvy about using the news media and modern technology to dramatize their opposition to or support for a Supreme Court nominee.

Participation in the process is prospective and it is costly. Groups engage in the process primarily because they wish to advance their policies by serving an informational role for senators. They also participate to increase their membership by gaining exposure through their effort (1) to place issues on the national political agenda and (2) to mobilize grassroots campaigns to support or oppose a particular nomination.[60]

How effective is group involvement in Supreme Court confirmation? When groups present a unified front, they can be effective. For one thing, strong interest group opposition typically leaves the impression that a nominee is unqualified and this can have devastating consequences on a nomination. For example, more than 300 liberal organizations lined up to oppose the nomination of Judge Robert Bork in 1987. More than one hundred conservative groups supported the nomination.[61] The Bork nomination was indeed a watershed event both in terms of the size of interest group involvement and in group tactics. Groups employed mass media advertising, grassroots mobilization, focus groups discussions, and polling.[62] The lopsided nature of the interest group opposition to Bork helped cement the negative tone of the debate in the Senate and Bork's eventual defeat. With the help of well-motivated and well-funded group research and the dissection of Bork's extensive writings, including commentaries on various Supreme Court decisions and on the Constitution, Bork was successfully portrayed as an ideological extremist bent on taking away precious rights of women and minorities in the United States. Caught off guard, his supporters had insufficient time to coordinate a counteroffensive. When Bork attempted to clarify his record and perhaps soften his ultraconservative image during Senate questioning, Senator Arlen Specter (R-PA) accused Bork of undergoing a "confirmation conversion." Bork was defeated by a vote of 42 to 58 on October 23, 1987. It was an embarrassing defeat for the Reagan administration.

*Ad Hoc Idiosyncratic Factors.* Senate confirmation of Supreme Court justices is a process where idiosyncratic and wholly unpredictable contextual factors may influence the voting decision in the Senate. Demographic variables are an example of these ad hoc idiosyncratic factors. They include age, race, gender, and religion. Others are nondemographic and include the region of the country where the nominee comes from. These idiosyncratic factors deserve mention in any discussion of Supreme Court confirmation because they have occasionally been found to influence the confirmation of justices. Theoretically, presidents can and indeed have relied on demographic factors as a guide to the nomination and senators have relied on them for their confirmation vote. But the chances that purely symbolic nominations will succeed in the Senate are very low in modern times. Even appointments based on region that were common prior to 1950 are now significantly less likely to succeed. But the mere possibility that idiosyncratic factors have played a role and now may still play a minor role suggests that appointment of justices to the Supreme Court is not based solely on merit.[63]

## CONCLUSION

We have come a long way in the history of the selection of justices to the Supreme Court. At one level, the process has undergone tremendous transformation in the sense that nominations are now a national event with gavel-to-gavel coverage in the national media. This was never the case during the 18th and 19th centuries. At the same time, some things about Supreme Court confirmation have stayed the same. The president and Senate still share responsibility over judicial appointments although the role of the Senate has been relegated to consenting on presidential picks rather than advising. Nevertheless conflict remains a cornerstone of Supreme Court confirmations. One dramatic change is the level of direct public involvement in the process. Advancements in communication technology have made it easier for grassroots organizations to mobilize their faithful to bring voices of concern or support to the attention of senators on matters of judicial selection.

Although many aspects of judicial selection are uncertain, this is clear: So long as the Supreme Court remains an influential force in American democracy, conflict will remain a central part of the process of selecting justices.

The rights revolution, which started in the aftermath of the New Deal, has awaken Americans to the personal connections that Supreme Court decisions have with their lives. They no longer simply take a back seat in the judicial theater to observe events as they unfold. Rather, many partake in the events by voicing their opinion to their elected officials in Washington. It appears that senators do listen and do respond. From that perspective, the selection of Supreme Court justices has become a wholly democratic process.

# Agenda Setting in the Supreme Court

During the great debates over ratification of the Constitution, Alexander Hamilton of New York expressed the hope that justices will act as general monitors, broadly supervising the other branches of government and the states and holding them firmly to the path of constitutional duty.[1] The unique authority possessed by the Supreme Court in its exercise of the power of judicial review leaves a trail of incontrovertible evidence that Hamilton's wish has been realized and that it continues to bear fruit with each passing term of the Court. The Supreme Court builds its agenda one case at a time, term after term in order to fulfill Hamilton's wish of monitoring the course of legal rights and freedom in American democracy.

There are two stages of decision making in the Court: the agenda-setting and the merit decision stage. In the agenda-setting stage, justices select which cases to hear during the term. This first stage and the activities surrounding it form the focus of this chapter. In the second, merit decision stage, justices make final decisions whether to reverse, affirm, or remand the judgment of the lower court in the cases selected for consideration. In many respects, the Supreme Court represents the structural embodiment of freedom and democracy in America. Visit many societies around the world and you will find that cultural inhibitions counsel citizens and groups to file lawsuits sparingly or only as a last resort when attempting to solve important civil and criminal disputes. In the United States, however, if we set aside the cost of litigation, there are virtually no cultural inhibitions for citizens, organized groups, labor unions, corporations, and state and federal governments to file lawsuits against one another. French commentator Alexis de Tocqueville is correct when, after touring the United States in 1835, he observed that nearly every important dispute resolves into a judicial one in America.[2]

The cases (or petitions) that come to the Court all seek one thing: resolution in the loftiest court in the land. Cases arrive in the Supreme Court in the thousands each year. They pour in throughout the year from large cities and small towns, from rich and poor individuals, from interest groups, labor unions, corporations, and other entities across the land. As recently as 2006, petitioners were filing roughly 169 cases per week. During that year, 8857 cases landed at the Court's doorstep. Almost all were supported by at least one outside organization having no direct association with the case but acting as a "friend" of the Court to provide information that might be useful to justices.

The information these friends provide is usually compiled and submitted to the Court in what is called *amicus curiae* or friend of the Court brief.

As one can well imagine, while the information that these outside briefs furnish the justices can prove useful in their decision making, it is rarely neutral or unbiased. After all, groups hoping to influence the Court's decisions typically have narrower policy or ideological objectives compared to the justices' collective and broader goal of advancing understanding of the law.

The Court is located just across from the nation's Capitol. A visitor to the Court is welcome by the magnificent white marble pillars of the majestic building. The façade on the Court's entrance presents image carvings of ancient philosophers extolling the virtues of good and evil and calling upon litigants to come forth and receive "Equal Justice under Law." The Court's exterior and the internal customs under which justices operate are designed to command respect and convey the seriousness of the enterprise upon which the Court embarks every term. Nine months out of the year, from the first Monday in October until the end of June the following year, the Court is in session, addressing the most complex and mature legal questions brought forth.

When the Supreme Court speaks, American citizens listen and this is reflected in the Court's ever-increasing caseload. Citizens listen because of two very simple reasons. The first is the Court's perceived aura of impartiality. The second is its tradition of taking the long view on how the nation should resolve conflicts. These two reasons are commodities upon which public admiration and support for the Supreme Court rest. While it is true that public attitudes toward the Court fluctuate, a residue of public deference, if not reverence, for the Court remains a major source of "psychic income" for the justices.[3]

For the two reasons stated above, citizens are willing to grant justices the legitimacy and power they need to make controversial judgments that, from time to time, even a majority of citizens might find troubling. For example, most citizens were dismayed in 2005 when the Court severely restricted the property rights of ordinary citizens in *Kelo v. City of New London*.[4] Justices ruled that a city government could seize private property for purposes of profit-making private redevelopment. The Court declared that such seizure constitutes "public use" under the Constitution. According to the majority opinion authored by Justice John Paul Stevens, a local government could not take a homeowner's private property "simply to confer a private benefit on a particular private party." But in the *Kelo* case, the justices reasoned that the New London, Connecticut, redevelopment project was "a carefully considered redevelopment plan," which would confer a tax benefit to the city. Through this decision, the Court afforded legislatures broad latitude to determine what public needs justify the use of the takings clause of the Constitution.

This chapter takes an in-depth view on how Supreme Court justices set the plenary agenda for the Court. It does so while recognizing important historical norms established to ensure the integrity of agenda setting, norms such as the rule of four and the discuss list. In order to fully understand what the Court's agenda entails during any particular term, we must understand how that agenda is informed by the past, that is, how did we get here from there? Accordingly, we address the following questions in this chapter:

- Historically, what kinds of legal issues have been brought to the Supreme Court?
- How and why has Supreme Court caseload increased over time?
- What is the process by which the justices select which cases to hear?
- What are the domains of influence on the Court's decision to hear a case?

## An Evolutionary Account of Supreme Court Agenda Setting

An old cartoon from the *New Yorker Magazine* shows the manager of a baseball team who, engaged in a heated argument with an umpire, repeatedly pokes the umpire in the chest saying, "I'll take this all the way to the Supreme Court."[5] The cartoon portrays a popular myth in American society, which holds that any controversy can ultimately be resolved in the U.S. Supreme Court.

While this portrayal has a kernel of truth when applied to the earliest period of the Republic when the Court heard all petitions filed, the reality is quite different now. Not any controversy can be resolved in the Supreme Court. First, the Court does not resolve petty controversies such as a quarrel between a team manager and an umpire over a bad call during a little-league baseball game. Second, there are substantial transaction costs at stake. It is difficult and expensive to bring a case before the Court. One must hire a lawyer (often multiple lawyers) credentialed to practice before the Court and in most cases pay substantial sums for the privilege of legal representation in the Court. These potential costs plus Court filing fees are enough to dissuade all but the most determined individuals or groups to appeal their legal controversies all the way to the highest court. Third, for those cases that make it all the way, the vast majority are denied review or, if reviewed, would not receive a decision that fully settles the matter. Cases heard by the Court comprise a very small fraction of the total number of cases filed during each term. Justices lack the time and resources to put into deciding a large number of cases well. Therefore, they consider only the most important cases necessary for developing or clarifying national law. We shall examine later how the Court wades through all the cases filed to determine the most important ones to hear.

*Agenda setting* can be defined as the process by which an institution such as the Supreme Court determines which cases to hear in order to define constitutional rights and exert influence on the direction of public policy. The Court sets its agenda through the small number of cases (currently about 100) the justices decide to hear during each term. The decision to take a case is often informed by policy concerns of the justices[6] but as we shall see later, this is only one of several determinants. The cases they take raise a variety of complex questions. For example, does a state have a constitutional obligation to protect young children from physical abuse by their own parents? Does the due process clause of the Fifth Amendment protect a woman who seeks to terminate her unwanted pregnancy in violation of a state statute? Is an inmate who has served more than 20 years on death row and claims to suffer psychological torture as a consequence protected under the Eighth Amendment prohibition against cruel and unusual punishment? Could the press be punished for printing an outrageous, malicious satire?

None of these questions can easily be answered and that is exactly how the Court likes it. Under the Constitution, the justices actually do not decide cases but "issues and controversies" brought before the Court. Justices do not arrive at work each day with a concrete plan to decide only certain kinds of issues and shove others aside. Instead, the issues they tackle are solely contingent upon the kinds of controversies that come through the golden gates of the courthouse.

Technically, the Court's plenary agenda is shaped by litigants: individuals, interest groups, corporations, and governments that bring cases. Litigants are not subject to the control of the Court in terms of what issues they may bring. However, from time to time, the Court sends signals through its opinions about what area of the law needs further developing and hence the kinds of cases it would like to consider.[7] But it is litigants themselves who must determine what issues to bring to Court and how to frame those issues.

Over the years, the nature of the Court's agenda has undergone significant transformation. As society evolves, issues brought to Court to effectuate legal and social change usually shifts in response. Similarly, when membership in the Court changes, the nature of the decisions announced by the Court often changes as well. This is a reflection of Charles Darwin's evolutionary theory. The central lesson of evolutionary theory is that biological systems of organisms *evolve* through a process of symbiosis. Within those biological systems are individual organisms that undergo *change*.[8] But the logic of evolutionary theory is not limited to biological systems alone. We can apply a similar logic to help us better understand how governmental institutions such as Congress, the Supreme Court, or administrative agencies evolve. In the case of the Supreme Court, we do so by viewing the entire Court as a system and individual justices as organisms within the system. It is the sum of what individual justices do in a given Court and how they behave in their relationship with each other and with society that dictate how the Court as a system evolves. Agenda setting is, therefore, an integral part of the Court's evolution.

## TRANSFORMATION OF SUPREME COURT AGENDA

We can understand the Court's evolution by examining how its agenda has shifted and changed since the Court's inception. Careful study of the Court's agenda reveals at least four major historical periods in which a specific constitutional issue domain commanded the bulk of the Court's attention and decision making.

## Federalism and States Rights

The first historical period covered the Court's first 100 years (1789–1889). Issues of federalism and states rights dominated the agenda during this period in response to nation-building efforts of national leaders. Federalism is the principle that defines the nature of the relations between states and the federal government.[9] It is a key feature of what makes the United States a republic, with the two entities (the state and federal governments) each operating under a separate (and unequal) constitutions. This era was one in which the Court helped define the contours of federal power and the structure of national government and institutions. Table 4.1 shows the issue areas emphasized by the Court in the four different historical time periods.

Under Chief Justice John Marshall (1801–1835), the Court worked hard to establish and legitimate judicial review and to vigorously enforce the contract clause of the Constitution toward a vision of centralizing power in order to nourish economic growth through free market capitalism. Many of the cases we discussed in chapter 1, including *Marbury v. Madison* (1803) and *McCulloch v. Maryland* (1819), exemplify the type of issues that preoccupied the Supreme Court during this time. In addition, after Roger Brook Taney (1835–1864) took the helm as chief justice, greater recognition was given to states rights as defined by the Ninth and Tenth Amendments. The Taney Court tolerated strong decentralization of the American political system; it also wrongly and tragically tolerated slavery. Slavery was a major issue of legal and political conflict during this period as exemplified by that scourge of the Court: *Dred Scott v. Sanford* (1857). Slavery ended officially and theoretically after ratification of the Thirteenth Amendment in 1865.

## Economic Regulation

After the nation fought a brutal civil war (1862–1865) to end the deplorable practice of human slavery and to preserve the union, the second era was ushered

**Table 4.1** Areas of U.S. Supreme Court Emphasis by Historical Period

| Period | Duration | Areas of Supreme Court Emphasis |
|--------|----------|--------------------------------|
| I | 1789–1889 | Federalism and states rights |
| II | 1890–1945 | Economic regulation, primarily promoting *laissez-faire* and nongovernmental interference in markets |
| III | 1946–1970 | Fundamental freedoms of civil liberties and civil rights |
| IV | 1971–present | Individual privacy, environmental safety, and a return to federalism |

*Source*: Author's compilation

in. Emphasis in the Court's agenda shifted from state-building and federalism to reconstruction and regulation of business activity by state and federal authorities. This economic regulation period started during the time of President Benjamin Harrison in 1890 and ended in 1938 as President Franklin D. Roosevelt led efforts to bring the Great Depression to a close and deal with human atrocities of the economic collapse at home and the war in Europe (World War II). The Supreme Court aggressively promoted the philosophy of *laissez-faire* capitalism—the view that the economic life of the nation is best served by nongovernmental interference, little regulation of business and economic activity, and by letting the invisible hand of the market operate freely and be self-regulating. The current crisis in the financial markets leading to the $700 Billion bailout of Wall Street firms has raised questions about the free market philosophy of little or self-regulation.

A number of important cases decided during the era of free market promotion exemplified the Court's agenda and decision making. *Lochner v. New York* (1905) was the first monumental free market case decided and it set the tone for the Court's promarket posture on economic regulation. That position can be summarized by Thomas Paine's aphorism that "government is best which governs least." In *Lochner,* the justices prevented New York and other states from regulating labor contracts between employers and their workers. Other key cases decided during this period include the "sick chickens" case, *Schechter Poultry Corporation v. United States,*[10] which invalidated regulations of the poultry established under the National Industrial Recovery Act of 1933 (NIRA) to normalize prices and wages in the poultry industry, safeguard union organizing, and prevent the transportation and sale of sick chickens.

Another key case was *Carter v. Carter Coal Company*[11] that involved regulation of the coal mining industry. In this case, the Court rejected congressional effort to regulate certain aspects of the coal industry under the commerce clause. Combined, the "sick chickens" case and the coal mining case significantly weakened the ability of the political branches of government to control the economy. The decisions greatly angered President Roosevelt and precipitated his Court-packing campaign to stop the Court from stifling recovery plans designed to dig the nation out of the Great Depression. Interestingly, the Supreme Court reversed course and started supporting the president's policies beginning with *West Coast Motel v. Parish* in 1937 after public anger about the interbranch conflict grew.[12]

## Civil Rights, Liberties, and the Foundations of Privacy Rights

The most turbulent and transformative period of agenda setting in the Court's 20th-century history started in 1938 during the time of Chief Justice Charles Evan Hughes and ended in 1969 when Chief Justice Earl Warren retired. Litigation during this period focused on methodically fighting injustices inflicted by racial segregation and gender inequality on large segments of Americans and on laying the groundwork for a right to privacy.

The Court recognized greater constitutional protections for various social groups including blacks, women, criminal defendants, environmentalists, and the elderly.[13] Disadvantaged groups that typically experienced great difficulty penetrating the political process and who once regarded the Supreme Court as unresponsive gradually found in the Court a partner willing to give voice and recognition to their policy and legal concerns. Thus this period was primarily focused on civil rights and liberties as exemplified by *Brown v. Board of Education* (1954), which ended racial segregation of public schools and *Baker v. Carr* (1962), which enforced the supremacy of the federal government over state wishes.

Toward the end of this period the Supreme Court firmly articulated the foundations for a right to privacy in *Griswold v. Connecticut* (1965). This case involved the distribution of contraceptives to a married couple for purposes of family planning in violation of state law. The Court ruled that it is unconstitutional for a state to proscribe the dissemination of contraceptives to married couples. The Court went on to derive the right to privacy from the "penumbras and emanations" of various amendments to the Constitution. The justices pointed specifically to the First Amendment freedom of association, the Third Amendment right against the quartering of troops in private homes during peace time, the Fourth Amendment right that creates a zone of privacy around the individual and prevents government from engaging in unreasonable searches and seizures, the Fifth Amendment protection against self-incrimination, the Ninth Amendment holding that rights not enumerated in the Constitution shall not be disparaged. The amendment thus grants citizens the power to create additional rights for themselves. Finally, justices also rested the right to privacy on the Fourteenth Amendment's guarantee of liberty. *Griswold* was the warning shot that would open an intense culture war that ensued in the next period.

## Consolidation of Privacy and States Rights

The fourth period dates from 1970 to the present. During that period, litigation shifted toward consolidation and expansion of the right to privacy enunciated in *Griswold*. A key decision during this period was *Roe v. Wade* (1973), which legalized abortion and defined a trimester scheme under which states may regulate abortion. A woman's right to choose is untrammeled during the first trimester (0–3 months) as the decision to terminate a pregnancy is solely up to her and her attending physician. During the second trimester (4–6 months), quickening has occurred and a woman's right is no longer "unlimited" and "must be balanced against the state." States, therefore, may place minimum restrictions on abortion right but cannot prohibit abortion. Finally, a fetus can survive outside the womb during the third trimester (7–9 months) and the degree of permissible state regulation is high. States can ban abortion outright unless to protect the woman's life from serious jeopardy.

*Roe v. Wade* was a divisive decision that galvanized various social and religious groups into further litigation. The key issues in contention are whether states should fund abortion, designation of who should provide consent before abortion is performed, what type of record keeping requirements can be imposed on doctors, and whether a waiting period should be imposed.[14]

For many, the issue of privacy is today synonymous with abortion rights. However, from a constitutional perspective, the issue goes far beyond abortion rights. For example, privacy also implicates unreasonable searches and seizure by law enforcement officials in their effort to fight and prevent crime and terrorism. It implicates physician-assisted suicide, pornography on the Internet, euthanasia, gay unions, and so on. Through its decisions in these areas, the Supreme Court shapes our national identity and the kinds of issues citizens discuss around the water cooler at work and around the kitchen table at home.

Moving forward, there is suggestive evidence that after backpedaling on states rights and federalism claims for decades the Supreme Court is aggressively adjudicating these claims again. This push toward federalism claims has for the most part benefited states. Several conservative appointments to the Court by conservative presidents Reagan, George H.W. Bush, and his son W. Bush are primarily responsible for this shift. That movement is, however, dampened by some big decisions such as *Bush v. Gore* (2000), which overruled the Florida Supreme Court and prevented vote recount during the 2000 presidential election stalemate. Overall, *Bush v. Gore* is an important clue that the Court is, at the very least, inconsistent in its march toward reaffirming state sovereignty in intergovernmental relations.

## SUPREME COURT CASELOAD

*A Brief History.* The number of petitions filed in the U.S. Supreme Court has grown phenomenally over the past several decades despite congressional reforms to limit the Court's jurisdiction. Although the rate of case filing in recent decades has been phenomenal, overall this is not at all a new development. Historically, the Court has witnessed periods of significant caseload growth but this is dwarfed by recent caseload trends. And when workload becomes too burdensome, the Supreme Court has found it worthwhile to form partnerships with other branches of government for solutions. As Chief Justice Charles Evans Hughes in 1939 stated during an address to a joint session of Congress, "in the great enterprise of making democracy workable we are all partners. One member of our body politic cannot say to another—'I have no need of thee.' "[15]

Several examples of cooperation between lawmakers and judges in resolving caseload problems exist. In 1891, roughly 100 years after the Court began operations, Congress enacted the Evarts Act, which expanded the U.S. Courts of Appeals.[16] The circumstances that led to the Act would be eerily familiar today. The population of the United States grew tremendously after the civil war, partly because of high immigration from Europe. Population booms usually lead to greater social friction and litigation as struggle to obtain limited resources intensifies among citizens. But in addition to population boom, Congress expanded federal jurisdiction, leading to a growth in case filings in the courts. The trial courts were particularly hard hit as they strained to keep abreast of filings and reduce delays in processing cases and disseminating justice. After many public presentations by the justices, Congress took action to relieve the Court of what was at the time a crushing caseload. The expansion of the courts of appeals permitting a larger second tier of appellate review was a decisive solution to the caseload crunch. For example, during 1890, 623 new cases were docketed. However, during 1892, a year after the expansion of courts of appeals, only 275 new cases were filed in the Supreme Court. The courts of appeals have shown their usefulness as an effective screening device for potential Supreme Court cases.

Until 1925 the Supreme Court heard almost every case that aggrieved citizens and groups brought before it. Appealing a case to the Court and having it decided was viewed as a matter of right rather than an issue at the discretion of the Court. Justices felt distressed by the situation and complained about a burdensome caseload. Many of these cases were frivolous. Several temporary solutions were proposed but found unsatisfactory. Then at the urging of Chief Justice William H. Taft, Congress, in yet another spirit of cooperation, enacted the Certiorari Act of 1925 (sometimes called the "Judges Bill" because it was largely crafted by members of the Court when they worked at the basement of the U.S. Capitol). Although the new law expanded which parties could seek review by filing a petition for a writ of certiorari, it gave justices almost complete control over the Court's docket and it reduced the number of mandatory appeals. When asked "why shouldn't every litigant have a right to get a decision on his case from the Supreme Court?" Chief Justice Taft responded that in each case, there had already been one trial and appeal: "Two trials are enough for justice."[17] Because of the Judges Bill, the Supreme Court now rejects about 98 percent of requests for review.[18] In 1988, Congress eliminated virtually all of what remained of the Court's mandatory jurisdiction, giving the justices a free hand in selecting which cases to hear.[19] Nevertheless, requests for review have continued to rise.

What does the Supreme Court caseload look like? How much have petitions grown and how has the Court responded? To address these questions, we shall focus on three general trends: (1) the growth in caseload; (2) number of petitions granted review; and (3) growth in the number of Supreme Court staff.[20]

## Supreme Court Caseload Increases

Throughout the Court's first 10 years in business the total number of cases filed did not surpass 100. But the number of cases grew slowly albeit unevenly over the next several decades. It was not until 1916 when Americans were fully engaged in World War I that Supreme Court petitions surpassed 660 during a single year. The slow pace of caseload growth in the Court has since changed. The social movements of the 1950s and 1960s brought about a dramatic increase in the number of petitions to the Supreme Court as groups fought for justice, fair wages, and political freedom.

Figure 4.1 shows the trend in the number of new petitions filed each term in the Supreme Court and the total number of petitions on the docket from 1880 to 2004. The total cases docketed include those carried over from the previous term. Clearly, there is an impressive upward trend in both

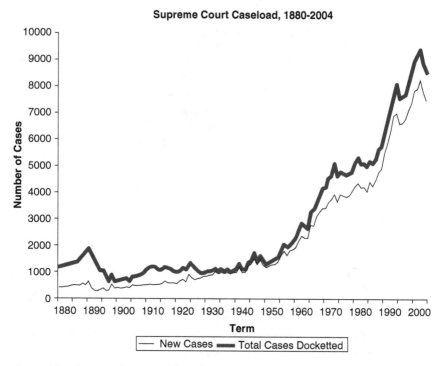

**Figure 4.1**    Supreme Court Caseload, 1880–2004.

categories, with the rate of increase growing sharply after 1960. A *docket* is comprised of all the cases filed that are awaiting Court action. The number is usually higher than the number of petitions filed during that term because of carryovers. This could mean several things. First, the Court might be experiencing difficulty staying abreast of case filings. Second, there are many cases in which further information is required from attorneys in order to clarify a particular point of law and reach a logical and defendable decision. As the figure shows, there has been a fivefold increase in the total number of petitions docketed from 1880 to 2004 and a tenfold increase in the number of new petitions during that time.

## Explaining Supreme Court Caseload Increases

We have determined that Supreme Court filings have increased dramatically and that the rate of increase was slow from 1880 up until the early 1950s. After that, the rate of increase accelerated. The question is what explains this dramatic increase in caseload since the 1950s? Empirical research points to three theoretical explanations.

*Institutional Theory.* The institutional explanation of caseload increases draws from research looking at activities inside the Supreme Court concerning how the Court develops its agenda by selecting which cases to hear.[21] According to this theory, Supreme Court precedents and the manner in which the Court processes and disposes of cases stimulate further litigation. For example, precedent can signal to potential litigants that the Court is highly motivated to achieve legal change in a particular area of law. This was indeed the situation in the 1950s and 1960s.

During this period, the Warren Court adopted a philosophy of expanding civil rights and granting access to individuals and groups that were typically shot out of the political process. The justices outlawed racial segregation in public education, signaling clearly their willingness to change legal policy concerning *de jure* (i.e., state authorized) discrimination. In doing so, justices established new areas of litigation, including forced busing of school children and remedial altering of attendance zones.

Busing was a politically unpopular solution to integration. Efforts to use busing to achieve integration led to community discord and civil unrest in the 1970s. For instance, a plan approved by a federal district court requiring busing to achieve racial integration in Charlotte, North Carolina, was strongly opposed by a majority of the Charlotte-Mecklenburg School Board. The resulting dispute between the Board and integration advocates, including parents such as Charlotte native James Swann, led to the case *Swann v. Charlotte-Mechlenburg Board of Education* (1971). In *Swann*, the Court upheld the power of district courts to use reasonable means to achieve racial balance in elementary schools, including teacher reassignment and busing of school children. Meanwhile, in Boston, riots broke out between integration advocates (who saw busing as a reasonable solution) and disgruntled parents (who saw busing as a state-sponsored assault on their community, families, and children).

Tackling racial segregation was only one dimension of an expanding caseload. The Court also decided a number of cases in the 1960s that recognized and expanded the rights of criminal defendants. Three decisions in particular motivated further litigation as prison inmates and criminal defendants sought judicial redress based upon these decisions. The first of these three cases *Mapp v. Ohio* (1961) incorporated the exclusionary rule, making it applicable to the states. The rule had never been this widely applied ever since it was judicially created in 1949 in the case of *Wolf v. Colorado* to safeguard Fourth Amendment rights, which according to Justice Robert Jackson "belong in the catalog of indispensable freedoms."[22]

By definition, the exclusionary rule postulates that evidence obtained by law enforcement officers during an illegal search cannot be used against a defendant in a criminal trial. The logic of the exclusionary rule is that government must not benefit from engaging in illegal activity in order to prosecute illegal activity. For years, the exclusionary rule barred only the federal government from presenting illegally seized evidence in Court. State authorities could use such evidence. This inconsistency was not only unfair to suspects it also made the exclusionary rule a prime candidate for abuse. Indeed, the abuse was so flagrant that the exclusionary rule was knick-named the "silver platter" doctrine because federal officials would seize evidence illegally and hand it over to state officials (presumably in a silver platter) so that state officials can prosecute the accused offender.

After the *Mapp* decision came down, defendants convicted and sentenced on the basis of evidence obtained unlawfully filed habeas corpus petitions in the Supreme Court, requesting reexamination of their cases and possible release from prison. The Court applied its *Mapp* decision retroactively, permitting thousands of inmates to file petitions for redress. Many ultimately gained their freedom. During the 1980s, the Court went on to create several exceptions to its *Mapp* decision; exceptions that critics say undermine the effectiveness of the exclusionary rule to deter police misconduct. One is the good faith exception announced in *United States v. Leon* (1984). The Court ruled that evidence seized on the basis of a faulty warrant, which officers had reason to believe was valid, can indeed be used in Court.

Three years after *Mapp*, the Court decided the second of the three truly important criminal justice cases: *Escobedo v. Illinois* (1964). Escobedo involved the right of the accused to be granted access to a lawyer before interrogation under the Sixth Amendment. Among the requirements of the Sixth Amendment is that "In all criminal prosecutions, the accused shall enjoy the right...to have the Assistance of Counsel for his defense." When Danny Escobedo was arrested by Illinois police in January 1960, the defendant was accused of murdering his brother-in-law for apparently physically abusing and mistreating Escobedo's sister. Police interrogated Escobedo for more than 24 hours, denied him access to food and water and his attorney. The Supreme Court explained that the interrogation stage is where the accused is most vulnerable in the justice system, the stage when legal aid and advice are most critical to the accused. The Court went on to establish a procedural safeguard requiring the presence of an attorney before questioning.

The case left many important procedural questions unanswered. One concerned how the new due process requirement of attorney presence before questioning would be enforced. In a society where most citizens who are entangled in the criminal justice system are ill-informed, how would the accused be made aware of their right to an attorney before questioning? The Supreme Court addressed this question two years later in 1966 in *Miranda v. Arizona*. The justices enunciated the now famous *Miranda* warnings, requiring that as soon as an individual becomes the target of a criminal investigation or before being placed in custody, officers must inform the accused prior to any questioning of his or her right, which includes the guarantee of effective assistance of counsel under the Sixth Amendment. Officers must warn the accused that "[Suspect] has a right to remain silent, that any statement he does make may be used as evidence against him, and that he has a right to the presence of an attorney, either retained or appointed."[23]

The defendant may waive these rights but only "voluntarily, knowingly, and intelligently."[24] Further, the Court stipulated that there must be no questioning if the accused "indicates in any manner and at any time of the process that he wishes to consult with an attorney before speaking."[25] Based on these three cases (*Mapp*, *Escobedo*, and *Miranda*), the Warren Court opened the courthouse gates, and habeas corpus petitions from prisoners poured into the Court.

The Warren Court's revolutionary treatment of the rights of defendants has spurned several Bill of Rights success stories. One telling example is the case of Clarence Earl Gideon, a poor and illiterate man who was charged with burglary in Florida.[26] Under Florida law, he was denied access to a lawyer for his defense because he was not facing a capital offense. Because Gideon was too poor to hire an attorney, he defended himself and was easily convicted and sentenced to prison. While in prison he produced a handwritten petition on prison stationary and submitted it to the Supreme Court. The petition was granted and the Court appointed attorney Abe Fortas to represent Gideon in the case *Gideon v. Wainwright* (1963). Several organizations filed amicus curiae briefs supporting Gideon. Gideon won his case and through it, the Court made the Sixth Amendment right to attorney applicable to the states. Hence, no longer are states permitted to try and convict criminal defendants and send them to prison without the assistance of counsel to assist in their defense unless the defendants refuse such assistance. These cases are representative only of the kinds of criminal appeals the Warren Court faced. Importantly, through its decisions in these cases, the Court unwittingly encouraged more litigation.

We conclude this discussion of institutional theory of litigation by noting that the Warren Court's revolutionary treatment of the rights of the criminally accused has been both reviled and praised by attorneys, judges, and policymakers. Opponents of the Court's criminal justice forays argue that justices of the Warren Court tied the hands of law enforcement officers and restrained their ability to apprehend and prosecute criminals in order to protect citizens. Supporters argue that without the exclusionary rule, *Miranda* warnings, and other safeguard principles, law enforcement officials would have little incentive to respect the law.

*Social Development Theory.* Another theory that explains the increase in the Supreme Court caseload is derived from research focusing on developments outside the Court. Social development theory holds that legal change is fundamentally predicated upon changes in society itself in terms of how individuals interact with one another.[27] In particular, social development theory relies on patterns of social interaction within the context of (1) population growth and (2) technological transformation to explain litigation increase. As society becomes more complex and more hierarchical, making communal relations more difficult to maintain, it becomes more likely that litigation and other formal means of dispute resolution would be utilized.[28]

The 1950s and 1960s provide a convenient window for demonstrating the essence of the social development theory. Population growth is retrospective in that it can inform us about our past. Although Americans strive for egalitarianism as a defining value, social class conflict has always been a part of society. The intense racial, gender, and class conflict that the nation experienced during the 1950s and 1960s can be attributed partly to population boom after World War II. On July 1, 1945, U.S. population was approximately 140 million. Ten years later, on July 1, 1955, total U.S. population had exploded to roughly 166 million.[29] It is no coincidence that the Court experienced its sharpest caseload increases during this period.

Technological transformations are a second dimension of social development theory. During the 1950s and 1960s, despite troubling social unrests, the nation was at the cusp of significant scientific and technological innovations. The creation of the National Science Foundation in 1950 to support scientific discoveries, the work of NASA and its monumental achievement of placing a man on the moon, the collaborative efforts that led to establishment of the Internet all generated optimism that spurred new business ventures and risk taking. Industrialization grew rapidly during this period with significant help from the G.I. Bill as returning soldiers went back to school to hone their technological and leadership skills. Many eventually joined the civilian labor force, started new businesses, which contributed significantly to economic growth. In the 1970s, the Internet became a reality and online communication took off in the 1980s and 1990s. It would be hard to conclude from even a cursory look at litigation trends that technological change did not contribute to the increase in Supreme Court caseload, especially in the area of commerce, indecency, privacy, and artistic expression.[30]

*Political Culture Theory.* Like the social development theory, political culture theory is based on external forces. But rather than relying on population growth and social and technological complexity in society, this theory relies on a culture of litigiousness to explain the explosion in Supreme Court caseload. According to this theory, litigation is a form of political participation, much like the act of voting. An important part of the culture of litigiousness is the activism of interest groups and their reaction to the large number of statutes enacted by Congress and the states. Traditionally, new legislation leads to more litigation as groups and individuals hurt by the new law seek redress in Court and those favored by the new legislation fight to preserve benefits conferred by it. Under the political culture theory then, winning in Court is not the main motivation for litigation. Instead, litigation is viewed as a way to shine a spotlight on an issue and bring it to the nation's attention.

## PETITIONS GRANTED REVIEW

Even though petitions have increased dramatically over time in the Supreme Court, the number actually granted review remains very small and has not changed much over the past several decades. Generally speaking, the Supreme Court grants review to roughly 1–2 percent of the cases filed, that is, between 80 and 125 cases. The number of paid petitions increased slowly from 1926 to 1980 and has been declining since then. In 1980, 2749 paid petitions were filed but only 167 (6 percent) were granted review. *In forma pauperis* cases (those filed by indigents unable to pay the required

$300 filing fee), on the other hand, have been on a rampage, recording a very dramatic increase overall. These cases are filed mostly by prisoners hoping to have their convictions reexamined by the Supreme Court and possibly overturned. During the 1960s, the Warren Court expanded the rights of criminal defendants and convicts to receive a fair hearing and this partly led to strong increases in Court filings from this group. *In forma pauperis* petitions are significantly less likely to be granted review. In 1980, for example, 2371 *in forma pauperis* cases were filed and only 17 were granted review.

Part of the explanation why only a small number of petitions overall are granted review is that Supreme Court justices do not perceive a real conflict in most petitions filed. Moreover, since justices do their own work (with the help of law clerks), they are easily overwhelmed if they take too many cases for decision. In addition, even though individual cases might be highly important to a prisoner, cases granted review by the Supreme Court must raise legal questions of the highest national importance. The vast majority of the petitions brought to the Court either in the paid docket or nonpaid docket never meet this importance requirement.

### Number of Court Employees

Finally, an important issue in considering Supreme Court caseload is the number of employees hired to process the petitions and keep the Court running smoothly before, during, and after the justices consider those petitions. Until 1930 the number of Supreme Court staff never reached 60. But since 1935, the Court has experienced a significant increase in its staff in reaction to overall caseload increases. Even so, the increase in staff has lagged increases in caseload.

The Supreme Court moved from its temporary site in the basement of the U.S. Congress to its permanent site across the Capitol in 1935. The move required the Court to hire additional personnel, including almost 30 positions for guards and janitorial services. After the move, the number of employees rose sharply, then experienced a small decline during World War II, and then resumed a steady increase. Overall, the number of Supreme Court employees has risen 733 percent from 55 in 1935 to 458 in 2005. But this is a small increase relative to the 853 percent increase in the number of cases on the docket in approximately the same period. The Court's docket has risen from 901 cases in 1935 to 8584 total in 2004.[31]

Court employees are responsible for processing these cases, directing their flow to the correct offices once they enter the courthouse, and for ensuring a smooth flow of communication about the cases within the building. Supreme Court personnel comprises of full-time permanent positions included in congressional appropriations each year. They include administrators, secretaries, couriers, guards, cleaning crew, law clerks, Clerk of the Court, and the Marshall. Individuals assigned to the care of the Supreme Court building and grounds under authority granted by Congress are not included in the Court employee count.

## GETTING CASES TO THE SUPREME COURT

Cases appealed to the Supreme Court have their source in state or federal trial courts or federal regulatory agencies. Trial courts are the original courts of record for purposes of appealing a case all the way to the Supreme Court. By tradition, cases that originate in the federal court system always remain within the federal system. Similarly, cases that originate from the state system tend to stay within the state system but not always. One example is prisoner petitions, which can move from a state court system to a federal court system based on a writ of habeas corpus if a federal or constitutional question can be raised.

State and federal judicial systems in the United States have three main levels. At the lowest rung of the judicial hierarchy are trial courts, the live blood of the American justice system. These courts are mainly responsible for holding jury or bench (i.e., judge) trials in civil and criminal cases, determining the facts of the case, and issuing a verdict of guilty or not guilty based on the application of law to the facts. Figure 4.2 shows the flow of cases from trial courts to the U.S. Supreme Court. Trial courts include the 94 federal district courts, U.S. Court of International Trade, state trial courts, as well as noncivilian courts such as military trial courts and the Foreign Intelligence Surveillance Court. Cases from these courts can be appealed to the regional courts of appeals or to intermediate state appellate courts (state cases only). Cases from the federal appeals courts can be appealed to the U.S. Supreme Court. However, cases from intermediate state appellate courts must first be appealed to the state's highest court, usually the State Supreme Court before they can be appealed to the U.S. Supreme Court.[32]

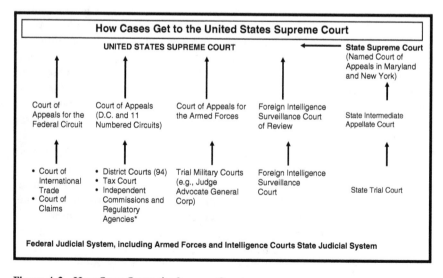

Figure 4.2   How Cases Get to the Supreme Court.

Getting a case to the Supreme Court involves resources. One needs money to conduct research to prepare the petition. Most litigants hire several attorneys or a law firm to represent them and this can be very expensive. In some cases, an interest group would sponsor the case and use it as a test case if doing so advances the cause that the interest groups seeks to champion. Many examples abound. *Roe v. Wade* was a test case sponsored by the National Organization for Women (NOW) to advance women's rights. The organization used its own resources to conduct the research necessary to prepare and file the petition; NOW also provided the lawyers who helped in arguing the case before the Supreme Court.

## PROCESSING OF CASES

When a case is appealed to the Supreme Court, the Court must first take jurisdiction. Jurisdiction is the power of a court, including the Supreme Court, to hear and decide a case and issue a remedy. The Supreme Court has two types of jurisdiction: *original and appellate.* Original jurisdiction is specified in Article 3 of the Constitution. Original jurisdiction means that the Court has the power to decide a case for the first time. Therefore, in original jurisdiction cases, the justices sit as both jury and judge, establishing the facts of the case, applying the law to those facts, and making a decision. Only one or two original jurisdiction cases are appealed to the Court each term and they typically concern disputes between two states, a state and the federal government, or dispute involving foreign ambassadors. Original jurisdiction is nondiscretionary. The Court cannot exercise gate-keeping powers and reject original cases if they have been properly filed. Justices are obligated to decide them.

A good example of an original jurisdiction case is the boundary dispute brought to the Court in 1998 between New York State and New Jersey over ownership of a portion of Ellis Island, the site of the Statue of Liberty. Until 1954, Ellis Island was the primary entrance point for new immigrants to the United States. Afterward, it became a lucrative tourist destination with New York providing maintenance for the site and collecting all the tourism revenue.

New Jersey sought to share in the tourism boom by claiming ownership of part of Ellis Island. Specifically, the dispute was whether submerged land on New Jersey's side of Ellis Island, which was eventually exposed and was then filed by New York, belonged to New York under an 1834 compact between the two states. That compact deemed Ellis Island part of New York but said nothing about ownership of submerged lands. The Supreme Court ruled, in *New Jersey v. New York*,[33] that since New Jersey had sovereignty over previously submerged portions of Ellis Island, and since the compact did not specify rights of ownership, New Jersey would retain sovereignty. The Court thus supported New Jersey's claim. By implication, part of the tourism revenue now must go to New Jersey. Territorial disputes between states are now less frequent than in times past. Consequently, few original jurisdiction cases show up at the Court's doorstep each term.

Most cases arrive at the Court under its appellate jurisdiction. Appellate jurisdiction is discretionary in nature, meaning that rather than being a matter of constitutional or statutory requirement, it is ultimately up to the Court to agree to hear a case. Cases coming under appellate jurisdiction have already been decided by a lower court and so a record has been established of the relevant facts involved. This is an important distinguishing feature between original and appellate jurisdiction cases.

The Court exercises appellate jurisdiction in three ways. First, a litigant filing under appellate jurisdiction may request a writ of certiorari ("cert" for short). The vast majority of the more than 9000 new petitions filed in the Court each year are petitions for a writ of certiorari. Second, a case can reach the Supreme Court through a mechanism known as certification, a rarely used method. *Certification* is a request for guidance on a legal matter filed by a lower appeals court to the Supreme Court. By an Act of Congress, lower appellate courts (usually represented by the chief judge) can file a writ of certification asking the Supreme Court to answer questions that would help clarify the law. The justices can then clarify the law or simply certify the case for automatic appeal to the Supreme Court. Because only lower appellate court judges can request a writ of certification, this option is not directly available to litigants and so the number of cases sent to the Supreme Court via certification is typically very small in any given term.

Finally, under appellate jurisdiction cases can be brought "on appeal." These are cases that Congress has determined are so important to the proper functioning of American democracy that, as a matter of right, a decision from the Supreme Court is warranted. Historically, these included cases in which a state trial court upheld a state law challenged as violating the U.S. Constitution. In judicial reforms passed by Congress and signed into law in 1988 at the urging of the Court, Congress eliminated virtually all appeals cases except those few appealed from a special three-judge district court panel often involving the Voting Rights Act of 1964.[34]

Petitions are submitted to the Office of the Clerk year round. The Court has precise guidelines for writing the petition and presenting its content. For example, petitions must be written on paper that is opaque, unglazed, 6 ⅛ by 9 ¼ inches in size, not less than 60 pounds in weight and have margins of at least three-fourths of an inch on all sides. Under Court rules, some exceptions are made for paupers (those who cannot afford the filing fee of $300 for most petitions). In that case, petitions can be written on 8 ½ by 11 inches paper.[35] In addition, the petition for certiorari must be presented in an order specified by Court rules. For example, the petition must contain "the questions presented for review," expressed concisely in relation to the circumstances of the case, without unnecessary detail. This must be presented on the first page following the cover; the brief must then present a list of all the parties to the proceeding. This is followed by a table of contents. This abbreviated description of the rules gives a glimpse of what is required in order to file a case in the Supreme Court. The main concern of the Court in setting these precise rules is to improve efficiency in its work by ensuring that the petition itself is legible and that information is presented consistently across petitions so that it can be easily accessed. Cases that meet the Court's precise filing requirements are then assigned a docket number and distributed to the justices' chambers.

To summarize, Article 3 of the Constitution permits the Supreme Court to decide cases of first instance (those that have not been decided by any other court) under its original jurisdiction. A very small subset of cases decided by the Court each term arrives at the Court's doorstep under original jurisdiction. The vast majority of cases arrive under its appellate jurisdiction, which includes those brought via a writ of appeal, certification, or certiorari.

## Deciding to Decide

The Court must first make a collective decision whether to grant or deny cert. Thus cases that have been properly filed must undergo additional screening. With the help of their law clerks, the justices would review the petitions and prepare for the cert conference where they would vote to grant or deny the case a hearing. For both the Court and litigants, this is a very important stage of the process of appellate review. Take the petitioner for example. A positive outcome at this stage means that the case has been selected for review and access to justice in the Supreme Court has been granted. A negative decision signifies that in the minds of the justices, the case is insufficiently important, the litigation has run its course, and so the lower court decision stands.

*The Discuss List.* Supreme Court docket was mandatory until 1925. Justices had to decide every case brought. Since then the history of the Court's obligatory jurisdiction in both law and practice can be described as "a tale of retrenchment rather than expansion"[36] as the number of cases actually decided has become smaller and smaller. It was during this period that Chief Justice Charles Evans Hughes established the tradition of setting up a discuss list, that is, a list of petitions that the chief thinks sufficiently worthy of the Court's attention. The list is circulated to other justices who can add cases to the list but cannot remove cases from it except those they themselves have placed on the list. The first known use of the discuss list was in 1931, according to the papers of Justice Harlan Fiske Stone.[37] In one memorandum sent by Chief Justice Hughes to Justice Stone, the Chief wrote: "My Dear Justice Stone: I enclose a list of petitions for certiorari to be presented to the Conference (week of October 7) simply by number and title. If you desire one of the cases on the list to be stated to the Conference, kindly let me know."[38] From the chief justice's perspective as the Court's administrator, the discuss list serves primarily an administrative function. But more generally, the discuss list holds possibilities for strategic behavior as well.

Based upon the recently released papers of Justice Harry Blackmun, we have learned more about the discuss list. It turns out that a justice can also add a case to the list by circulating a memo to the other justices indicating a desire to add a particular case or set of cases to the list.[39] Occasionally a justice would withdraw a case he or she has placed on the list often without stating a reason, but apparently reflecting a change of mind about the cert worthiness of the petition. Justices who withdraw a case from consideration may be motivated by strategic reasons. A justice acts strategically by adjusting his or her behavior in anticipation of how others will act in the future. For example, Justice O'Connor may withdraw from consideration a case she has placed on the discuss list if she determines in retrospect that there will be insufficient votes on the merit to achieve her desired policy objective. Cases not placed on the discuss list are assumed to be *dead-listed*, meaning no justice considers them important enough or appropriate for discussion in the cert conference.[40] Therefore, for litigants who seek a decision on the merits in the Supreme Court, getting on the discuss list is the first major hurdle that they must overcome.

## Preparing for the Certiorari Conference

The cert conference is one of two secret conferences Supreme Court justices hold during seven two-week sessions throughout the term. You would recall that the cert conference is to discuss and vote on which petitions the Court would hear during that term. Justices usually come to the conference armed with discussion points about the cases. They would attempt to convince their colleagues why the cases they have placed on the discuss list deserve a hearing. To help them prepare for conference, justices rely significantly on their law clerks. Law clerks are like junior associates in a law firm. They assist justices with researching cases, preparing bench memos, and writing opinion drafts of cases that have been argued in Court.

*The Certiorari Pool.* During the Burger Court, a procedural change known as the "cert pool" was introduced into the agenda-setting process to assist justices in preparing for conference. Initiated in the early 1970s, cert pool was the brainchild of Justice Lewis Powell. It is the practice of using law clerks to review petitions and distill their most essential legal questions and arguments. Justices willing to participate in the cert pool each contribute a law clerk to the pool and receive in return a common "pool memorandum" on each case from a single clerk. In other words, once in the pool, law clerks divide the petitions among themselves and each prepares an evaluation of the assigned petitions based upon the records and briefs. The evaluation would then be distributed to those justices participating in the cert pool. In this way instead of the justice reading every petition in preparation for the cert conference, he/she needs only to read the summary evaluation prepared by the clerk. Thus the chief advantage of the cert pool is that it enhances efficiency and flexibility for justices. In addition, it has the virtue of ensuring that each petition receives a careful reading from one clerk, which might be impossible were each justice's clerks to review every petition.

From a litigants' perspective, however, the cert pool does come with certain disadvantages. One is that justices deny themselves the opportunity to truly master the details of the case on their own terms before casting their cert vote. Another disadvantage is that, from the perspective of legal change, law clerks can have too much power and influence in the cert decision and hence on the development of the law, which is not altogether a positive development. Finally, according to Kenneth Starr, former clerk to Chief Justice Warren Burger and independent counsel in the Whitewater investigation, law clerks in the cert pool face "a hydraulic pressure to say no."[41] It is harder for a clerk to run afoul with the justices by recommending a denial of certiorari than by recommending a grant, which might later be dismissed as improvidently granted, possibly bringing disgrace upon the clerk.

To avoid such problems, justices do read the pool memos carefully, relying on the judgment that comes from experience, and sometimes asking their own clerks to add comments and suggestions. Ultimately, the responsibility over the petition lies with justices. And as Justice Ginsburg indicated, "When in doubt, we do read the petitions and responses." Partly for the disadvantages stated, Justice John Paul Stevens has long opted out of the cert pool custom. In 2008, he was joined by Justice Samuel Alito.[42]

Decisions made at the cert conference constitute a vital part of the gatekeeping authority of the Court. Only Justices can attend the conferences. This policy is designed to provide an environment where justices can feel totally free and uninhibited to communicate their views without fear of public criticism or embarrassment. Therefore, what transpires behind the closed doors of the conference room constitutes one of the best kept secrets in Washington DC.

*The Handshake.* The Supreme Court Bench comprises a mixture of complex and oftentimes difficult personalities who must work together as professional colleagues over a lifetime. In light of the important questions justices face each day (many of which challenge their core beliefs), how do they get along? More importantly, how do they keep from harboring personal grudges that might threaten the fabric of their interpersonal relationships and possibly jeopardize their performance on the bench? The answer can be found in the ritual of the handshake. Members of the Court shake each other's hand as a show of friendship and collegial bonding before the start of each gathering to conduct official business. Shaking hands with one another of the justices also communicates forgiveness for whatever anguish a justice might have caused another in previous encounters. Thus the handshake discourages vendettas, promotes camaraderie and peace in the Supreme Court family.

*Observing the Rule of Four and Notifying Petitioners.* Following the handshake that signals the start of the certiorari conference, justices would take their seat at a rectangular table in the conference room located adjacent to the chambers of the chief justice. The conference table is not as large as one might expect, given the size of the Court and the weighty issues debated there. As Justice T. Marshall described, "it is a small table...just big enough for the nine of us."[43] There the justices discuss all matters freely and openly before casting their votes. If four of the nine justices vote to consider a case, then the case is granted cert and placed on the Court's plenary calendar.[44] This is called the *rule of four*. It is of immense procedural importance. If the Court were to require fewer than four votes to grant cert, then many more cases would meet that lower threshold for consideration and the justices would then have to give consideration to far more cases than they perhaps can handle, ultimately leading to rushed or poor decisions. On the other hand, if the Court were to require more than four votes for cert, then the vote on the final decision stage (the merit state) would in all practical purposes be preordained. Thus the rule of four reminds the justices that the case is not over and it forces justices to give more careful consideration to the legal arguments laid out in the briefs and as pointed out by counsel during oral argument.

Once a case has been selected for consideration, the Clerk of the Court would notify the successful petitioners and invite them to file legal brief on the merit. This begins the long process of deciding the outcome of the case. The appellant (the party that lost the case in the lower court and is now appealing) has 45 days to file the brief on the merit; the respondent (the defendant) has 30 days to file a response after receiving the appellant's brief. The Court is under no obligation to notify petitioners whose cases have been denied cert nor is the Court under any obligation to explain why a case was granted or denied cert. For now, it suffices to note that the Court's own rules specify that petitions for a writ of certiorari would be "granted only for compelling reasons." Lawyers and litigants must, therefore, discern whether their case presents a compelling reason as explained in rule 10 of the Court (see the next section). Indeed, according to one notable observer of the Court's cert process, H.W. Perry (1991, 221), "justices do not want lawyers or anyone else to know precisely what it is that makes a case certworthy." This blunt characterization of the American Court's certiorari process is not unique. The Supreme Court of Canada, for example, is equally reticent about spelling out precisely what makes a case cert worthy. The Canadian Supreme Court uses such vague and elastic terms as "public importance" or "significance" as the jurisprudential basis for deciding whether to grant leave to appeal a lower court decision.[45]

Since the Court has made it a practice of not notifying petitioners denied review, how do these petitioners learn about their cert decision? Before the electronic age, petitioners learn of the Court's decision if they do not receive an invitation to submit briefs on the merit as the term draws to a close. During the Internet age, however, petitioners can learn of the Court's decision by reviewing the calendar of cases scheduled for consideration in the Court's official Web site.

## CONSIDERATIONS AFFECTING CASE SELECTION

Why are some cases granted cert while others are denied? Despite the lack of communication from the Court itself about why justices deny cert, this has not stopped political scientists and legal scholars from researching considerations affecting cert worthiness.[46] As Donald R. Songer pointed out, an explanation of the Court's cert decisions must begin by recognizing that justices have a great many cases to review in a relatively short time.[47] As their workload increases, it is logical to infer that they would devote relatively less time than deserved to review case material before making a decision. One study estimated that at most the justices spend an average of 9.5 minutes to review a paid petition for certiorari and considerably less time to review *in forma pauperis* petitions.[48] This is not to suggest that the justices are callous and uncaring in their decisions, but rather that justices must find a way to separate the serious, nationally important disputes from the frivolous and often localized ones. This concern led Joseph Tanenhaus and his colleagues in the 1960s to develop an explanation based on cues found in the petitions themselves.

## Cue Theory

Cut theory is an important theory devised to understand case selection in the Supreme Court. It posits that Supreme Court justices look at easily identifiable cues that alert the justices to the cert worthiness of a petition.[49] These cues can be categorized into legal and political cues.

*Legal cues* are set forth in Rule 10 of the Court. This rule is written by the Supreme Court to its own specification as a guide to the cert decision. The rule reads as follows:

> Review on writ of certiorari is not a matter of right, but of judicial discretion. A petition for a writ of certiorari will be granted only for compelling reasons. The following, while neither controlling nor fully measuring the Court's discretion, indicate the character of reasons the Court considers:

(a) United States Court of Appeals has entered a decision in conflict with the decision of another United States Court of Appeals on the same important matter; or has decided an important federal question in a way that conflicts with a state court of last resort; or has so far departed from the accepted and usual course of judicial proceedings, or sanctioned such a departure by a lower court, as to call for an exercise of this Court's power of supervision.

(b) When a state court of last resort has decided an important federal question in a way that conflicts with the decision of another state court of last resort or of a United States Court of Appeals.

(c) When a state court or a United States Court of Appeals has decided an important question of federal law which has not been, but should be, settled by this Court, or has decided an important question in a way that conflicts with applicable decisions of this Court.[50]

We can infer from this description that legal cues specify whether the petition raises a real legal conflict. From the Court's perspective, a real conflict is one that is justiceable, where the litigants have a real stake in the outcome, and involves a genuine legal disagreement between different state courts of last resort (interstate conflict), different courts of appeals (intercircuit conflict), different judicial panels within the same circuit court (intracircuit conflict), or between a lower court and the Supreme Court (hierarchical conflict). When a petition satisfies one or more of these conditions, the Court is likely to find it compelling enough to warrant a hearing and a decision.

*Political cues* can be described as those nonlegal factors that when found in a case enhance the probability of the case being granted cert. A political cue exists when (1) the U.S. government is a direct party in the case; (2) the petition involves a civil liberties and a civil rights issue; and (4) the lower court decision is inconsistent with the policy preferences of the Supreme Court.[51]

*The Federal Government as Party.* The U.S. government regularly appears before the Supreme Court as a direct party to a case. The solicitor general (SG) is responsible for spearheading any effort by the federal government to bring a case to the Supreme Court. It is assumed that the federal government represents the citizens of the United States and so a case brought by the SG carries weight in the Court.

The Office of the Solicitor General is part of the U.S. Justice Department and the SG, who is the third-ranking member of that department, has primary responsibility to represent the U.S. government in the U.S. Supreme Court. In that role, the solicitor general also assists the Supreme Court by screening federal government cases for appeal to the Court thereby saving the Court precious time and resources. The SG maintains two offices, one in the Justice Department and the other in the Supreme Court building. Some scholars have gone as far as to describe the SG as the tenth justice by virtue of the important legal function the SG performs for the federal government and the Court.[52] The SG is a quintessential repeat-player in the Court and is a very successful advocate indeed. Research indicates that over 70 percent of the cases brought by the SG to the Court are granted cert and as we see in chapter 6, the SG's winning record on the merits is also very impressive.

*Civil Liberties Issue.* Civil liberties is a generic category that combines several different aspects of the Constitutional provisions contained in the Bill of Rights, including criminal procedure, First Amendment rights (freedom of religion, speech, press, and association), privacy (e.g., abortion, contraception, the freedom of information Act and related statutes, attorney-client and doctor-client privileges), due process (noncriminal guarantees dealing with fair treatment). On average, petitions implicating multiple civil liberties provisions are significantly more likely to be granted cert than those involving a single constitutional provision. One example of a case raising multiple provisions is *Employment Division of Oregon v. Smith* (1990), which involves the inhalation of peyote (a hallucinogenic drug) by Smith for religious purposes. Smith was fired and was denied unemployment benefits after he informed his supervisor at a drug counseling program that he had used peyote. The cases raised both free speech and free exercise of religion claims. Court upheld Smith's denial of benefits.

*Civil Rights Issue.* Civil rights cases are those that arise because the government seeks to classify people for public policy purposes on the basis of race, age, indigence, residence, military, or handicapped status, sex, or national origin, presumably in violation of the Fourteenth Amendment. In an effort to fight discrimination, the Supreme Court looks with intense suspicion laws designed to categorize people or single them out for either favorable or unfavorable treatment without compelling reason. Such cases are significantly more likely to be granted cert although since the Rehnquist Court fewer and fewer civil rights cases have been granted as the Court shifts its emphasis to other areas.

*Lower Court Decision Inconsistent with Supreme Court Policy Preferences.* There is strong evidence that Supreme Court justices are policy-minded elites[53] and as such have strategic designs on petitions at the jurisdictional stage. Indeed, we know based on substantial empirical research that when deciding which cases to decide, Supreme Court justices consider how other justices will vote at the merit stage and then cast their own certiorari vote accordingly in order to maximize the chances that their desired policy position will prevail on the merits.[54] The Court practices an error correction strategy whereby, as policy-minded human decision makers, justices vote to grant cert in cases whose lower court decisions they dislike on policy grounds.[55] Thus strategically, justices would grant cert in order to reverse the disliked judgment of the court below. But for every lower court decision a Supreme Court justice dislikes, there are many that the justice favors and would wish to affirm authoritatively. Accordingly, an alternative voting mechanism called defensive denials is one whereby a policy-minded justice would vote to deny cert when the Supreme Court is expected to reverse on the merit a lower court decision that the justice favors. Such action seeks to prevent the Supreme Court from possibly reversing and, therefore, nationalizing a lower court decision that the justice favors.

Cue theory predicts that the greater the number of legal and political cues that can be found in a petition, the more likely will that petition be granted cert. But the theory has some important shortcomings too. For one thing, the theory is time-bound. That is, the theory works only at certain historical intervals. For example, not many people would expect civil liberties to be a strong predictor of certiorari decision during the *Lochner* era when the Court was focusing on issues of economic regulation. Also, the theory is incomplete in that it omits other important factors that influence judicial decision making at the jurisdictional stage such as interest groups.

*The Number of Interest Organizations.* Interest groups are an important force in judicial decision making, especially at the jurisdictional stage. Interest groups serve two key functions. First, the number of interest groups filing amicus curiae briefs in a case represents a signal to the Court about the political salience or importance of the case.[56] A large number of amicus briefs accompanying a case communicates to the Court that the issue is politically salient of a large segment of the American people. A small number does not necessarily suggest a lack of substantive or legal importance, but simply a lack of widespread political interest by citizens.[57]

Interest groups also serve another role, an informational one, in Supreme Court decisional process.[58] Under Rule 37.1, the Court admonishes amici to furnish new and relevant information: "An amicus curiae brief which brings relevant matter to the attention of the Court that has not already been brought to its attention by the parties is of considerable help to the Court. An amicus brief which does not serve this purpose simply burdens the staff and facilities of the Court and its filing is not favored." The Court appreciates legal briefs from these third parties and reviews the briefs carefully for information and potentially insightful viewpoints and policy implications not raised by the direct parties in the case.

In addition, groups can raise questions and issues from different perspectives that the direct parties in the case either might have overlooked or ignored because it is not in their best interest to draw the Court's attention to those issues. But the Court is fully aware that those filing amicus curiae briefs often are in Court to take sides, not necessarily to present neutral or unbiased information. Nevertheless, these briefs are still useful because they keep the direct parties in the case honest about what information they furnish the Court and about how important the legal issues are to the American people.

## CONCLUSION

The central theme of this chapter is to assess and explain how the Supreme Court builds its agenda. The chapter examines agenda setting from a historical perspective thereby taking account of where the Court has been in order to understand where it is headed. After decades of frustration and complaints about its excessive workload, the Supreme Court was finally able to persuade Congress to remove mandatory jurisdiction, making it possible for justices to control almost completely their own workload through the number and kinds of cases they agree to hear. A look at the Court's caseload overtime shows clearly an upward trend. Several explanations account for that increase, including institutional reasons whereby the Court's own decisions specify the kinds of dispute justices might be willing to address in future; social and technological complexity brought on partly by population growth and technical innovations; and finally, the growth of congressional legislation including the rights revolution and laws to fight the war on drugs. As case filings have grown over the years so has the need to hire more employees to process the cases. Consequently, the number of workers employed by the Supreme Court has grown phenomenally since 1935 when the Court moved to its current location across from Congress.

Over 9000 cases are appealed to the Court each year. Justices must winnow through these cases to select the few (100 or so) that are designated for consideration. Justices work closely with their law clerks to make their selections. Both legal and political factors account for the Court's decision to take a case. Although the Court formally gives more credence to legal factors such as the presence of a real legal conflict between two or more appeals courts or within a single appeals court, social science research suggests that the Court also is significantly influenced by political and ideological considerations, including the number interest groups represented in the case and the presence of the federal government as a party to the case. In the next chapter, we consider the origins and importance of oral argument in the decisions that justices make on the merits.

# 5

# ORAL ARGUMENTS IN THE U.S. SUPREME COURT

During his address to members of the American Political Science Association in 1960, association President Carl Brent Swisher noted that justices of the U.S. Supreme Court obtain their information for decisions from a variety of sources. He suggested that "Among the nine [justices] one may get his illumination primarily from the oral argument, another from the briefs, another from the discussion in conference, another from independent research, and still another from conversation with his law clerk or gossip with his secretary."[1] Although all these sources of information are important in their own unique ways, some have not received the attention they deserve in scholarly analyses. Among these is oral argument. In this chapter, we focus entirely on oral argument as an important source of information for Supreme Court justices.

## WHY ORAL ARGUMENT?

The basic motivation for this chapter is the simple fact that most textbooks on the judicial process devote only a paragraph or two to a discussion of oral argument in the Supreme Court.[2] This is unfortunate because it leaves an overall impression that oral arguments are inconsequential in the Supreme Court. As we see throughout the chapter, this impression is utterly short-sighted and incorrect.[3] To change that fundamental impression is the centerpiece of this chapter.

There are several reasons why students of American judicial process should pay attention to oral argument. First, oral argument is the central activity that gives structure to what the Supreme Court does. According to Chief Justice John Roberts, oral argument "is the organizing point for the entire judicial process."[4] The justices read the briefs, conduct the research, and hold discussion with their law clerks to prepare for oral argument. The voting conference is held shortly after oral argument. Therefore, since the exchange with attorneys is still fresh on the minds of justices, conference discussions often turn on what transpired during oral argument.

Second, oral argument confers public legitimacy to Supreme Court decisions. It is a hallowed event that gives the public a window into the internal dynamics of the Court. Throughout the Court's decision-making journey in any given case, oral argument is the only activity in which the general public is given an opportunity to observe the justices at work. From that perspective, oral argument gives us a sense of how the justices operate as a small group and it bestows the justices with a reassuring sense of public approval for their actions. Furthermore, oral argument represents the only time that lawyers from both sides of the dispute come face to face with justices to engage in a dialogue about the law, as well as the legal and policy implications of the dispute.

Finally, oral argument is the point where justices hold the first discussion of the merits of the case with their colleagues. Because justices desire to form their own opinions of the case independently, they rarely discuss the merits of a case with each other before oral argument. Only in the most extraordinary cases do justices discuss the merits before oral argument (or conference in those cases where oral argument is not held). Thus oral argument is the first point where justices communicate with each other about the merits of the case but then only through the back-and-forth questioning of the attorneys.

Justices as well as the petitioner, the respondent, and their lawyers are all vividly aware that there is much at stake during oral argument. Each litigant hopes to emerge victorious after the give-and-take of oral argument is over and the case is decided. But beyond the desire to emerge on the winning side, by and large, litigants recognize that the case represents something momentous: an opportunity to define the course of legal history and to influence the lives of millions of Americans who might be similarly situated now and in future. This, in a way, explains why justices study the case carefully before oral argument and why both sides of the dispute expend considerable amount of time and money researching the case, seeking the assistance of third parties, and holding moot court sessions. At the very least, oral argument is a short period of intensely focused dialogue between justices and attorneys in which justices frequently arrive at tentative decisions that often correlate with their final vote on the merits.[5]

To enhance our understanding of the nature of Supreme Court advocacy, we must first gain an appreciation of the evolutionary beginnings of oral argument and how the nature of oral argument has been transformed across time. How did the tradition of oral argument begin? Are there other institutional traditions that have supplanted oral argument in importance in the Court? Whether one thinks oral argument is consequential or not (and there are some who think not), asking where this tradition originates and how it has changed is nevertheless an important question because it teaches us about the continuity and transformation of institutional culture in the Court.

We begin the discussion in this chapter by examining the evolution of oral argument. The basic argument advanced is that the underlying reason for the evolution of oral argument is to foster efficiency in the way the Court performs its job of securing and assigning meaning to the Constitution. The chapter is organized around the following questions:

- What is the evolutionary foundation of oral argument in the Supreme Court?

- How important is oral argument in the outcome of Supreme Court cases?
- How can lawyers make effective oral argument?
- What are the emerging trends in Supreme Court practice with regard to oral argument?

## EVOLUTIONARY FOUNDATIONS OF ORAL ARGUMENT

Historically, the nature of oral argument in the U.S. Supreme Court has undergone significant transformation. That transformation is driven by the need for efficiency or the desire by justices to maximize the quality of information provided by litigants before the Court. The nature of the transformation is most apparent in (1) the time allotted for oral argument; (2) the nature of advocacy before the Court (e.g., oratory and the expectation justices have for the lawyers); and (3) the comparative importance of oral argument versus the legal brief.

### The Origins of Oral Argument

For the United States, the late 18th century was a period of infinite hope and expectation, punctuated by abundant uncertainty. It is, therefore, not surprising that during the Supreme Court's first and second years in operation (1790 and 1791), a sense of uncertainty prevailed among attorneys over the rules of practice in the Court. This was especially true on the question of how argument should be presented to justices. Should it be orally or in writing via legal briefs? There was little guidance from the Court at the time or from existing legal documents to address this important question. The Constitution had created the Supreme Court and defined its original jurisdiction. Moreover, the Judiciary Act of 1789 had established guiding principles that pointed the way forward for the Court, specifying, for example, the number of justices to sit on the Court and the nature of the Court's appellate jurisdiction. The 1789 act, you would recall from chapter 1, also established the basic structure of the federal judicial system. But by design, both the framers of the Constitution and the authors of the judiciary act left vague the details of practices and procedures of the Supreme Court. The need to establish and maintain workable rules of practice would fall upon the shoulders of justices themselves.

To address the prevailing uncertainty in the rules of practice, the attorney general of the United States at the time Edmund Jennings Randolph, as leader of the Supreme Court bar, filed a motion with the Court on behalf of the bar, requesting clarification as to what procedural rules attorneys should follow. On August 8, 1792, Chief Justice John Jay and the associate justices responded by issuing a proclamation adopting for the Supreme Court the rules of practice of the courts of King's Bench, and of chancery, in England:

> This court consider[s] the practice of the courts of king's bench, and of chancery, in England, as affording outlines for the practice of this court; and that

they will, from time to time, make such alterations therein as circumstances may render necessary.[6]

By adopting the rules of practice used at the courts of King's Bench, the U.S. Supreme Court departed from what was an apparent objective of the Judiciary Act of 1789: to place a decidedly American imprimatur on legal practice in the new Nation.[7] The Court was motivated by the pressures of the moment to undertake what seemed like a betrayal of nationalist impulses that provided the essential underpinnings of the Judiciary Act of 1789. But, in fact, the Court's objective in adopting the English rules was simply to provide guidance for attorneys. Adoption of the English rules was meant as a temporary measure to be replaced in future with procedural rules uniquely American. By following the King's Bench procedures, justices were certain that at the very least attorneys could resort to English books that explain the proper legal practices and decorum lawyers were supposed to employ.[8]

As it turned out, there was a long-standing tradition in which advocates at the King's Bench presented their argument orally to the courts. For example, in the House of Lords (the highest court in England), advocates would typically state orally the decision of the lower court and then proceed with an extended presentation of the facts, along with any precedents on which they rely in making their argument. This process of presenting material orally to the English courts foretold how oral argument was structured in the U.S. Supreme Court during the late 18th and early 19th centuries. The history thus suggests clearly that it was the adoption of the King's Bench rules that sets the wheels in motion toward the current tradition of oral argument in the U.S. Supreme Court and in the lower federal and state courts. But the rules of oral argument were not maintained in their original form over time. They underwent several important changes.

## Changing the Rules of Oral Argument in the Early Court

The substantive rules surrounding oral argument have been modified numerous times during the course of Supreme Court history (table 5.1). Many of the most important and enduring changes took place during the Marshall Court (1801–1835). It was during the Marshall Court that initial steps were taken to limit the time allotted for oral argument and the number of attorneys per side that were permitted to present argument. More details about these rules are presented later in this section. But ultimately, the cumulative impact of the rule changes points to two outcomes apparent in the Court's current practice: movement toward shorter oral arguments and voluminous legal briefs.

As a matter of course, adoption of the King's Bench rules of practice gave way initially to extremely long oral arguments in the Supreme Court. Oral arguments usually lasted for several hours, sometimes several days, before a case was submitted for a decision. For example, as discussed later in greater detail, the case of *McCulloch v. Maryland* (1819) was argued for six days by

**Table 5.1**  How Supreme Court Rules Involving Oral Argument Have Evolved

| Year | Type of Rule Adopted |
| --- | --- |
| 1792 | Kings Bench rules |
| 1795 | Statement of materials of the case requested by justices but was misinterpreted or ignored by attorneys |
| 1812 | Court limits oral argument to only two attorneys per side |
| 1821 | Court requires parties to submit written briefs |
| 1833 | Court signals but did not mandate it will accept entire argument via written briefs |
| 1849 | Court limits oral argument to two hours per side (excerpts permitted for the most important cases, e.g., *Ex Parte Miligan*); requires counsel to file abstract of points and authorities. |
| 1879 | Rules changed to admit women to the Supreme Court Bar, permitting them to present oral argument. |
| 1884 | Mandates all briefs include argument |
| 1911 | One and a half hour allotted for oral argument, except cases on the summary docket (those not justifying extended time) and so are allowed only 30 minutes. |
| 1927 | Court allots one hour per side for oral argument except cases in the summary docket that are allotted 30 minutes per side. |
| 1955 | Until this year, oral arguments were held five days a week. Rule changed so that orals are held Mondays, Tuesdays, and Wednesdays in two weeks out of each month, while Thursdays and Fridays are for conference deliberations.[1] |
| 1970 | Court shortens oral argument to 30 minutes per side in most cases, with exceptions granted for the most important or complex cases. |

*Source*:  Author's compilation from U.S. Reports, various rule amendments, Epstein et al. (2007)[2] and Gressman et al. (2007).[3]

*Notes*:

1. Henry J. Abraham. 1998. *The Judicial Process*, 7th edition. New York: Oxford University Press, p. 208
2. Lee Epstein, Jeffrey A. Segal, Harold J. Spaeth, and Thomas G. Walker. 2007. *The Supreme Court Compendium*. Washington DC: CQ Press
3. Eugene Gressman, Kenneth S. Geller, Stephen M. Shapiro, Timothy S. Bishop, and Edward A. Hartnet. 2007. *Supreme Court Practice*, 9th edition. Arlington VA: Bureau of National Affairs

six of the most renowned attorneys of that era. That case solidified the supremacy of the federal government over state governments.

In addition to long arguments, the Court's caseload was small and attorneys were not required to file legal briefs to discuss the blue print of their cases. For those who took the initiative of filing briefs, such briefs or declarations were quite short and succinct, usually no more than three or four pages long.[9] The length of the early briefs filed by petitioners or respondents is miniscule compared to the lengthy legal briefs of today, which, under Rule 33 of the Court, can be 50 pages long for each litigant for briefs on the merits and 30 pages for briefs submitted at the certiorari stage by the petitioner or respondent.[10]

Briefs played a minor role in the informational needs of the Court during the 19th century. Therefore, in order to make decisions, the Court's information had to come from another source that is trustworthy and reliable. Without any doubt, that source was the oral argument.

Unlike in modern courts where justices form their first impressions of a case through legal briefs as well as information supplied by friends of the court, justices relied primarily on oral argument during the 18th century to form their first impressions of the case and decide how they would vote. Because oral arguments were unlimited in length during this period in Court history, the strategy frequently employed by attorneys was to quote long swatches of history from treaties and opinions handed down by the English Courts. Some lawyers even resorted to quoting verses from the Holy Bible to make their point to the justices.[11]

In 1795, the Court made a somewhat feeble attempt to change the rules of oral argument by giving "notice to the gentlemen of the bar, that hereafter [the justices] will expect to be furnished with a statement of the material points of the case." This rule might be interpreted by members of the modern Supreme Court bar as an invitation to file a legal brief. But the documentary history of the late 18th century reveals that there was virtually no written submission by attorneys. Instead, lawyers interpreted the new rule as requiring them to "fill their oral presentations with citations and long excerpts of learned treatises in support of the argument."[12] This, attorneys did exceedingly well. It was also customary during this period for oral argument to be presented by multiple attorneys representing their side.

## Consequences of Long Oral Arguments

By virtue of their education and professional training, lawyers are programmed for argument. Allowing multiple lawyers to argue each side of a cause without the constraint of a time limit is simply an invitation for a protracted fight. It is, therefore, not hard to understand why oral arguments went on for so long. But although long arguments resonated with the justices because of their potential to supply justices with abundant information for decisions, long arguments have consequences. First, they can test the patience of individual justices. For example, Chief Justice Roger B. Taney once complained that Luther Martin, a renowned advocate of the 19th century, was a "profound lawyer" but that Martin "introduced so much extraneous matter, or dwelt so long on unimportant points, that the attention was apt to be fatigued and withdrawn, and the logic and force of his argument lost."[13] Second, when a justice falls ill and had to miss multiple days of oral argument, the Court often had to reargue the case afresh, clearly disrupting the Court's argument schedule. From this perspective, long oral arguments are an inefficient way of obtaining information about a case and they can inevitably lead to delayed justice.

In 1812, the Marshall Court took initial steps to limit the duration of oral argument. Justices restricted argument to only two attorneys per side.[14]

Exceptions were granted for truly important cases such as *McCulloch v. Maryland* (1819) in which the Court allowed a total of six advocates to present argument, including Attorney General Joseph Hopkinson, Walter Jones, Luther Martin (all arguing for McCulloch) and William Pinkney, Daniel Webster, William Wirt (all arguing for Maryland). These were the greatest Supreme Court advocates of that era.[15] As noted above, oral arguments were held for six days in *McCulloch*. Supreme Court historians believe that the two-counsel rule drove the growing trend toward specialists who now dominate oral advocacy in the Supreme Court.[16] By limiting argument to two attorneys per side, the Court managed indirectly to reduce the cumulative time it takes to argue a case before it was submitted for discussion and vote in conference.

## THE NATURE OF ORAL ARGUMENT DURING THE 19TH CENTURY

Oral arguments covering several hours and oftentimes several days or weeks was the norm throughout the 19th century. At that time and under prevailing oral argument tradition, being considered a good Supreme Court lawyer required not only strong intellectual power, excellent communication skills, but also physical stamina and a willingness to withstand long durations in a test of wit. Many lawyers of this earlier dispensation felt energized by the long hours and often were impatient during quiet spells. When Justice Louise D. Brandies was a practicing attorney, for example, he indicated as much in a letter to his brother, Alfred, in 1887: "I really long for the excitement of the contest—that is a good prolonged one covering days or weeks. There is a certain joy in the draining exhaustion and backache of a long trial, which shorter skirmishes cannot afford."[17]

### The Triumph of Oratory

Quite a part from lengthy oral arguments, another distinguishing aspect of oral argument during the 19th century was the high level of oratory employed by counsel. Oratory simply means eloquence in public speaking.

Linguistically speaking, the 19th century was a century of oratory, as politicians and lawyers excelled in the skillful use of the spoken language to communicate their messages and dazzle their listeners. To some extent, oratory is a key aspect of the evolution of oral argument in the Supreme Court. Whereas oration was expected of lawyers in the 19th century, this is much less so today. Oratory was commonplace not only in the hallowed hearing room of the Supreme Court but throughout the corridors of the legislative and executive branches of government. Unlike today where, by dint of media pressure, electronic sound bites are a favored communication style of politicians, oratory was the treasured attribute of political elites in the 19th century. Since many of the great judicial advocates of that time were themselves politicians,[18] it is not surprising that Supreme Court oral arguments became extensive exercises in oratory, which came to be expected by the justices.

The most successful lawyers in the Court were those who typically could meet justices' expectation for oratory within the context of a logical legal argument. Oratory was, therefore, a tradition that was encouraged and nourished by the justices through the allocation of longer time intervals for oral argument. Unlike today where opposing litigants each receive only 30 minutes to present a case, making it extremely difficult for lawyers to engage in rhetorical flourish, it was possible for counsel to engage in oratory during the 19th century because they were allowed ample time to develop their argument slowly and methodically. In addition, justices were more ideologically unified and so attorneys faced fewer questions and interruptions from justices during oral argument compared to today, where in most argument sessions, questioning usually starts almost immediately counsel starts to speak.

Although oratory was an enduring tradition in the Supreme Court, meaningless oration is discouraged by justices. For example, Justice Robert Jackson warned advocates before the Court that "The memorized oration, or anything stilted and inflexible, is not appropriate."[19] In essence, oratory is most effective when it appears spontaneous to the listener even though it might have been rehearsed or memorized. Renowned lawyers used spontaneous oratory to win the hearts and minds of justices.

### Daniel Webster's Oratory in *Dartmouth College v. Woodard* (1819)

In the annals of famous advocacy before the Supreme Court, Daniel Webster stands out as one of the giants. Webster has been described by fellow lawyers as an "excessively clever" advocate, although Webster saw himself as a poor student of the law whenever he looked into the mirror. Webster had the gift of understanding the pulse of the Court and he was often able to arm justices with arguments that would eventually become part of the pillars of our constitutional framework.[20] As a hobby, Webster read poetry and literature to clear his mind from law books. This actually turned out to be an excellent complement to his professional work and partly explains his powerful oratory. Indeed, several examples of his oratory have been documented.

*Dartmouth College v. Woodard* (1819) is one case in which Daniel Webster displayed his characteristic oratory.[21] The *Dartmouth* case came to the Supreme Court from New Hampshire at a time when there was vigorous debate about the role of colleges in American life, their relationship to the state, what they should teach, how they should be governed, and how and by whom charitable gifts would be used.[22] The case started in 1816 as a conflict between the college president, John Wheelock, and the board of trustees over faculty appointments, the local church, and the president's duties and prerogatives. After the board became less acquiescent to his management of college affairs, Wheelock went public, writing and distributing an 88-page pamphlet in which he described the board of trustees as "Federalist conspirators bent on destroying popular government."[23]

The Republican-controlled New Hampshire legislature rallied to Wheelock's defense and took control of Dartmouth, a private Ivy League college. The legislature accomplished this by passing legislation in 1816 amending a 1769 charter between the college and the British Royal Crown. That charter called for a 12-member board of trustees to govern the college and to appoint the board's successors. However, the legislature felt that the trustees were ideologically more attuned to the attributes of a monarchy than to the foundations of American liberty. The amended charter introduced some significant changes: increasing the number of trustees of the college from 12 to 21, creating a board of overseers to review important decisions of the trustees, and empowering the state governor to appoint the nine new trustees and to fill positions on the board of overseers. Since the new law abridged the old charter, it violated the contracts clause of the U.S. Constitution.

The legislature's action did not sit well with the incumbent trustees because it effectively took power away from them and gave it to the state. The legislature claimed that it took this action to protect the college from financial disarray. The incumbent trustees sued William H. Woodard (secretary and treasurer of the college) to win back control. Woodard was named in the action because the 1816 act designated him trustee with responsibility over college records, seal, and account books. After losing at the lower court levels, the trustees brought in Daniel Webster (a Dartmouth alumnus) as their lead attorney along with two associates, Jeremiah Mason and Jeremiah Smith.

During four hours of legal argument in which he debated the Constitution and its protection of contractual rights, Webster impressed upon the Court what the policy consequences of its decision will be. If the justices ruled in favor of New Hampshire (i.e., for Woodard), Webster informed the Court that every private college in the nation will be at risk of a legislative takeover whenever a majority of legislators deemed it necessary (even for political or noneducational objectives). Webster concluded with an impassioned plea for the justices to save Dartmouth and other private institutions similarly situated from state domination:

> Sir I know not how others feel, but for myself, when I see my Alma Mater surrounded like Caesar in the senate house, by those who are reiterating stab upon stab, I know not for this right hand have her turn to me and say *Et tu quoque mi fili!* And thou, my son![24]

Several of the justices and many in the audience were deeply moved. As was often the case when he appeared before the Court, Webster's oratory won the day. Webster's experience shows many contrasts with modern Supreme Court practice in terms of the duration of oral argument and the level of oratory.

## The Push for Shorter Oral Arguments and the Rise of the Legal Brief

In the 20th century, the expectation of oratory is no longer an overarching feature of Supreme Court advocacy. This is primarily because the amount of time allotted for oral argument has been dramatically curtailed. Nowadays, unless the Court directs otherwise, each side is allotted only 30 minutes to present its case. The significance of this trend is that it makes every minute more precious. Justices no longer expect to be dazzled and entertained with oratory. Instead, they most appreciate a logical and straightforward legal argument that provides relevant information for their decisions. It is for this reason that during oral argument, justices spend significant amounts of time questioning the lawyers and pressing for clarification of vexing issues raised in the case.

In 1833, the Court made an important move toward shorter oral arguments. The Court signaled that it would accept entire legal argument via written briefs if counsel chooses to submit it. The Court suggested that "in all cases brought here on appeal, writ of error, or otherwise, the Court will receive printed arguments, if the Counsel on either or both sides shall choose to submit the same."[25] Although the rule was hortatory rather than mandatory, it signaled the emergence of the legal brief and continued the slow movement toward shorter arguments. The logic here is that with legal briefs, justices would have access to written information about the case and minimize the need for lengthy oral arguments. This push toward shorter oral argument coincided with the rise of other sources of information for justices, namely the amicus curiae briefs (different from the litigants' briefs). The very first amicus curiae brief filed in the Supreme Court by a nongovernmental entity was submitted by Kentucky Senator Henry Clay (acting as a citizen) in the case *Green v. Biddle* (1823),[26] which expanded the contracts clause (U.S. Constitution, Article 1, Section 10) to encompass public as well as private agreements. However, it was not until the 1930s that amicus curiae briefs became a regular feature of Supreme Court case material.

Justices now have access to voluminous amount of information via both case briefs and amicus curiae briefs that they rely upon for decisions. Clearly, Amici participation has fluctuated considerably over the years but with a generally rising trend. However, the Rehnquist Court experienced a drop in the number of amici participation due to a significant decline in the number of cases, particularly in civil rights cases, the Rehnquist Court accepted for full review. Nevertheless, orally argued cases without any amici participation are increasingly rare in the Supreme Court.

Daniel Webster's experience seems to suggest that oral arguments are influential in the final decision on the merits. Nevertheless, a number of scholars have argued that oral arguments are little more than window dressing, that oral arguments carry no substantive effect on how justices make decisions, and that oral argument "does not provide reliable clues as to how a given justice may vote."[27] This is a provocative thesis supported by many attitudinalists, scholars who adhere to the belief that justices are guided by personal values and ideological preferences when deciding cases.[28] Because preferences are known to be stable over time and because justices spend so little time in oral argument, the case is made that oral arguments do not have much influence in the final disposition of cases now as they did during the 19th century. Indeed, many attorneys also question whether oral arguments really make a difference, especially if the case has been fully briefed. As Chief Justice Rehnquist noted, "It would seem that inside of a hundred years the written brief has largely taken the place that was once reserved for oral argument."[29] What we can conclude from Rehnquist's observation is that oral arguments were more influential in earlier periods than in modern Court eras.

The Supreme Court did not mandate submission of written briefs until 1821. And after instituting this requirement, the briefs submitted were typically very short and their information content was so low that it rarely dictated the final decision. In other words, briefs failed to meet the informational needs of the Court. According to the Court, the brief was to contain "the substance of all material pleadings, facts, documents, on which parties rely and the points of law and fact intended to be presented at the argument."[30]

In 1833, the Marshall Court further refined the rules of oral argument. Justices introduced a rule signaling that the Court would accept entire argument via written brief if counsel chooses to submit it. The rule thus permitted lawyers weak on eloquence but not necessarily weak on intellect to bypass oral argument entirely. This rule essentially made oral argument optional and it survived until 1980 when the justices changed it under Rule 38.1, noting that the Court is "reluctant to accept the submission of briefs, without oral argument, any case in which jurisdiction has been noted or postponed to the merits or certiorari has been granted. Notwithstanding any such submission, the Court may require oral argument by the parties."

One of the most important changes came in 1849. The Court mandated counsel to file abstracts of points raised in the case and to identify the controlling legal authorities. But more importantly, the Court limited oral argument to two attorneys per side. Then in 1884, the Court mandated that all briefs include detailed argument. Around the turn of the century, the Court changed the rules yet again that issues raised in a case could be adequately explored during a one-hour oral argument session for each side of the case. In 1970, the Court officially limited the time allotted for oral argument to 30 minutes per side.

Under Rule 28.3 of the current Court, except in extraordinarily complex cases, 30 minutes per side is the time allowed for oral argument. Request for extra time must be filed no more than 15 days after the petitioner's or appellant's brief on the merit has been filed. Examples of cases in which extra time was awarded include *AT&T v. Iowa Utility Board*,[31] which was a complex commercial utility case. The Court permitted two hours of oral argument to allow justices to fully digest the various intricate facets of the case. In 2003, a highly important constitutional challenge to the McCain-Feingold federal campaign finance law was argued for four hours in the case of *McConnell v. Federal Election Commission* (2003).[32]

## Disagreement over the Importance of Oral Argument

Citizens, law students, and even many professional lawyers often wonder whether oral arguments actually influence justices' decisions independently of the legal brief. This concern is raised by the false assumption that if justices simply spend time to read legal briefs, their questions or concerns will be answered, obviating the need for oral argument. But even among informed observers of the Court, there is disagreement over whether oral arguments are important in shaping the Court's final decisions. Two political scientists known for their penetrating analysis of the Court Jeffrey A. Segal and Harold J. Spaeth acknowledged in their revised influential work on the Court that we lack systematic information on the impact of oral argument. They have recorded their exasperation by simply stating that the extent to which oral argument affects justices' votes is "problematic."[33]

In spite of what judicial scholars may have concluded about the influence of oral argument, Supreme Court justices themselves are in the best position to inform the general public about whether or not oral arguments are influential in their deliberations and decisions. But to be clear, even justices themselves have sent mixed signals. For one thing, Chief Justice Earl Warren regarded oral arguments as "not highly persuasive."[34] And Chief Justice William Rehnquist noted that overtime, legal briefs have supplanted oral argument in importance: "…inside of a hundred years the written brief has largely taken the place that was once reserved for oral argument."[35] However, some other justices have found oral arguments to be highly useful and indeed an indispensable part of appellate decision making. Justice William Brennan is an example of justices who find oral argument influential in the Court. For Brennan, "Oral argument is the absolute indispensable ingredient of appellate advocacy…Often my whole notion of what a case is about crystallizes at oral argument. This happens even though I read the briefs before oral argument; indeed, that is the practice now of all the members of the Court." Justice Brennan was making an oblique reference to Justice Felix Frankfurter who insisted on not reading briefs prior to oral argument because he believed that oral argument "has a force beyond what the written word conveys."[36]

But just because some justices endorse oral arguments as important does not mean we should accept these statements uncritically. Indeed, without convincing empirical evidence, doubts would remain over the influence of oral argument on decisions on the merits.

Fortunately, from recent empirical analyses of oral arguments, convincing evidence has emerged showing that oral argument is indeed influential in the decisions justices make, especially when it pertains to policy considerations. Timothy R. Johnson has supplied statistical evidence indicating that a significant minority of the main arguments in majority opinions come from discussions during oral arguments.[37] Others have shown significant correlations between oral arguments and justices' final responses to those arguments.[38] Before he became chief justice, John Roberts, himself a successful advocate before the Court, went as far as to predict that "the secret to successful advocacy is simply to get the Court to ask your opponent more questions."[39]

Clearly, oral argument is important and valuable in a number of ways. First, oral argument gives justices the only opportunity during the term to obtain information directly from attorneys representing the litigants. They obtain this information by asking questions of the attorneys or having them respond to justices' comments and hypothetical situations. Often those questions seek clarification about material presented in the briefs or to seek information concerning important issues not addressed in either the petitioner or respondent briefs. After all, the legal brief is a strategic tool in that materials presented there are usually those that attorneys and their clients choose to emphasize to the justices. Information potentially damaging to a client is usually omitted even though such information might determine the outcome. Important issues not raised in the party's brief usually come to the attention of the justices through amicus curiae briefs. During the 1992 term, for example, 64 percent of amicus briefs supporting petitioners and 70 percent of amicus briefs supporting respondents offered information not contained in the direct litigant's brief.[40] Justices usually seek clarification or contextual understanding of such information during oral argument. Thus, from the justices' perspective, oral argument serves as an information-gathering device.

Second, students of the Court appreciate oral arguments as important exercises because internal institutional politics that typically take place behind closed doors can play out during oral argument. In this sense, justices use oral argument as a vehicle for communicating their own views of the case to other justices in the hope of winning them over when the case is deliberated in conference or shortly thereafter. Therefore, we must remember that oftentimes when Justice Antonin Scalia questions counsel about a juridical standard or the potential policy implication of a potential ruling, he is actually speaking to other members of the Court who might be wavering on the issue. Seen in this perspective, justices use oral argument not only as an information gathering device but also as a tool of information dispersal to their colleagues.

## Who Participates in Oral Argument?

Roughly 4500–5000 new applicants are admitted to the Supreme Court Bar each year. Only those so admitted are allowed to file briefs and practice law before the Court. Whereas many attorneys join the Supreme Court Bar because they wish someday to practice before the Court, most of those joining do so for its symbolic value and the prestige it bestows. Indeed, the vast majority of attorneys who maintain membership in the Supreme Court Bar never actually practice law before the Court.

The demographic representation of new entrants to the Supreme Court Bar varies each year but is usually dominated by men, consistent with the legal profession. Women constitute roughly 25 percent of new members of the Supreme Court bar each year. Overall, women total only about 8 percent of the Bar as of 2006. The remaining 92 percent are men.[41]

What are the prospects for change in these dismal statistics? The trend in law school admission and graduation rates suggests that real change is afoot.

In recent years, law schools across the United States have reported a steady, and in some cases, dramatic increases in women enrollment. The number of women law school graduates since the 1990s has also shown a corresponding increase. Thus, one would expect the proportion of women in the Supreme Court bar to show significant improvement in the coming years.

The first woman (Belva Lockwood) was admitted to the Supreme Court bar in 1879 based on the power of her own congressional lobbying efforts. A year later, she sponsored the first African American admitted to the Bar (Samuel Lowry of Huntsville Alabama). There are more women members of the Supreme Court bar than African Americans. Indeed, the percentage of African American members of the bar remains smaller than most other groups, and black lawyers in private practice rarely appear before the Court to experience what one black lawyer who did argue in the Court called "a moment of glory."[42]

Several factors account for the dearth of African American lawyers appearing for argument at the Supreme Court, including problems in recruiting and retaining black lawyers at top law firms where they typically experience difficulty in making partner; the rise of a small group of lawyers who focus on Supreme Court advocacy and who advertise heavily and thus take business away from small time lawyers; the decline in civil rights cases granted cert, an area of the law where black lawyers are highly concentrated. Finally, the dwindling number of cases overall granted cert also limits opportunity for black lawyers to participate in litigation before the Court.[43]

Research suggests that geographic representation of oral advocates in the Court is very lopsided, with 94 percent of lawyers in recent years coming from Washington DC Metropolitan area as opposed to only six % from outside the beltway.[44] This speaks to the growing concentration of Supreme Court advocacy expertise in the DC Metropolitan area. Most DC-area lawyers who argue in the Court are repeat players and they include the quintessential repeat player: the solicitor general (SG). Repeat players enjoy a greater credibility and, therefore, a greater likelihood of winning cases than lawyers outside the beltway who tend to be one-shotters. For his part, the SG is a true Washington insider with long-standing dedication to the rule of law. The incumbent focuses on developing legal principles by representing the federal government in the Supreme Court.

Beyond representing the federal government, the SG often participates as amicus curiae on behalf of third parties. Thus, between 1953 and 2004, the solicitor general participated in oral argument as amicus in 309 of 2839 cases (approximately 11 percent). Although there are fluctuations from one term to another in the number of cases where the SG participated in oral argument as amicus, the trend is decidedly upward.

## THE LINK BETWEEN ORAL ARGUMENT AND CASE OUTCOMES

Is there any evidence of a direct impact of oral argument on case outcomes? The short answer, according to many justices, is yes. But for many years, scholars lacked reliable empirical evidence to corroborate this affirmative response. More recently, that evidence has emerged. Empirically, the question of whether oral arguments directly influence case outcomes can be answered through a variety of methods.

First, one could systematically select a sample of Supreme Court justices themselves or their law clerks and ask them directly whether, how, and when oral arguments are influential. The advantage is that responses would come directly from those who actually use information exchanged during oral argument in crafting Court decisions. The difficulties with this option is that it is difficult for researchers to win a coveted interview with one Supreme Court justice, let alone a sufficient number of justices to make a clear and convincing case about the influence of oral argument. Only a handful of scholars including H.W. Perry have scored interviews with some justices and law clerks, and in these interviews, they have focused on broad questions of judicial philosophy and procedure rather than on oral argument and its impact.

Second, one could listen to the taped recordings of oral argument, paying particular attention to the responses offered by attorneys to questions or issues posed by the justices to determine whether those responses were employed as rationale for the Court's majority, concurring, or dissenting opinions.[45] The advantage of this method is that it would reveal the most direct evidence of the impact of oral argument on justices' decisions. The difficulty with the technique is that it is time consuming and inefficient. Also, there is the potential risk of audible problems with taped recordings.

Third, one can find an instance in which a justice actually rates each attorney's performance during oral argument under the assumption that such performance will likely affect justices' evaluation of the credibility and value of the information received, and ultimately how justices vote on the merits. Lending support to the plausibility of this technique is strong empirical evidence indicating that more experienced advocates win more and often in the Court than the less experienced advocates, even after accounting for the resource status of the party they represent.[46] Apparently, the experienced advocate understands which strategy works best, how to prepare for oral argument, and what potential pitfalls to avoid during oral argument.

Judicial scholars have used all three methods to determine the influence of oral argument in the disposition of cases. Of particular interest for us is the third option. It turns out that during his 24-years on the Court Justice Harry Blackmun (1970–1994) made it his personal interest and hobby to assign performance grades to attorneys appearing before the Court for oral argument. Blackmun graded lawyers for style and substance and employed three grading scales at different periods: A through F from 1970 to 1974 (with "A" being the best argument); 1 through 100 from 1975 to 1977 (with 100 being the best); finally 1 through 8 from 1978 to 1994 (with 8 being the best).

Political scientists Timothy Johnson, Paul Wahlbeck, and James Spriggs have standardized these different grading scales into one scale by determining how far away each grade was from the mean grade in that particular scale. They transformed the letter grades by assigning numeric grades: A becomes 95, A– becomes 90, B+ becomes 87, B becomes 85, B– becomes 80, and so on. Finally, using the technique of regression analysis they regressed these grades on several variables that act as proxies for attorney credibility and the quality of the information presented. These factors include litigation experience, solicitor general's involvement, and attorney type (e.g., law professor, former Supreme Court law clerk, and federal government attorney other than solicitor general).[47] The researchers reported that Justice Blackmun's scores represent a reasonable measure of oral argument quality.

Having determined that these grades are reliable, the authors examined whether oral argument grade actually has an impact on the Court's propensity to reverse the lower court decision. Johnson, Wahlbeck, and Spriggs reported that the relative quality of competing attorneys' oral arguments sharply influenced justices' votes on the merits, even after accounting for factors such as the complexity of the case and whether or not the lawyer attended an elite law school.

This influence is seen more clearly when the difference in argument quality between the competing attorneys increases. For example, when the petitioner's attorney is better than the respondent's attorney, there is a 78 percent chance that a justice will vote for the petitioner. The chances decrease to only 39 percent when the respondent's lawyer is better. In short, their analysis "demonstrates that nearly all justices are influenced by the quality of oral arguments, but those justices who are ideologically closer to a lawyer's position have an enhanced tendency to support that lawyer if he or she presents better oral advocacy than does the opposing counsel."[48] Given this basic finding—that justices are more likely to rule in favor of clients whose attorneys make better oral argument—an important question naturally arises, namely, what can attorneys do to present effective argument and improve their odds of winning in the Supreme Court? We address this question in the following section.

## Making Effective Oral Argument in the Supreme Court

An effective oral argument is one that is credible, legally relevant, yet remains truthful to the cause of the lawyer's client. In the Supreme Court, sound and credible legal arguments can help win cases.

Political scientists who conduct research on the role of information in decision making have shown that the credibility of an information source is crucial for persuasion and for achieving influence. Credibility usually hinges on whether information recipients believe the sender to be knowledgeable and truthful on the subject of the message. If the recipient believes the sender to be ill-informed, any information conveyed is likely to be heavily discounted or dismissed as being possibly inaccurate, false, or misleading.[49]

The question is: How does a motivated attorney achieve credibility in the eyes of the justices? There is no single best formula. But it suffices to say that an attorney can achieve credibility through careful preparation, planning, and rehearsal. Indeed, the Supreme Court demonstrated its faith in careful preparation as far back as 1929 when the Court reminded attorneys in *New York Central Rail Co. v. Johnson* that "the attempted presentation of cases without adequate preparation, and with want of fairness and candor, discredits the bar and obstructs the administration of justice."[50]

Oral argument is an artistic performance. It must be approached as such. Therefore, detailed preparation must be joined with careful planning and rehearsal. Planning encompasses the strategy that the advocate brings to the act of oral argument. Rehearsal is the act of sharpening the rhetoric of the presentation. These, therefore, are the key ingredients necessary for building confidence sufficient to give the advocate total command of the factual and legal nuances of both sides of the case. Winning requires paying attention to these ingredients.

In a recent speech at Northwestern University Law School, Chief Justice John Roberts offered an additional ingredient: humility. Asked by an eager second-year law student what advice he had for beginners on how to present effective oral argument before the Supreme Court, Roberts took special delight and was emphatic in his response. He, after all, is someone who built a solid reputation as an effective Supreme Court litigator, having argued nearly 40 cases for the U.S. Justice Department and winning about 70 percent of them. Now being on the other side of the bench, Robert has a prized perspective. The chief justice noted that one of the spectacular mistakes a lawyer can make is to cast aspersions at the opponent's argument by telling the Court that the case is easy or that the opposition's argument is completely asinine or bogus and so it should be ignored. Instead, Roberts advised counsel to recognize and acknowledge that justices have a difficult decision to make and that the other side has raised some strong points (because they almost always do) and then to elevate the conversation by explaining to the Court why their own argument is superior in light of the Constitution, precedent, or statute.[51] Chief Justice Roberts also advised advocates to listen carefully to the question justices ask before attempting a response. Undoubtedly, since time is important, the best response is one that actually addresses the question raised by the justice rather than one that is off point or is exceedingly rushed and in the process fails to allay the justice's concerns.

Oral argument is a ritualized battle of wits between confident opponents, and the basic responsibility of the advocate is to convey relevant information regarding the case and to explain why justices should rule in favor of the lawyer's client. At the end of the day, a winning argument is one that forces the justice to ask "How can I possibly rule against this lawyer?" An individual justice is likely to ask this question if the attorney answers all the questions asked and answers them confidently when asked rather than later. Delaying or postponing an answer can be misinterpreted as evasion or lack of confidence in the answer.

In order to maintain an effective presence during oral argument, an attorney must be absolutely prepared to face nine of the smartest people in

American society. That means leaving no proverbial stone unturned and no hypothetical issue unexplored before coming to Court. It also means taking the opportunity to exploit weaknesses in the opponent's presentation or answers to questions justices asked. Full preparation takes time and effort, which must be directed toward understanding completely the facts of the case and the nuances of every potential legal argument and its policy implications.

Some lawyers are renowned for their force of intellect and incredible poise and steadiness during oral argument. These lawyers can occasionally escape with little preparation and still win a case in the Supreme Court. Indeed, renowned attorney John W. Davis who argued numerous cases in the Court during the 1940s and 1950s is known for spending only the one hour time span during his train ride from New York City to Washington DC to examine legal briefs in cases he is scheduled to argue before the Supreme Court. Even with that short amount of preparation, Davis went on to win a majority of his cases. The larger lesson here is that most attorneys are not John W. Davis. They must spend numerous hours studying the basic points and legal nuances of the case to summon the confidence to stand before the Court and advocate for their client.

When justices take their seat in the hearing room (the chief justice first; associate justices follow in order of seniority), they come prepared to focus their attention entirely on one case for 30 minutes. Woe to the attorney who is ill-prepared for this encounter. If the ill-prepared attorney is lucky and has Justice Antonin Scalia on his or her side, the justice may take over the argument as he has done on many occasions.[52] Relying on members of the Court for advocacy assistance, however, is never a smart strategy. It reveals a disturbing lack of preparation and is ill-advised.

The consequence of weak preparation can be steep. At a minimum, a lawyer can be embarrassed, at worse a tarnished reputation or even a temporary loss of consciousness can ensue as happened to one lawyer during oral argument in *Hazel-Atlas Glass Company v. Hartford Empire Corporation*. During argument in *Hazel-Atlas*, a commercial fraud case, the justices were a bit confused about the facts. Argument focused on one particular affidavit on the record. Justice William O. Douglas demanded to know "who drafted this affidavit." Apparently, overcome with embarrassment, the lawyer fainted, hitting his head on the table as he fell on the floor. The Court adjourned and a doctor was summoned. When argument resumed, the lawyer stood up, looked straight at Justice Douglas and said that he had drafted the affidavit.[53] Clearly, it is no legend that some attorneys have fainted during oral argument in the Supreme Court because they were ill-prepared for the exchange. The justices are well prepared for oral argument. They prepare by examining the case briefs, amicus curiae briefs, bench memos prepared by their law clerks, and conducting their own research about the issues presented in the case. It behooves every advocate, therefore, to prepare extremely well before approaching the lectern to speak when the Court is in session. But the best preparation is one that is grounded in a belief in a lawyer's own calling. That belief is best described in a story told by Justice Robert Jackson in 1951:

> Once upon a time three stone masons were asked, one after the other, what they were doing. The first, without looking up, answered, "Earning my living." The second replied, "I am shaping this stone to pattern." The third lifted his eyes and said, "I am building a cathedral." So it is with the men [and women] of the law at labor before the Court. The attitude and preparation of some [lawyers] show that they have no conception of their effort higher than to make a living. Others are dutiful and uninspired in trying to shape their little cases to a winning pattern. But it lifts up the heart of a judge when an advocate stands at the bar who knows that he [or she] is building a Cathedral.[54]

Generally speaking, if Justice Jackson is correct, an attorney is more likely to be successful as an advocate when he or she considers oral advocacy as part of a higher calling that should be pursued zealously.

## Trends toward Specialization of Supreme Court Advocacy

Numerous trends have emerged in Supreme Court advocacy over the past several decades. Among these is occupational specialization. In the legal profession, occupational specialization is the concentration of practice in a particular field of law, where an individual devotes more than 50 percent of one's time to that field of law, and gains total expertise in that field of law. The occupational specialist as opposed to the occupational generalist is one of the hottest trends in the legal profession; this is especially true of advocates before the Supreme Court.

Ever since the Supreme Court permitted lawyers to advertise their legal services in *Bates v. State Bar of Arizona* in 1977, the United States has witnessed an explosion in the specialization of legal services. Increasingly, this trend is being exported to other countries, including China, Australia, and Canada. Subject-matter specialization by lawyers started to increase in the 1960s in response to a number of factors, including the quantity and complexity of legal knowledge and the need for lawyers to reassert market control in the face of intensifying and often ruthless competition.[55] At first specialization was limited mostly to lawyers employed in government or commerce and industry. But overtime specialization spread to all other areas of law, and has affected the nature of litigation itself, especially appellate litigation.

Traditionally, a lawyer in private practice who represented a client at the district court level, say in an asbestos contamination case, would remain lead counsel in the case all the way to the Supreme Court. By the 1970s, this tradition began to crumble. Once a case reaches the stage of appealing to the Supreme Court, many small time lawyers found themselves dropped as lead counsel in favor of Washington representation. Today, the specialized structure of appellate practice means that not only individuals but also law firms can concentrate in particular areas of the law and in specific levels of the judicial hierarchy, including state and federal trial courts, courts of appeals, and the Supreme Court.[56] It is hardly surprising nowadays to find large law firms that specialized in Supreme Court practice in the areas of bankruptcy, estate, labor, corporate or tax law. These specialized law firms and their expert advocates win more cases in the Supreme Court and so they are highly sought after for representation often by wealthy clients primarily because of their advocacy experience and past successes in the Court. It proves that nothing succeeds like success. Where are these specialized large law firms located? They are found all across the nation's urban landscape but are most heavily concentrated in large metropolitan areas, including Chicago, Houston, Los Angeles, New York, and especially Washington DC where they are in close proximity to the Supreme Court.

One disadvantage of the trend toward specialization of advocacy is that it highlights an informal process of advocacy that is ruthlessly less democratic than is desirable when confident small-time lawyers are shot out of the opportunity to appear before the highest Court. More importantly, the trend robes justices of a richer diversity of opinions and ideas in the development of the law.

It might seem odd to some that after cultivating a relationship with a trial attorney, many litigants opt for new, presumably more specialized, counsel on appeal. What is the rationale? Well, the first rule of persuasion is to place yourself in the position of the person making the decision in your case. The justice reviewing the case will be reviewing a cold case with a fresh perspective. Therefore, there are advantages to having an attorney on appeal who can place himself in a similar position as the justice in order to bring objectivity and a fresh perspective in evaluating the facts and law in the case. It would be difficult, though not impossible, for the attorney who lost the case below to develop such an objective evaluation. In addition to hiring a different lawyer, hiring a specialized appellate lawyer can bring other advantages. The specialized attorney is more likely than the occasional appellate advocate to keep abreast of emerging trends, new concepts, and new standards of review that may be crucial in winning the case.

Another emerging trend in specialization of Supreme Court advocacy is at the state level. Traditionally, the state attorneys general assume full responsibility for preparing a case for appeal to the Supreme Court and then conducting the oral argument. In recent years, states have established offices for appellate advocacy or office of state solicitor general whose primary job is to write appellate briefs and represent the state during oral argument before the Supreme Court. The states, of course, have a very successful model on which to draw. Since 1870, the federal government has had such a specialized office—the Office of the U.S. Solicitor General. This new development in Supreme Court advocacy has something of a snowball effect. If one side hires a Supreme Court specialist to present oral argument, the other side is motivated to hire a specialist or create one. As Chief Justice John Roberts noted, "this is just a variant of the old adage that one lawyer in town will starve, but two will prosper."[57]

## CONCLUSION

Oral argument in the Supreme Court is not different from information transmittal in other American institutions such as state legislatures, Congress, and the executive branch where elite decision makers respond to those making appeals to them. The debate over the usefulness of oral argument in Supreme Court decisions has raged for over 50 years. Even among lawyers and justices, there have been mumblings that oral arguments are not influential and that justices have a predetermined outcome on their minds before oral argument starts. If this were true, oral argument would be merely a formality and a huge waste of precious time. This chapter has attempted to dispel that notion and to place oral argument in its proper place as an influential informational gathering tool for the decisions that Supreme Court justices make on the merits. Although legal briefs have supplanted oral argument as the first impression-formation point in a case, oral argument remains important because it is the only way that justices obtain immediate, direct, and unvarnished information from litigants through their attorneys. This shows that the capacity for quality oral argument to sway the outcome of a Supreme Court case should never be underestimated.

# 6

# DECISION MAKING ON THE MERITS

Judging inevitably has a large individual component in it, but the individual contribution of the good judge is filtered through the deliberative process of the Court as a body.

Chief Justice William H. Rehnquist[1]

The great fundamental decisions that determine the course of society must ultimately be made by society itself.

Robert M. McCloskey[2]

The most important mechanism through which the Supreme Court makes a lasting contribution to the development of law and ignites policy debate in American society is the final decision on the merits. Decisions are reached through an interpersonal process involving bargaining and accommodation, and reflect the collective wisdom and collaboration of all the justices. Once final decisions are reached, they are communicated through the written majority opinion, the structural embodiment of the Court's work.

This chapter extends the detailed discussion of oral argument in chapter 5 by examining what transpires after oral arguments have been conducted and the case has been submitted for a final decision. Specifically, we address the five following questions:

1. What happens during the Court's secret conference on the merits?
2. What factors influence the final decisions justices make?
3. What theoretical approaches to judicial decision making can help us to better understand Supreme Court decisions?
4. What considerations attend the Court's selection of a justice to write the majority opinion and what are the opinion writer's core responsibilities?
5. Overall, how divided is the Court and what explains the level of divisiveness?

As Chief Justice Rehnquist noted in the above quotation, decision making in the Supreme Court is a deliberative process, involving all nine justices and the assistance of their law clerks. Because of the back and forth communication required to bring a case to a final resolution, long delays are often unavoidable. In difficult cases, it can take more than four months after oral argument before justices solidify their positions on a case and communicate their decision to the public. One explanation for the delays is fluidity. At any time from the final conference vote to when the final decision is announced, justices reserve the right to change their vote and join any alternative voting coalition that may have formed around the case. Fluidity is cherished and expected by the justices. For them, it is judicial independence in practice.

The questions asked in this chapter are among the most important for a deep understanding of judicial process in the U.S. Supreme Court. Therefore, they are discussed in detail in three parts. Part 1 uses *DeShaney v. Winnabego* as a case study for examining the lead up to the secret conference vote and as a primer for enumerating the factors that influence conference votes. Part 2 gives a general analysis of theoretical approaches for understanding Supreme Court decision making. Part 3 examines the architecture of opinion assignment and the level of discord within the Court.

## PART 1: CASE STUDY OF THE *DeSHANEY* CASE

*DeShaney v. Winnabego* began as a family dispute in 1984 and went all the way to the Supreme Court. It involves the serious and emotional problem of child abuse, including family rights and state intervention. The case began in the small town of Oshkosh in Winnabego County, Wisconsin. A four-year-old boy named Joshua DeShaney was rushed to the local emergency room at Mercy Memorial Hospital after receiving a severe beating and violent shaking by his father, Randy DeShaney, a U.S. Air Force veteran. Joshua's mother, Melody DeShaney, was not living in the house at the time. She was divorced from Randy in 1980 and had relinquished custody of Joshua to Randy thereafter.

As soon as Joshua was taken to the hospital, doctors performed emergency neurosurgery. The procedure revealed evidence of brain trauma. In addition to the brain trauma, doctors discovered that Joshua had sustained several repeated brain injuries apparently received over a long period of time. The cumulative effect of these episodes of physical abuse left Joshua permanently brain damaged and was declared severely mentally retarded. Doctors concluded that Joshua would remain in this debilitated condition for the rest of his life.[3]

Randy and Melody DeShaney's marriage ended after just a few years. It was a dangerously turbulent union in which Randy was reportedly physically and verbally abusive. Following the divorce, Melody took Joshua and moved to Phoenix, Arizona, to start a new life. Randy remained in Oshkosh and eventually remarried. It was not long before Melody realized that she no longer could raise Joshua. She was 21 years old, lonely, and poor; she was living an unsettled life. Therefore, she decided to surrender legal custody of Joshua to Randy and his new wife, Christine, hoping that by living with two parents among an extended family, Joshua would have a "nice kid life."

On several occasions, police officers were summoned to the DeShaney residence to settle a private family dispute. Meanwhile, the Winnebago County Department of Social Services had received successive reports of abuse in the household and a child protective worker from the department was assigned to supervise the family. On one occasion several months before the final beating on March 8, 1984, the county social services department took temporary custody of Joshua after he was hospitalized for a suspicious head injury and hospital staff observed extensive bruises on his body. Randy explained that the bruises were the result of an "accident" suffered by the four-year-old when he played with his friends. Although authorities in the Department of Social Services suspected abuse, they were uncertain that they possessed sufficient evidence of parental abuse to place Joshua in foster care. Joshua was eventually released to his father and no charges were brought.

Throughout their interactions with the DeShaneys, caseworkers were guided by a model of social work taught and practiced during the 1980s known as the "family preservation model." Under this model, the primary responsibility of the social worker is to maintain the family structure.[4] Both the child and the abusive parent are viewed as clients and a punitive attitude on the part of case workers is strongly discouraged. The assumption is that parents are best qualified to nurture their own children and that ameliorating the emotional hardship faced by a family will facilitate a safe and secure home environment. Unfortunately, this rosy scenario failed to materialize in the DeShaney home.

Melody DeShaney felt that social workers were negligent in their responsibility. In her view, social workers acted with careless disregard for Joshua's welfare when they released him to his father after suspecting that Joshua was suffering physical abuse at home. She had little recourse but to go to Court and fight for her son's future. She hired an experienced local attorney (Donald J. Sullivan) and filed a civil lawsuit in the U.S. District Court for the Eastern District of Wisconsin against the Wisconsin Department of Social Services (DSS) for negligence, arguing that the county, through DSS, failed to protect her son from her abusive ex-husband and violated her son's rights under the due process clause of the Fourteenth Amendment.

The primary question raised at trial was whether the state of Wisconsin has a constitutional obligation to protect children (such as Joshua) from their abusive parents. As the plaintiff, Melody and her attorney had the responsibility of proving that a "special relationship" existed between Joshua and DSS.

The "special relationship" theory is part of an evolving body of personal injury law. It enables a plaintiff to convert a common tort into a federal civil rights action. Under the theory, a state acquires an affirmative duty to protect an individual from harm done by a private party if the state placed the individual in a situation where he cannot defend himself. Examples of situations where courts have found a "special relationship" include when a police officer in Chicago left children stranded on a highway at night in freezing temperatures, leading to their hospitalization after their uncle (the driver of the vehicle in which they were traveling) was arrested and taken away (*White v. Rochford*);[5] when a profoundly mentally retarded man was involuntarily committed to a state hospital in Pennsylvania and eventually was physically assaulted by staff and fellow patients (*Youngberg v. Romeo*);[6] when prison guards knowingly exposed inmates to risk of physical assault by other inmates (*Spence v. Staras*);[7] and when prison officials denied an inmate urgently needed medical care (*Benson v. Cady*).[8] In all these situations, courts have concluded that the state assumed a custodial relationship with the victims.

Under Wisconsin law, only case workers have the authority to remove a child from an abusive home. At the district court, DeShaney's lawyer argued that a special relationship existed because the state had created essentially a virtual institution to which Joshua was confined, one from which caseworkers failed to remove Joshua after suspecting abuse. The district court rejected that argument, noting that Randy was responsible for the abuse not state workers. Disappointed with the verdict, Joshua and his mother appealed to the Court of Appeals for the Seventh Circuit in Chicago where the case was decided by a panel of three judges.

There are 13 circuit courts in the United States and their sphere of responsibility is regional. The lone exception is the Court of Appeals for the Federal Circuit (located in Washington DC), which enjoys a nationwide geographic jurisdiction but focuses on a narrower set of cases, including patent and trademark, customs duties, and international trade.

Generally speaking, appeals court cases focus on questions of law, not questions of fact. *DeShaney* was no different. In an opinion authored by Seventh Circuit court Judge Richard Posner, the court largely agreed with the district court's application of the law and, therefore, ruled against Melody and Joshua DeShaney. Posner reasoned that DSS was "blameworthy" in the poor performance of its caseworkers but that poor job performance did not "appreciably increase the probability of Joshua's injuries."

Melody DeShaney and her lawyer reviewed their options and decided to appeal to the U.S. Supreme Court. Attorney Sullivan submitted legal briefs to the Court, requesting certiorari. The Court granted cert and took jurisdiction after the required minimum of four justices, in this case Justices Harry Blackmun, William Brennan, Thurgood Marshall, and Byron White, voted to hear the case. The clerk of the Court placed the case in the argument calendar and lawyers for the appellant (DeShaney) and respondent (State of Wisconsin) were invited to submit briefs on the merits and report to Court for oral argument.

### Role of Lawyers, Interest Groups, and the U.S. Solicitor General

Oral arguments in *DeShaney* were presented on November 2, 1988. As usual, oral arguments were civilized but pointed, centering on general principles such as the state's obligation to citizens, with only passive remarks being made about Joshua and his plight.

In their preparation for argument, lawyers on both sides sought help from interested third parties such as interest groups. At the Supreme Court level, third-party organizations can advance a litigant's cause by simply sharing information and know-how or by working directly with that litigant on crafting an effective petition or oral argument. They also serve a useful informational role for justices through their amicus curiae briefs by addressing important issues that the direct parties to the case might have overlooked. Empirical evidence suggests that information provided by groups through amicus curiae briefs is accepted and used by the Court, especially when the information is also raised by the petitioner in the case.[9]

DeShaney's lawyers sought assistance from the Children's Rights Project of the American Civil Liberties Union (ACLU), an interest group known for fighting to safeguard and promote individual rights and liberties. In addition, the ACLU submitted an amicus curiae brief urging reversal of Judge Posner's decision. The Massachusetts Committee for Children and the Youth also submitted a brief urging reversal.

For its part, the state received support from a coalition of interest groups representing several state and local governments that submitted amicus curiae briefs foretelling the financial disaster of a decision in favor of DeShaney. They claimed that it would greatly expand liability for state and local governments in constitutional rights violations alleged by citizens. The importance of amicus briefs is demonstrated by their capacity to sway judicial opinion, especially when briefs are submitted by groups with public visibility and sustained effort to restructure public policy in a particular area.[10]

Empirical studies suggest that a lawyer's previous advocacy experience in the Supreme Court can make a meaningful difference in preparation, presentation, and likelihood of success in subsequent cases.[11] DeShaney's lawyers Donald Sullivan and Curry First were inexperienced in Supreme Court advocacy. "Donald Sullivan and I," Curry First would later admit, "in terms of experience at the Supreme Court and with this issue, were completely . . . out of our league."[12] The DeShaney lawyers were facing other distractions: Sullivan was running for a seat in the Wyoming state legislature. Yet, they never transferred leadership to a more experienced team of lawyers.

Studies on litigation outcomes have furnished incontrovertible evidence that money and other resources matter significantly. With ample resources, a litigant can acquire the best legal talent, making it possible for the "haves" to come out ahead of the "have nots."[13] For their part, the State of Wisconsin and its lawyers, unhindered by financial strain, made a capital investment by enlisting the services of a boutique Washington DC law firm Onek, Klien, and Farr that specializes in appellate and Supreme Court advocacy. This was a dream team of lawyers. Attorney Joseph Onek clerked for Justice William Brennan and later served as deputy counsel to President Jimmy Carter. Attorney H. Barton Farr clerked for Justice William H. Rehnquist just a few years earlier and was also an experienced advocate before the Court. Finally, Attorney Joel L. Klein was a well known Washington lawyer who eventually became counsel to President Bill Clinton during his impeachment trial in the Senate. The three lawyers played mostly advisory roles but Wayne M. Yankala who actually argued the cause for Wisconsin was a rising superstar in legal circles. Clearly, the state hired top talent with substantial Supreme Court experience to represent its cause.[14]

In addition, the state benefited from the support of the U.S. solicitor general's office. Deputy Solicitor General Donald B. Ayers (who himself clerked for Justice William Rehnquist 12 years earlier) presented the federal government's position on the case and filed an amicus brief supporting the State of Wisconsin.

Generally speaking, the solicitor general occupies a special place in Supreme Court decision making. The incumbent enjoys a repeat player status and expertise unmatched by most lawyers before the Court. Consequently, the SG exerts significant influence on the justices' decisions. By one estimate, roughly 70 percent of the cases in which the SG formally supports one party resulted in victory for that party. During oral argument, Ayers informed the Court that the Fourteenth Amendment bestows *negative rights*, meaning that the amendment was created to limit state power over individuals rather than requiring states to take specific action to benefit individual citizens. Ayers' argument resonated with a majority of justices and his main argument was adopted by Chief Justice Rehnquist who wrote the majority opinion in the case.

But justices were not unanimously convinced by the SG's argument. At one point during orals, Justice Harry Blackmun leaned forward from his leather chair and lamented Joshua's fate into the microphone: "Poor Joshua!" These words reverberated across the courtroom and now stand as an enduring symbol of the emotional toll the case generated. Blackmun, a moderately liberal member of the Court, sensed that Joshua's case was lost because, in his view, oral argument was focusing on tangential questions far removed from Joshua, his fate, and his medical situation. Blackmun felt helpless to save the case.

## State Action and the *DeShaney* Case

To address the due process and equal protection questions posed in the case, the justices first must consider whether there is *state action*. Most provisions of the Bill of Rights and the Fourteenth Amendment are designed to protect private individuals against governmental action. There are a number of situations that constitute state action for which harm done to individuals can result in punishment being imposed on the state or its political subdivisions such as cities, counties, or agencies. For example, the Court has ruled that state action exists when a private entity performs a governmental function (*Marsh v. Alabama* 1946). Also state action may exist when the government is involved with, or encourages, private action that injures or invidiously discriminates against a private citizen (*Shelly v. Kramer* 1948). These incidents are actionable against the state.

In *DeShaney*, the question was whether Wisconsin's welfare policy as implemented by social workers placed Joshua in jeopardy within his own home (a question of due process). The second question raised in the *DeShaney* controversy was whether the federal Constitution requires a state to intervene in a private domestic dispute and offer security to those who might be in danger (a question of equal protection). In order for DeShaney to prevail, the Court must find that a special relationship existed that would obligate the state to take responsibility for Joshua's injuries.

## THE CONFERENCE ON THE MERITS

Following oral argument, justices retreat to an oak-paneled room on the second floor of the Supreme Court building. Inside this magnificent room is an elegant mahogany table and nine leather chairs, where they hold a secret conference to discuss the merits of the cases. Some of the most politically transformative decisions in American government are made here. The establishment of the right to sexual and reproductive privacy, the end of formal racial segregation, the use of money as a form of political speech in elections, the declaration against abuse of executive privilege, and even the settlement of the 2000 presidential election, all took place in this conference room.

To maintain strict secrecy and avoid leaks, no one other than the justices is allowed into the conference room during the biweekly deliberations. This closed-door policy discourages hesitation and encourages frankness. In the words of Justice William O. Douglas, "If [justices] are true to their responsibilities and traditions, they will not hesitate to speak plainly and frankly on the great issues coming before them."[15]

We learn years afterward from the personal papers of retired justices on what transpires behind the closed doors. We know for sure that the sitting arrangement at conference is strictly by seniority. The chief justice sits at one end of the table and the most senior associate justice sits at the other end. For the remaining placements, the three next most senior justices sit on one side and the four most junior on the other. The most junior justice sits at the corner next to the door and is responsible for the mundane task of answering the door and receiving missives.[16] The junior justice maintains a link to the outside world as the doorkeeper, and also reports a record of the justices' votes to the clerk of the Court to be shared with the outside world.

Seniority also guides discussion and voting. By a tradition dating back to 1801, the chief justice presides over the conference discussion and has the privilege of announcing his vote intention first. In *DeShaney* as in other cases, Chief Justice Rehnquist first introduced the case and discussed the important legal issues raised, their implications for society, and how he planned to vote. Rehnquist voted to affirm the lower court, a vote against DeShaney. The most senior associate justice, William Brennan, spoke next and voted to reverse and hold the state accountable to Joshua. Conference deliberation usually proceeds in this fashion until the most junior justice speaks last and indicates a vote choice. The justices then table the issue and advance to the next case. The process is repeated until all scheduled cases have been discussed.

In *DeShaney*, Justice Blackmun's lamentation of "Poor Joshua!" proved prescient. Joshua had lost his case in the Supreme Court by a vote of 6 to 3. Chief Justice William H. Rehnquist wrote the majority opinion and was joined by the other conservatives on the Court. The liberals William Brennan, Harry Blackmun and Thurgood Marshall dissented.

## Opinion Types

Every term, the Court produces a wide variety of opinion types, depending on the configuration of the vote or the complexity of the issues involved in the case. The coalition of five or more justices that comprises the majority would normally write a *majority opinion*. This is the opinion that establishes legal precedent and becomes the controlling policy statement of the Court regarding the issue in question. The minimum five justices must agree about the outcome of the case and about its rationale before the case can command full precedential value.

Failing that the Court issues a *"judgment of the Court."* This signals disunity in the Court and can limit enforcement and compliance by lower court judges and members of implementing populations.[17] Judgments of the Court are infrequent. From 1946 to 2006, they reached double digit in only four terms.[18] They are most common in highly salient issue areas such as civil rights and liberties where a high level of ideological content exists.

Individual justices in the majority coalition (or a combination of them) can write a *concurring opinion* agreeing with both the result and rationale or simply to emphasize or embellish a point of law stated in the main opinion. This is called a *regular concurrence*. Moreover, justices who agree with the result but disagree with the rationale stated by the majority may write a concurring opinion (either individually or jointly) explaining their different reasons for voting with the majority. This is called a *special concurrence* and is found often in cases decided via a judgment of the Court.

Occasionally, justices issue a *per curiam,* which is a short unsigned opinion by the Court. Because it lacks the attribution of authorship to specific justices, it is considered a decision issued from the Court as an institution. As an opinion type, a *per curiam* does also command precedential value. The Court uses this method of decision in cases that are less complicated and do not involve novel issues of law.

Finally, justices who disagree with the outcome of the case and by implication the rationale stated in the majority opinion can write a *dissenting opinion,* explaining their disagreement and its reasons. It serves as a means of clarifying the law by enhancing the quality of majority opinions, stimulating intellectual exchange among justices and, ultimately, safeguarding American democracy.[19] The dissenting opinion is, therefore, a valuable tool for speaking to a future Court in hopes of correcting the errors of the moment. Oftentimes, future Courts do listen. For example, Justice John Harlan's dissent in *Plessy v. Ferguson* (1896) was the basis of the majority decision in *Brown v. Board of Education* (1954). Similarly Justice Hugo Black's dissent in *Betts v. Brady* (1942), which denied Smith Betts (a poor but literate white man) an attorney for his robbery defense in Maryland, became the basis of the majority opinion in *Gideon v. Wainwright* (1963), which granted an attorney for Clarence Earl Gideon (a poor but illiterate white man) refused an attorney for his robbery trial in Florida.

## *DeShaney* and the Idea of Negative Rights

In *DeShaney*, the justices decided against Joshua 6 to 3 in an opinion authored by Chief Justice Rehnquist. The Court answered the two questions raised (regarding state action and state constitutional obligation in private matters) in the negative and failed to find a "special relationship" between DSS and Joshua. The majority concluded that there is no state action involved because the State of Wisconsin did not create the circumstances that led to Joshua's physical abuse. Had Joshua been placed in a foster home and the abuse occurred, then the state would have been potentially liable.

The Court further ruled that states do not have a constitutional obligation to provide services to its citizens or to control the behavior of parents toward their own children. This is the crux of the idea of "negative rights." Chief Justice Rehnquist noted that the Constitution bestows "negative rights" to citizens, rights designed to protect citizens from the awesome powers of the state, rather than requiring states to intervene in people's lives. Within the meaning of negative rights is the belief that parents have a right (and can expect) to go about their business in the privacy of their own homes without governmental intrusion. Therefore, under the Constitution, the Wisconsin Department of Social Welfare is not liable for the deplorable, shameless, and abusive behavior of an intemperate father toward his own son.

## Potential Influences on the *Deshaney* Decision

In taking decision in *DeShaney*, justices were swayed by a set of political and legal factors. These factors inform the various theories of Supreme Court decision making examined in Part 2 of this chapter.

*Political Factors.* The first political factor is ideology of the justices. Think of ideology as a summary measure of a justice's values or preferences over a range of social or political issues. It is a complex indicator that can allow us to predict and explain how a justice will decide a particular case.

It is hardly coincidental that although nine justices listened to the same oral arguments, considered the same legal briefs, and examined the same Constitution, statutes, and case facts, most conservative justices considering the *DeShaney* case voted with the majority to affirm the lower court decision, denying the benefits sought by Melody and Joshua DeShaney. Conversely, all the liberal justices voted to reverse. How could that be? It is quite reasonable to assert that the ideology of the justices played a potentially decisive role in their decision. It is not that the conservative justices are heartless and callous about Joshua DeShaney's well-being. Rather, it is that they subscribe to a philosophy of government that is different from that of liberal justices. Within a capitalist democracy, conservatives believe that the government that governs the least is the best so as to encourage cherished American values like individual responsibility. Therefore, for conservative justices on the Court, Randy DeShaney should take full responsibility for his deplorable actions toward his own son. The overriding philosophy of liberals such as Justices Brennan and Blackmun is that in order for the promise of American democracy to be realized, government has a role to play in promoting safety and showing compassion by helping families and particularly citizens who are incapable of protecting themselves. By understanding this ideological divide, we can begin to appreciate why the justices voted the way they did.

The second factor in decision making is the role of the solicitor general of the United States. The SG made a strong, impassioned argument urging a decision in favor of Wisconsin in *DeShaney*. This argument apparently helped convince at least some of the justices to support the state. Indeed, the similarities in logic between the SG's oral argument and Rehnquist's majority opinion, especially with regard to the idea of negative rights, give strong indication that the SG helped to sway the outcome of the case in Wisconsin's favor.

The third political factor in this and other Supreme Court decisions concerns amicus curiae briefs submitted by organized groups and by attorneys general from several different states. There is suggestive evidence that these amici played a useful role in the *DeShaney* verdict by furnishing information useful to the Court, particularly information about the potential implications of a decision one way or another. For example, many state attorneys general raised the concern that a decision in favor of DeShaney would open the floodgates of litigation against local communities with devastating financial consequences for future state budgets.

Somewhat related to amici is the last potentially important political factor: public opinion. A number of scholars have found evidence that public opinion plays an influential role in Supreme Court decision making on the merits.[20] But it is unclear what precise impact public opinion had in the *DeShaney* outcome. What is clear is that the dissenters deliberately used language free of impartiality, language designed to generate public outrage about the case such as the expression "poor Joshua!"[21]

*Legal Factors.* Finally, we cannot overlook the fact pattern of the case and legal factors involved. Based upon Justice Blackmun's rather emotional exclamation of "poor Joshua!" there is reason to believe that the sad facts of the case influenced at least some justices to show a proclivity toward Joshua's case, especially justices on the liberal end of the ideological spectrum. As Justice Blackum later explained during an interview with his former law clerk and now Yale Law Professor Harold Hongju Koh, "This youngster was subjected to the punishment by a brutish father, and the social service agencies knew this and did nothing about it..."[22] He went on to state in his dissent that he would adopt a "sympathetic reading" of the Fourteenth Amendment, "one which comports with fundamental justice and recognizes that compassion need not be exiled from the province of judging."

Legally speaking, some scholars have found support for the proposition that law influences justices through jurisprudential regimes or legal standards such as strict scrutiny, state action, undue burden, which are seen to guide and constrain decisions in subsequent cases.[23] The majority predicated its *DeShaney* opinion on a narrow reading of the Fourteenth Amendment's state action doctrine and on precedent (*Youngsberg v. Romeo,* 1982) defining the characteristics of a special relationship. In his majority opinion, Rehnquist admonished his colleagues to withstand the "natural sympathy" that a case like *DeShaney* may command. By and large, the Court fulfilled its obligation of patrolling the boundaries of the Constitution, and decided to protect the states.

## PART 2: THEORETICAL APPROACHES TO SUPREME COURT DECISION MAKING

The factors enumerated above can be considered an integral part of numerous theoretical approaches that have guided scholarly inquiry into Supreme Court behavior. In continuing with our evolutionary theme in this book, we examine extant approaches in the historical order in which they were developed as explanatory tools of judicial behavior and the factors emphasized by researchers when they test these theories. The chief theoretical approaches are (1) the legal model; (2) the behavioral/attitudinal model; (3) the strategic model; and (4) the neoinstitutional model. We employ the terms theory and model interchangeably. Both are abstractions that enhance deeper understanding.

A theory can be defined as an interrelated set of concepts that help us to understand the political world around us. That world may include a defining historical event such as the election of an African American president or a series of events such as Supreme Court decisions to incorporate the Bill of Rights to the states. A model is an abstract representation of reality; it is not reality itself. For example, a model could represent the causal relationship between theoretical concepts either in statistical, mathematical, or diagrammatical form.

### The Legal Model

The legal model holds that Supreme Court justices decide cases such as *DeShaney* v. *Winnabago* by carefully examining legal precedent, intent of the framers, plain meaning of the Constitution (or statutes), and balancing of societal interests in light of case facts.[24] Under the legal model, justices rely on one or more of these concepts to resolve legal controversies. The belief is that the legal model lends continuity and predictability to the law, especially for those who must interpret it and those who must abide by it.

To its core adherents, this approach to decision making is completely predicated upon legal precepts. Accordingly, justices are the dispassionate oracles of the law who view the Constitution or statutes each as a bounded historical entity from which meaning must be derived without deviation and without the influence of sympathy, bias, or inarticulate premises. This approach considers legal interpretation to be a nondiscretionary exercise, a process (akin to a scavenger hunt) of discovering which law governs the case rather than inventing it. When Justices speak, it is the Constitution that speaks through them and not the justices themselves trying to wield authority through their personal moral predilections. The approach is purely mechanistic; it rejects the view of the Constitution as a living document to be interpreted in light of contemporary transformations in society.

The most popular mode of legalistic analysis is *interpretivism*, defined as "the belief that the text of the Constitution or intent of the framers should bind Supreme Court justices."[25] Under this mode of analysis, important new rights such as the right to privacy, which received no explicit mention in the Constitution, would not be established as it was in *Griswald v. Connecticut* based upon the "penumbras and emanations" of different parts of the Constitution.

In an interpretivist's world, the Court is not an engine of social change because such a vision was not definitively articulated by the framers. The Court's early abominations on racial servitude, including *Dred Scott v. Sanford* (1857) that shamefully constitutionalized slavery and *Plessy v. Ferguson* that legalized racial segregation and tacitly unleashed the injustices and inhumanities of Jim Crow upon African Americans, would today remain the law of the land. In consequence, *Brown v. Board of Education* would not exist and America would remain a socially and racially backward nation on the international stage. Clearly, interpretivism promotes stability in the law but in doing so succeeds in stifling social progress.

Interpretivism is not necessarily a conservative ideology although it is often misconstrued as such because most commentators, politicians, and justices who subscribe to interpretivism are colored with conservative stripes. But exceptions exist. One interpretivist who was not a conservative ideologue based on his voting record is Justice Hugo Black, an absolutist and civil libertarian who vigorously supported adherence to text and intent. It was Black who coined the phrase "no law means no law," referring to the First Amendment's command that "Congress shall make *no law* respecting an establishment of religion, or prohibiting the free exercise thereof..."

There are important strengths and weaknesses associated with each aspect of the legal model. We discuss these in the next section.

## Strengths and Weaknesses of the Legal Model

*Adherence to Stare Decisis.* This concept means that justices let stand decisions rendered in the past (i.e., precedent). They do so through what is known as *legal reasoning*. The process involves three steps. First the justice making the decision observes a similarity between the current case (A) and a previous case (B). Second, the justice invokes the rule of law inherent in case B. Finally, the justice applies that rule of law to reach a decision in case A.[26]

One strength or advantage of adhering to previous rulings is that it gives uniformity and predictability to the law by limiting the possibility that justices would decide cases on a momentary whim or with a wholly individualistic sense of right and wrong.[27] In theory, these strengths comport with Alexander Hamilton's challenge to Supreme Court justices in *The Federalist Papers* #78 that they should be "bound down by strict rules and precedent" and for justices to devote themselves to a "long and laborious study" of "the records of precedent" in order to reach principled decisions.

Another potential strength of precedent comes from examining how the Supreme Court actually treats and uses precedent. Justices consider adherence to *stare decisis* to be "a cardinal and guiding principle of adjudication."[28] The Court is exceedingly reluctant to overrule precedent and many, including justices, assert this is sound policy that safeguards the Constitution's longevity. During the half century between 1954 and 2005, the Court altered its own precedent a total of only 138 times. In the process of overruling its own precedents, the Court declared an act of Congress, state law, or territorial ordinance unconstitutional in 31 of these 138 cases (45 in both the Warren and Rehnquist Courts, 48 in the Burger Court).[29] Most importantly, when the Court does overrule its own precedent, it cites another precedent as authority. For example, in the 1975 case of *National League of Cities v. Usery*[30] the justices overruled amended provisions of the 1974 Fair Labor Standards Act, which extended federal minimum wage and minimum hours protection to all state employees. The issue raised in the case was whether states can constitutionally object to congressional authority to regulate interstate commerce. Ruling that the amended provisions violated the Eleventh Amendment, the justices overruled *Maryland v. Wirtz*[31] and cited a 1975 precedent, *Fry v. United States*[32] as authority. Justices are justified in overruling precedent because their constitutional duty demands it. The Constitution is the principal legal authority justices are sworn to uphold and defend rather than the gloss that previous justices might have placed upon its meaning.

There are also weaknesses associated with adherence to precedent. First, despite public discussions of its importance, justices may not necessarily rely on precedent for decisions. Some political scientists have argued that precedent is used only as an afterthought, as a cloak for justices' ideological preferences.[33] These scholars further assert that "precedents lie on both sides of most every controversy."[34] From the tremendous variety of decisions the Supreme Court has rendered during its lifetime, litigants can find precedent to support their own side in any dispute. Indeed, a simple perusal of any constitutional law text book proves this point. Under these circumstances, the Court's duty at the very least is to proceed by analogy toward an appropriate precedent but there are no set rules for making that determination. More importantly, the mere possibility of there being one or multiple precedents on each side of a dispute diminishes the overall importance of precedent as a basic determinant of Supreme Court decision making.

Second, in the practice of Constitutional interpretation Supreme Court justices are free to discount or even to set aside precedent in order to prevent absurd consequences for citizens. According to Justice William Brennan, "Constitutional interpretation for a federal judge is, for the most part, obligatory [and] Justices must render constitutional interpretations that are received as legitimate." It is the power to make legitimate decisions rather than to adhere to a particular precedent that is obligatory. Thus justices recognize that precedent does not have controlling influence on their decisions because precedent can be wrong or illegitimate. Judge Frank Coffin of the U.S. Court of Appeals for the First Circuit similarly expressed skepticism about the power of precedent when he stated that "if precedent clearly governed, a case would never get as far as the Court of Appeals: the parties would settle."[35]

Finally, a detailed scholarly analysis of the significance of precedent in Supreme Court decision making provides a third reason for skepticism about the role of precedent. In their 1996 empirical study, Jeffrey Segal and Harold Spaeth hypothesized that if precedent matters, it should influence subsequent decisions of members of the Court. If a justice dissented from a decision establishing a particular precedent, that same justice should vote to uphold the precedent when subsequently applied to a future case. But that was not what they found. Of the 18 justices they examined, only 2 justices were occasionally constrained enough by precedent as to subjugate their preferences to precedent.[36]

*Plain Meaning.* Analysis based on plain meaning assumes that the Constitution and statues are written in clear and unambiguous language. And so plain meaning commands justices to limit their interpretation to the language or words used in the Constitution or statutes. As Justice Joseph Story stated in his widely circulated "Rules of Constitutional Interpretation" (1833), "Where the words are plain and clear, and the sense distinct and perfect arising on them, there is generally no necessity to have recourse to other means of interpretation."[37] A long line of justices who ascended to the bench after Justice Story also assert forthrightly that interpretation begins with analysis of plain meaning of the text.[38]

In many ways this aspect of the legal model makes sense. But there are two problems. First, law is replete with ambiguities and linguistic infelicities for which situational factors might require flexibility in its interpretation. Second, the legal model's "failure to specify the point at which plain meaning terminates and one of the other variants begins"[39] is troubling.

With regard to the importance of situational factors in interpretation, take the First Amendment's command that "Congress shall make no law ... abridging freedom of speech." Interpretation based on plain meaning would lead one to the result that "No law means no law" as Justice Hugo Black had repeatedly reminded other justices. Thus the Supreme Court must strike down any congressional or state legislation that restricts free speech, even political speech, whether in war time or in peace time. Yet the Court occasionally forages in a territory such as national security where it could not resist the impulses to restrict speech. For example, the command of plain meaning failed when, during an era of intense patriotic fervor in the nation, the Court in *Schenck v. United States* unanimously upheld the conviction of socialist Charles Schenck for speaking out against the conscription of soldiers during World War I because presumably his speech presented "a clear and present danger," a substantive evil that Congress has a right to prevent.

Sometimes the difficulty of deciphering plain meaning moves beyond the Court and spills over to the larger society, causing tremendous confusion among the masses. The Second Amendment presents a telling example. It states: *"A well regulated Militia, being necessary to the security of a free State, the right of the people to keep and bear Arms, shall not be infringed"* (emphasis added.)

Do the words of this amendment confer a constitutional *individual* right, permitting citizens to purchase and own firearm? Alternatively, do the words bestow a *collective* right, authorizing firearm ownership only for individuals who are members of a state militia and who have successfully undergone a state-sanctioned and well-structured training program on firearm operation? Through an intense national campaign, gun enthusiasts and especially the National Riffle Association (NRA) have successfully promoted gun ownership as an individual right and have won millions of adherents including members of state and federal legislatures and even Supreme Court justices such as Antonin Scalia. The gun lobby's campaign shrewdly focuses on the second part of the amendment: "the right of the people to keep and bear Arms shall not be infringed" while ignoring or downplaying the first: "A well regulated Militia being necessary to the security of a free State." Unfortunately, for many decades the Supreme Court was astonishingly reticent about this important yet controversial issue. Justices have decided perhaps only a half dozen cases on the Second Amendment in over 200 years of constitutional adjudication.[40] Apparently, they concluded this was an issue best left to politicians. Of course, the Court's decision in *District of Columbia v. Heller* (2007) that the Second Amendment bestows an individual right to firearm ownership challenges that conclusion.

*Framers' and Legislative Intent.* The act of following the original intent of the framers as a decisional principle is known as *originalism*. As used throughout the book, *original intent* means construing statutes and the Constitution in accordance with the intent and preferences of those who originally enacted and promoted the law. To originalists, the Constitution and statutes have human intentions rather than being a mere statement of compromise or a verbal memorandum. Supporters of a jurisprudence of original intention such as former Reagan Attorney General Edwin Meese and Justice Antonin Scalia argue that the approach would depoliticize the judiciary and "produce defensible principles of government that would not be tainted by ideological predilection."[41]

According to Justice William Brennan, an antioriginalist, the approach "demands that Justices discern what the framers thought about the question under consideration and simply follow that intention in resolving the case before them."[42] Analysis of intent is, therefore, a backward-looking process, requiring justice to examine carefully the statements and records left by the drafters of the Constitution or statutes and to accord due deference to the judgment of those who constructed the original compact.

Intentions are latent and unobservable predispositions. They "are highly subjective and personal things. They are not like badges pinned to a coat lapel. They lie deep in the hearts and minds of [people]. They are not always clearly stated by those who have them, nor even capable of clear and specific formulation. The words used to convey them seldom do so perfectly."[43] Assuming that intentions can be properly substantiated and identified, how might justices decipher it? For framers' intent justices can draw wisdom from *The Federalist Papers*, a compilation of essays of events during the Federal Convention of 1787 in Philadelphia. To understand legislative intent, justices can simply scour the congressional record and legislative history for developments that transpired during consideration and drafting of legislation. Fortunately, Congress does maintain complete records of all official communication and activities occurring in each chamber, including hearings, members' floor speeches, and individual votes on bills.

But generally speaking, relying on original intent presents a number of vexing problems. First, no amount of combing through the historical records can give thoroughly reliable and irrefutable answers concerning intention of the framers. For one thing, the *Federalist Papers* are not a perfect representation of the framers' intentions. The papers are a product of human recollections and a random set of notes that Madison, Jay, and Hamilton collected from other participants in the convention. It is, therefore, highly likely that the papers represent a rather incomplete account of events since many attendees left early and missed certain significant discussions.

Most discussions of original intent refer to the original framers who actually were present at the Federal Convention. This would exclude a number of very influential Americans of that era who were absent from the convention proceedings including Thomas Jefferson (away in France at the time), Patrick Henry, John Jay, John Adams, and Samuel Adams. Yet, the extensive writings of these men on the Constitution, especially Thomas Jefferson, are readily referenced by later generations as proof for positive intention of the original framers when plausibly these authors were merely interpreting the written Constitution "so as to bend it to [their] own ideas of sound public policy"[44]

The second problem with the intent argument is that most issues covered in the Constitution were hotly debated, and are etched into the Constitution only as statements of compromise rather than a summary of the framers' intentions. Justice Brennan summarized the problem inherent in the jurisprudence of original intent as "little more than arrogance cloaked in humility." Specifically, "it is arrogant to pretend that from our vantage we can gauge accurately the intent of the framers on application of principle to specific, contemporary questions."[45] Moreover, the records of the constitutional convention are sparse and at the very least constitute ambiguous evidence of intent.

Third, the original document is overlaid with a dense and growing encrustation of constitutional rules and amendments by numerous new framers who appeared in later years and have placed their own unique intentions upon the Constitution. Naturally, this raises the question of whose intention is most germane—that of the original drafters, the new framers of later years, members of the early Congress, or the ratifiers in the various states? No clear answer exists that the Constitution possesses a single unifying intent. Neither does legislative intent exist. Its elliptical nature has led some scholars to characterize legislative intent as an oxymoron: "an internally inconsistent, self-contradictory expression" that does not have a specific meaning.[46]

*Balancing of Interests.* The balancing approach is invoked when individual rights are weighed against the regulatory interest of government in resolving legal claims. In considering the Court's application of balancing, it is useful to note that constitutional rights do not always travel in the same direction. Sometimes they are in conflict, moving in opposite directions. Consequently, advocates of the balancing approach take a position that is more ad hoc, more case-specific than philosophical. To them the factual context of the case becomes critically important. As a result, Supreme Court decisions can vary tremendously because at times individual activity is given more weight whereas at other times government effort to regulate individual behavior is given more weight. In that sense, the balancing approach provides justices with flexibility and convenience.

However, application of the balancing approach can pose analytical problems. First, there is no objective criterion specified by the Court for determining when justices would invoke balancing. Second, more often than not, reliance on balancing leads to a decision favoring the government. In the next section, we examine three instances where balancing leads to favorable outcomes for individuals or underdogs. Then we review examples where the application of balancing leads to decisions favoring the government.

## Balancing Approach and Underdogs: *Sherbert, Yoder,* and *Sheppard*

In the area of fundamental freedoms such as free speech, religious exercise, and establishment, the Court usually applies the strictest scrutiny when deciding cases. The individual usually wins in religion cases when government regulation is not secular and government cannot demonstrate a compelling interest that is supported by the least restrictive (or least intrusive) means for achieving the interest. Conversely, government typically wins when regulation is secular in purpose and the government demonstrates a compelling interest supported by the least restrictive means for achieving the interest.

In *Sherbert v. Verner*, the question was whether state unemployment benefits could be denied to a Seventh Day Adventist (Adell Sherbert, a South

Carolina Textile Mill worker) who claimed she was fired because her religious beliefs prevented her from working on Saturdays. In assessing the constitutionality of her denial of benefits, the Court employed the balancing test by considering whether the free exercise of religion had been burdened by the state's denial of benefits and whether the imposition was supported by a "compelling state interest." The Court concluded that the states' avowed interest in reducing fraud was unimpressive and that the state failed to show that other methods for stemming fraud would not work. Consequently a decision was issued in favor of Adell Sherbert.

In *Wisconsin v. Yoder*—an establishment clause case—a balancing approach was employed. In this case, Wisconsin law requiring compulsory school attendance for children until age 16 was challenged by Amish families as a violation of their religious faith. The Amish culture detests worldly possessions and interpersonal competition typified by high school experience. Consistent with the standards of review employed in *Sherbert,* the Court declared the Wisconsin law unconstitutional at least as applied to the Amish. In a concurring opinion joined by Justices Brennan and Stewart, Justice Byron White wrote: "Cases such as this one inevitably call for a delicate balancing of important but conflicting interests."[47]

All too common, freedom extended to the news media to investigate and report on criminal activity can lead to prejudicial publicity, jeopardizing individual right to a fair trial. In *Sheppard v. Maxwell* (1966), Dr. Samuel Sheppard, a renowned osteopath living in Cleveland, Ohio, was accused of murdering his pregnant wife, Marilyn. Adverse publicity about the murder filled the airwaves and local newspapers, portraying Sam Sheppard as a liar and an unfaithful husband.[48] A front-page editorial in a Cleveland newspaper asked "Why is Sam Sheppard not in jail?" On the day of jury selection, another newspaper headline further inquired: "But who will speak for Marilyn?" Finally, photographs and names of the sequestered jurors were repeatedly published in various newspapers. Sheppard was convicted and his conviction was upheld by a higher court. He appealed to the Supreme Court for federal habeas corpus relief. The Court agreed with Sheppard that prejudicial publicity had tainted the trial procedure and ordered his release from custody.[49] Government interest was not in contention in this case. Instead, the Court balanced the interest of the media to report newsworthy events against that of the accused individual and sided with the individual.

In all three examples, a claim of fundamental rights violation was raised and was decided in favor of the underdog. In none was there a serious threat to public safety. The Supreme Court is a pragmatic institution that (like elected politicians) places a premium on public safety. Individuals often have a relatively harder time in this area while states find it somewhat easier to demonstrate compelling interest in order to win. In cases where public safety is central, justices are inclined to balance the scale of justice in favor of the government. The following examples illustrate this tendency.

## Balancing Approach and Public Safety: *O'Brien*, *Branzburg*, and *Leon*

The 1968 case *United States v. O'Brien* provides another example of how the Court uses the balancing approach but one where the individual fared poorly. The case concerned the Constitutional rights of David O'Brien and three others to symbolically protest the Vietnam War by burning their government issued draft cards. The Court upheld the defendants' conviction and facilitated the government's administrative convenience in managing the war effort and protecting the security of the United States.

In *Branzburg v. Hayes* (1972) the Court denied claims of a reporter's privilege to withhold testimony from a grand jury inquiry concerning the reporter's knowledge of criminal activity he had observed and written about. The Supreme Court applied the balancing approach and ruled in favor of the government. In the Court's view, the government's responsibility to prosecute serious crimes trumps reporters' privilege to protect informants even though this might place a chilling effect on news gathering activities.

Finally in *United States v. Leon* (1984), a case dealing with Fourth Amendment protection against unreasonable searches and seizures, the justices carved out an exception to the exclusionary rule, which was established in *Weeks v. United States* (1914) and made applicable to the states via *Wolf v. Colorado* (1949). The *exclusionary rule* stipulates that evidence seized illegally by law enforcement officers will be excluded from a criminal proceeding. To permit the use of such evidence in Court, Justice William R. Day reasoned in *Weeks*, would make a mockery of the Constitution. At its core, the exclusionary rule was designed to deter official police misconduct and to remove inducements for unreasonable invasion of privacy during police search for incriminating evidence.

The *Leon* case started in Burbank, California, in 1981. Police officers received a tip from a person of unproven reliability identifying two individuals, Patsy Stewart and Armando Sanchez, as drug dealers. Officers conducted a comprehensive investigation and surveillance of the suspects' movement and houses. In the process, they identified Alberto Leon and his friend, Ricardo Del Castillo, as participants in a drug dealing operation. A police detective then drafted and signed an affidavit to obtain a search warrant, which was duly issued by a neutral magistrate. Empowered with the search warrant, officers searched the suspects' houses and cars, seizing a wealth of illegal substances.

During the trial, this evidence was introduced into the record. But defense attorneys objected, arguing that the search warrant was invalid because the original tip lacked credibility, that as a result the detective lacked sufficient probable cause to request the warrant. The government did not contest these facts but argued that good evidence should not be disregarded based upon a merely defective warrant if officers acted in good faith in believing that they had a legitimate warrant. The government lost its case at the lower court levels and appealed to the Supreme Court, which granted certiorari and took jurisdiction.

The Supreme Court faced the question of whether exclusionary sanction is appropriately imposed in this case. In response, the justices applied a balancing analysis of the competing goals of (1) deterring official misconduct by excluding defective evidence and (2) permitting inherently trustworthy tangible evidence albeit defective that would expose the truth and enhance public safety. Justices came down on the side of the exposing of the truth, that is, in favor of the government. Writing for a six-person majority, Justice Byron White noted that unbending application of the exclusionary rule would impede the truth-finding function of our courts. Thus the Court established the "good faith" exception to the exclusionary rule under the Fourth Amendment.

Many other examples abound of the Court tending to favor the government in cases where the balancing approach is employed, especially in the criminal justice area. Quite often, public opinion weighs heavily in the justices' mind as the Court adjusts to an evolving standard of decency. The problem is that no objective criterion has been announced by the Court for when and why balancing will be used, thus reducing the approach to a mere tool of convenience invoked willy-nilly for resolving constitutional issues on a case-by-case basis. This oversight was echoed by the dissenting justices in *Leon* (Justices Brennan, Marshall and Stevens) who accused the majority of being disingenuous by ignoring an objective assessment of the facts and instead drawing the American people into a "curious world" where costs of excluding illegally seized evidence are "exaggerated" while the benefits of such exclusion "are made to disappear with a mere wave of the hand."[50]

*Summary of the Legal Model.* The legal model assumes that justices accept the authority of the law and are motivated by a strong sense of obligation to expound it dispassionately. The model argues in favor of the supremacy of legal doctrine as the foundation for proper judicial decision making. It entertains no extralegal influences (i.e., those outside the legal realm). It rejects the possible influence of discretion in judging and it ignores that justices are individuals with foibles and limited cognitive abilities. In light of this inflexibility, many social scientists believe that the legal model fails to explain judicial behavior. They have instead emphasized other approaches such as the behavioral approach, which emphasizes the "personal element" in judging. The most popular variant of this approach is the attitudinal model.

## The Attitudinal Model

Since the 1940s, political scientists have taken significant steps to demonstrate the "personal element" in judicial decision making. The effort emanates from the "realistic" or behavioral school of jurisprudence, which argues that "law is simply the behavior of the judge, that law is secreted by judges as pearls are secreted by oysters."[51] The attitudinal model is the bedrock theoretical principle of the realistic school and in the past several decades, the model has played a major role in how scholars understand the Supreme Court and its justices.

The attitudinal model has its empirical and theoretical foundation in the work of C. Herman Pritchett during a period when political scientists were fully engaged in an intellectual effort to introduce science into the study of law and legal processes. Pritchett's pioneering work entitled *The Roosevelt Court* carefully and systematically examined the dissents, concurrences, bloc voting, and ideological configurations surrounding the Court's nonunanimous decisions from 1937 to 1947. This work was further elaborated and formalized by Walter Murphy and Glendon Schubert, focusing on elements of justices' strategies (Murphy) and scaling of their attitudes (Schubert).[52] Thus while Pritchett is credited with ushering in the behavioral revolution in the scientific study of the Supreme Court, it was Murphy, Schubert, and, later David W. Rhode and Harold J. Spaeth,[53] who provided the initial theoretical elaborations and formalization of the theory using psychometric methods.

Early public law scholars—those who concentrate their teaching and research on normative questions concerning constitutional, administrative, and international law and their relationship to American politics[54]—were content to labor over the doctrinal esoterica of constitutional and other laws, painstakingly undertaking studies steep in "arcane lawyer-babble of case names."[55] Pritchett was more fascinated with the prospect of uncovering the political (and some would say more unpredictable and, therefore, more interesting) nature of judging by focusing on the personalities of justices themselves. How did Pritchett formulate the behavioral approach? His detailed analysis of voting blocs in the Supreme Court led him to surmise that while it is a happy coincidence that voting outcomes in many cases were unanimous, this state of affairs applied only to a small subset of the cases and, therefore, masked severe division of opinion "the conscious or unconscious preferences and prejudices of the Justices."[56]

In other words, Pritchett recognized that judging necessarily involved the exercise of discretion and that Justices' attitudes or policy preferences were the anchors dictating their legal choices on important questions. Although Pritchett did not formulate a complete theory of Supreme Court decision making, he nevertheless made his assumption quite explicit: "justices of the United States Supreme Court, in deciding controversial cases involving important issues of public policy, are influenced by biases and philosophies of government...which predetermine the position they will take on a given question."[57] In other words, justices are motivated primarily by their own policy preferences. Justice William Brennan voted the way he did because he was extremely liberal; Justice Clarence Thomas votes the way he does because he is extremely conservative.

The *attitudinal model* as formulated has a deceptively simple but powerful logic. It postulates that justices come to the Supreme Court with their values and ideological preferences fully formed and that, in light of contextual case facts, these values and preferences exercise overwhelming influence on their decisions.[58] Thus the attitudinal model is a complete and adequate representation of Supreme Court behavior though not an absolutely complete explanation for the justices' votes. A complete explanation of justices' votes would account for the role of law, historical tradition, institutional norms, fact pattern of cases, strategic considerations, environmental influences, and the personal element in judicial decision making. In one empirical testing after another, the attitudinal model has proven its mettle. Scholars have demonstrated that regardless of the composition of the empirical model constructed, justices' attitudes or ideological preferences overwhelmed other independent variables in explanatory power.[59]

Unlike the legal model, which views the Constitution as law and emphasizes the internal logic of opinions justices write, the attitudinal model views the Constitution as an event or a series of events to be studied, analyzed, and explained. Those events are manifested in the votes of Supreme Court justices and so the focus of the model is on the behavior of the justices, either as individuals (microanalytics) or as a group (macroanalytics). The model works because it assumes justices are preference-oriented; as such their motivations are unwittingly aided by ambiguities and uncertainties inherent in the nature of our Constitution and in statutes crafted by legislative majorities. In short, the model works because law is ambiguous. In the next section we demonstrate how the model works.

## How the Attitudinal Model Works

The attitudinal model works through the interaction of attitude objects (classes of litigants that justices encounter on paper, such as children, pilots, military veterans, death row inmates) with attitude situations (the dominant legal issue the cases raise, such as negligent state action, denial of retirement benefits, and discrimination).[60]

The following example demonstrates how the attitudinal model works. Imagine two equal protection cases A and B involving severe child abuse in two different states. The case stimuli are as follows. In Case A, the government of a Southern state has enacted legislation requiring social service workers to take *adequate* measures to protect children (attitude object) from physical and emotional abuse. Upon learning of an abuse, social service workers made a reasonable effort to protect the child by providing periodic counseling for the abusive parent and frequently monitoring the family. However, they did not remove the child from the abusive home, believing the parent was responding positively to counseling and that keeping the parent and child together was important.

In Case B, the government of a Midwestern state similarly enacted a law requiring social service workers to take *aggressive* action to protect children from physical and emotional abuse. Upon learning of an abuse, social workers moved quickly to remove the child from the abusive home and to place him in the custody of a foster parent. Unfortunately, in both cases, state involvement (the attitude situation) failed to end the child abuse. In Case A, the abusive parent found ways to continue tormenting his child whereas in case B, despite their careful selection of a foster parent, caseworkers were unaware of a hidden history of child abuse by the foster parent's subsequent live-in partner. That partner went on to physically assault the child on numerous occasions following the child's placement in the foster home. In both cases, the nonabusive biological parent of the child sued the state for negligence in taking proper care to protect the child from abuse and for violating the child's rights under the equal protection clause of the Fourteenth Amendment.

There is reason to believe that state involvement exists in both cases but in varying degrees. Therefore, we can array the two cases as shown in figure 6.1 based on the level of potential tort negligence confronting the state. Because in Case B the state actively removed the child from his home and placed him in foster care, there is a higher probability that state action existed under the Fourteenth Amendment. Consequently there is a potentially higher level of state negligence in Case B than in Case A, where the child was left with his parent. Accordingly, Case A is placed to the left of Case B in the diagram.

Similarly, we can array justices on an ideological spectrum according to their ideal points. Assuming that based upon independent newspaper editorials written about justices when they were nominated to the Court, we know justices' ideological positions on a number of policy issues. This prior knowledge leads us to believe that Justice X is liberal on social issues, Justice Y moderate, and Justice Z conservative. We can position the ideal point of Justice Y in between the ideal points of Justice X and Justice Z on the ideological space labeled state negligence. If, say, a third case of child abuse was brought where the state took full custody of the child by placing him in a state-operated rehabilitation institution for abused children with round-the-clock care, then the case would be placed to the right of Case B and to the right of Justice Z because the state is maximally liable for behavior within the institution. According to the attitudinal model, justices would decide the cases based on the interaction of their ideological attitudes and the case facts. They would thus reject a claim of equal protection (i.e., state negligence) in a case located to the left of their ideal point and affirm cases located to the right of their ideal point.

Given the arrangement in figure 6.1, Justice Z has the highest ideological threshold for finding a state negligent under the Fourteenth Amendment. Therefore, Justice Z would vote to deny plaintiff's claim of equal protection in both cases. To Justice Z, the state should not face liability for a violation suffered when the claimant was not fully under its custody. Justice Y would vote to award petitioner's equal protection claim in Case B (where caseworkers took limited custody by placing the child in foster care) but reject the same in Case A (where the child was left in his parent's home). Justice X would vote for the petitioner's claim of equal protection in both cases. For Justice X, the child was helpless and needed protection, which the state was in a position to provide but failed. It is thus more important to focus on the child's medical situation and to hold the state liable for failing to take every precautionary measure necessary to safeguard the welfare of the child. Using this mode of analysis, we can explain and predict

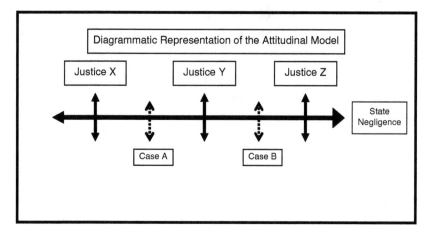

**Figure 6.1**   Diagrammatic Representation of the Attitudinal Model.

individual justice's votes in a wide variety of issue areas that come before the Court.

What is the logic controlling the reliance on preferences in Supreme Court decision making? First, Supreme Court justices are at the pinnacle of their legal careers. There is no higher judicial office to which they aspire; they are positioned as final arbiters of the Constitution, a reality succinctly captured by Charles Evans Hughes' aphorism that "We are under a Constitution, but the Constitution is what the judges say it is."[61] Second, under Article 3 of the Constitution, federal judges' salaries cannot be reduced for any reason and so justices can make decisions without fear of financial reprisal. Finally, there is no higher authority that can overturn Supreme Court decisions except the people through a constitutional amendment, which is an incredibly difficult result to obtain. For these reasons, justices can safely rely on their attitudes and preferences to guide their decision making. The theory works most powerfully in the Supreme Court, less so in lower courts because fear of reversal constrains lower court judges from straying too far from the law and relying on their attitudes.[62]

The claims of the attitudinal model have come under severe criticism even as the model gains adherents across the social, psychological, and physical sciences worldwide. Critics charge that the attitudinal model is derivative— that is, when modeling judicial behavior, scientists rely on voting patterns to explain how justices will vote. As such scientists engage in circular reasoning by ignoring the substance of legal opinions and the claims of authority that guide them, focusing instead on the individual justice making the decision.

Attacking scientific theories is nothing new. It is a routine part of scholarly endeavor, which should not be taken personally. Sir Isaac Newton who discovered calculus and refined Galilleo's theories of motion during the 18th century learned this lesson the hard way when he suffered emotional damage from attacks on his work. After his discovery— that colored light (red, green, and blue) and not white light was pure and immutable contrary to previous thinking— was denounced as "radical theory" by members of the Royal Society of England, the embittered Newton became reclusive and lashed out saying, "A man must either resolve to put out nothing new, or become a slave to defend it."[63]

Defend it, proponents of the attitudinal model have done. The criticism holds some merit but it applies more to the pioneers of the attitudinal model than to modern revisionists who have taken pains to address various criticisms of the model.[64] To be sure, the resilience of the U.S. Constitution has been continually reaffirmed for over 200 years. Scientific study is unlikely to make the Constitution disappear and it will always serve as the institutional center of controversy in American politics.

## Rational Choice/Strategic Approach

The rational choice or strategic approach to Supreme Court decision making considers as its pivotal characteristic the interdependence of actions and relationships among various institutional actors, including justices, members of Congress, the president, and interest groups. Justices are viewed under the strategic model as individuals whose decisions are constrained by the choices they expect other justices and political actors to make. They act strategically under these conditions to maximize their preferred outcome when expounding the law. In short, the argument of the strategic approach is that judicial choices are best understood as strategic behavior rather than merely a response to ideology, preferences or legal tradition.

The strategic approach was originally developed by scholars working in economics and finance when they employed rational choice theory to understand human interactions in competitive free market settings. Human interaction is goal-directed, and it is a necessary but not sufficient condition for strategic behavior. Research that started in the 1960s and continue into the present through the papers of former Supreme Court justices suggests that human interactions within the Court via intellectual arguments, internal bargaining over the scope and language of opinion drafts, and even formal lobbying and threats to expose a dispute within the Court show justices being exceedingly capable of exerting influence on the actions of their colleagues and vice versa.[65] This raises the plausibility of strategic behavior in the Court.

What are the necessary conditions for strategic behavior? They are four. There must be (1) a set of players, for example, Supreme Court justices or members of Congress interacting in a game of strategy; (2) a set of formal or informal rules understood by all individuals playing the game; (3) strategies, which players keep secret until deployed; and (4) payoffs or rewards gained from deploying one's strategies. Because most political processes take place in multiple stages, players find it beneficial to behave strategically (sometimes making suboptimal choices) in the initial stages and then acting more sincerely in the final stage. In this way, players are better positioned to maximize their preferred outcome.

We have seen in chapter 2 that the retirement decision is one area where strategic behavior can occur. But strategic behavior can take place in other decisional aspects of the Court besides retirement. The agenda-setting stage is another. Chief Justice Rehnquist has admitted that "There is an ideological division in the Court and each of us has some cases we would like to see granted, and on the contrary some of the other members would not like to see them granted."[66] Agenda setting is, therefore, tailor-made for strategic maneuverings as if each justice is engaged in a kind of competitive law practice against other justices. For example, when the affirmative action case of *Regents of the University of California v. Bakke* (1978) was appealed to the Court, the two staunchest supporters of affirmative action Justices William Brennan and Thurgood Marshall voted strategically against hearing the case even though, from an ideological perspective, the lower court decision was consistent with their preferences and they should have been eager to grant certiorari and nationalize the ruling.[67] But they lacked the votes to win a majority on the merits. Their vote to deny certiorari was, therefore, predicated upon their expectation that a potentially winning coalition of five or more justices exist to place a lid upon affirmative action programs nationwide.

This discussion of strategic behavior is not intended to suggest that Supreme Court decision making is a game in the ordinary sense of the word. Indeed, making choices in the High Court is serious business, which scholars have modeled as a game.[68] Because of the importance of interdependency of action, the strategic model makes an explicit assumption that is similar to that of the attitudinal model, that justices are motivated by individual preferences and so act rationally to achieve those preferences.

## Neoinstitutionalism

The last of our theoretical approaches is neoinstitutionalism. Starting in the 1980s, scholars have witnessed in political science and other social sciences a resurgence of interest in the role of institutions in understanding political behavior and outcomes.[69] Within political science, this new research tradition is increasingly making its mark in the subfield of judicial politics, especially research focusing on the nation's highest court.

In the broadest sense, *institutions* are the "rules of the game" in politics and society;[70] they are "the humanly devised constraints that shape human interaction."[71] They could be formal (taking the form of constitutions, legal doctrines, treaties, or congressional legislation) or informal (taking the form of cultural norms, network of relationships, or judicial tradition).

In the social sciences and law, there is widespread agreement that institutions matter tremendously![72] In particular, institutions provide numerous advantages that help us understand politics and the Court. For example, institutions impose structure on the independent choices justices make; they impose order and discipline in an otherwise inchoate world. Thus more broadly, institutions help to organize our political world by maintaining order, promoting civility, and structuring interaction among groups, ideas, and interests. In essence, institutions constitute the structural foundation of politics. If you have ever imagined living in a society devoid of rules or where there is a total breakdown in enforcement of rules, not much imagination is required to conclude that pandemonium and chaos would be the result. Institutions help avoid such potential disasters. Institutionalists, therefore, recognize that rules or norms not backed by enforcement are simply worthless.

Therefore, the main tenet of the neoinstitutionalism approach is that political action is viewed as the fulfillment of duties and obligations based on a stable set of rules that provide incentives and impose order and constraint

**Table 6.1**  Summary of Key Theories of U.S. Supreme Court Decision Making

| Theory | Main Tenets | Analytical Emphases | Advantages | Disadvantages |
|---|---|---|---|---|
| Legal Model | Supreme Court decisions are based on precedent, Framers' intent, plain meaning of Constitution/statutes, balancing of individual versus government interests and case facts | Constitution, legal doctrines derived from judicial opinions and historical tradition. Case analysis is the method of choice. | Fosters predictability and uniformity in the law | Static and mechanistic; ignores the importance of justices social background and political values |
| Behavioral/ Attitudinal Model | Supreme Court decisions are a choice based on individual attitudes, values or preferences, and subjective expectations in light of case facts | Ideology, political outlook/worldview. Empirical/statistical analysis are the methods of choice | Holds a realistic view of judging; takes human imperfections into account; parsimonious | Circular reasoning because justices votes are used to explain future vote choices; ignores the value of legal principles in judging |
| Strategic Model | Supreme Court decisions are the result of an interdependent choice based upon objective expectations about the behavior of other justices or political actors | Individual self-interest motivations; mathematical logic and empirical analysis. Game theory is the method of choice. | Purely deductive, logical reasoning | Makes many unrealistic assumptions (e.g., actors must be individuals) and places too much emphasis on individual self-interest as motivating force; de-emphasizes bounded rationality |
| Neoinstitutional Model | Supreme Court decisions/political actions are a fulfillment of duties and obligations based on a set of rules/norms that impose constraints on individual or group behavior | Political structure of government, institutional rules and informal norms; relations between the Court and other stations of power in government and society. Mixed emphasis on both normative (case study) and empirical methods | Imposes order and discipline on political choice; Legitimization of choice is a desired objective. Combines elements of the above models. | Lacks specificity in method of analysis |

*Source:* Author.

on justices' behavior. Generally speaking, the analytical emphasis of neoin-
stitutionalists is to engage the political structure by relying on some elements of historical tradition and relations between the Court and other
stations of power in government and society. In this sense legitimization
(i.e., support from outside the Court) is a key organizational imperative for
the Court; legitimization serves both as a source of judicial restraint and as
justification for particular decisions. Legitimization is especially prized when
the Court faces highly controversial decisions or where it is asked to reverse
a landmark ruling.[73]

Table 6.1 presents a summary of the main characteristics as well as advantages and disadvantages of the four theories discussed so far.

The neoinstitutional model requires further elaboration to capture its two
main intellectual pathways or tracks in political science research. One track
of neoinstitutional research on the Supreme Court mirrors the rational
choice approach while the other bends toward historical analysis.

### Rational Choice Institutionalism versus Historical Institutionalism

*Rational Choice Institutionalism* is an approach employed by rational choice
scholars to understand developments in government instrumentalities such
as the Supreme Court. This approach argues that political outcomes such as
Supreme Court decisions are the result of strategic choices that are rooted in
enlightened preferences of justices. Decision making is understood to reflect
a relativity of judgment among judicial actors.

*Historical Institutionalism* is an approach employed by social scientists to
develop a deep contextual understanding of political outcomes or events by
analyzing the cultural processes and the history of human interactions that
produce those outcomes. Specifically, it is an "'interpretive' approach to
studying the Supreme Court [based] on historical and ethnographic
analyses."[74]

The two approaches overlap somewhat in that both agree that institutions
matter and both are interested in explaining political phenomena, though
not to the same quantitative levels by virtue of their different methodological
styles. Historical institutionalists favor *depth* of analysis through process-
tracing of singular or smaller set of cases or events; rational choice institutionalists favor *breadth* through strategic modeling using game theory.

Using an inductive style, the analytical trajectory of historical instititu-
tionalists is first to identify an outcome or event of great political importance
such as the constitutional development of the right to privacy or incorpo-
ration of the Bill of Rights and then attempt to construct an in-depth explanation of it by tracing the process through which the event occurred and
what impact it has. To historical institutionalists, then, political outcomes
are the result of a complex process enabled by institutional rules, cultural
norms, legal tradition, and a network of human interaction. The benefits of
the approach are that it enables scientists to develop an understanding not

only of "how judicial attitudes are constituted and structured by the Court as an institution"[75] but also how the Court affects, and is affected by, the larger political system in the process of generating the event or outcome in question. Under this framework, then, institutions serve as intervening variables, not as the only plausible explanation for political choice or legal change.

Rational choice institutionalists, on the other hand, are fundamentally interested in uncovering the underlying logics or hidden truths (laws) upon which the game of politics is played in the United States and elsewhere.[76] The general theoretical principles (logics) of rational choice institutionalism are invoked in terms of a game (e.g., tit-for-tat or prisoners' dilemma). We have already learned that institutions structure the rules of the game of politics and determine how players constitute their strategies and what choices they ultimately make. Rational choice institutionalism emphasizes the primacy of discovering the "logic" of politics. Only then do they employ those logics or general principles to explain specific political events or Supreme Court outcomes. In this sense, their analytical style (theory and then explanation) is purely deductive. Critics of rational choice institutionalism such as Theda Skocpol of Harvard University find the theory problematic because "rational choice theorists too often presume that actors must be individuals, rather than looking for groups or organizations that in some way act together. Worse, some rational choicers are so taken with formal deductive modeling that they necessarily avoid messy historical changes and real life political processes."[77]

## PART 3: ARCHITECTURE OF OPINION ASSIGNMENT AND DECISIONAL TRENDS

The majority opinion issued by the Supreme Court constitutes the structural embodiment of the Court's power and policymaking. It is the primary instrument through which the Court most authoritatively formulates legal principles and communicates them to society. Because Court decisions hold serious immediate and historical importance, the majority opinion is written with utmost diligence and analysis, and with an eye toward achieving clarity within a process of deliberation involving all the justices but primarily the justices in the majority. Justices consider it an honor to be picked to write the majority opinion and have their names forever associated with that case as author.

After justices cast their votes in conference, the chief justice is responsible for assigning someone to write the majority opinion if the chief votes with the majority. The chief can self-assign the opinion or pick any member of the majority coalition. If the chief does not vote with the majority, however, the most senior associate justice voting with the majority assigns the majority opinion. Ultimately, the majority opinion is the product of collective effort, involving seasaw negotiations, bargaining, and accommodation of the ideas and interests of other justices. The majority opinion writer cannot dictate the views of other justices but does exercise significant agenda control authority in terms of what suggestions to accept, what legal issues to press, and whether to "push the envelope" regarding the depth and scope of the decision. But the writer must be mindful of the primary goal: produce an opinion that maintains a minimum winning coalition of five justices.

## Opinion Assignment Factors

There are many factors that affect opinion assignment. Most of these are geared toward enhancing institutional legitimacy and compliance with Court decisions.

*Self-Assignment.* The opinion assigner can self-assign to himself or herself. Under the assumption that the opinion assigner exercises agenda control over the content of the opinion, self-assignment allows the assigners to write opinions that would best reflect their own set of values and preferences on the case while maintaining the majority coalition.[78] Empirical research suggests that self-assignment by chief justices and associate justices is commonplace. Table 6.2 shows the assignment pattern of chief justices from Earl Warren to John Roberts. When we examine orally argued cases with signed written opinions, it is clear that opinion assignment is driven strongly by the chief justice. Chief justices assign 84 percent of the cases decided during the period, 1953–2006. The rest are assigned by the most senior associate justice in the majority. The chief justice receives little input and faces little interference from associate justices over opinion assignments except in rare instances where an associate justice may protest a given assignment. When it comes to

**Table 6.2**   Majority Opinion Assignment Behavior of Chief Justices, 1953–2006

| Chief Justice (Period) | Number of Cases* | Chief Justice Assignments | Self Assignments |
|---|---|---|---|
| Earl Warren (1953–1969) | 1561 | 1319 (84%) | 170 (13%) |
| Warren Burger (1969–1986) | 2270 | 1912 (84%) | 258 (13%) |
| William H. Rehnquist (1986–2005) | 1815 | 1487 (82%) | 212 (14%) |
| John G. Roberts (first term only, 2005–2006 ) | 76 | 68 (89%) | 9 (13%) |
| Total Cases | 5722 | 4786 (84%) | 649 (14%) |

*Orally argued cases with written opinion, including tied votes and judgments of the Court but excluding per curiam opinions. Case citation used as unit of analysis.
*Source*: The Supreme Court Judicial Database (Harold J. Spaeth, Principal Investigator, 2006).

self-assignment, chiefs have done so approximately 14 percent of the time on average, as is shown in the table. This figure is remarkably consistent across the four eras examined, suggesting that modern chief justices care about equalizing the task of crafting the majority opinion.

The assignment pattern in politically salient cases is somewhat different compared to regular cases. The most popular measure of case salience is publication of the opinion on the front page of the *New York Times* at the time the decision was announced.[79] In salient cases, chief justices are significantly more likely to self-assign. For example, in the highly salient *DeShaney* case, Chief Justice Rehnquist voted with the majority and self-assigned the opinion. A similar pattern can be found in truly transformative precedents such as *Marbury v. Madison* (1908), *Brown v. Board of Education* (1954), and *Miranda v. Arizona* (1966).

According to political scientist Saul Brenner, from 1801 to 1989, chief justices self-assigned 35 percent of all salient cases. From citizen and mass media perspectives, self-assignment by chiefs brings weight and authority to the opinion and may even engender greater compliance. It is partly for these reasons that Chief Justice John Marshall assigned the vast majority of opinions to himself, though these alone are not the sole reasons. He self-assigned partly to help unify the Court and the nation. As a matter of constitutional development, however, self-assignment by chiefs does not make an ounce of difference. Beyond the symbolism, a Supreme Court precedent is a Supreme Court precedent no matter which justice wrote the opinion. But historically, significant variation in opinion assignment among chief justices does exist, with some chiefs self-assigning significantly more than others. Such variation is important because it reveals differences in leadership styles, either a centralized (John Marshall) or decentralized (Earl Warren) style of leadership that a given chief adopts.

*Ideology.* Chief justices and senior associate justices assign opinion writing to other justices based upon ideological closeness with them. This was clearly demonstrated during the Warren Court where Chief Justice Earl Warren favored like-minded liberals William O. Douglas and Hugo Black with the highest assignments (176 and 162 opinions respectively). A similar assignment pattern emerged during the conservative Burger Court. Justice Harry Blackmun (a moderate conservative) was Chief Justice Burger's go-to-justice early on during Blackmun's career on the Court). But Blackmun was subsequently overtaken by another conservative, former NFL quarterback, Justice Byron White, after interpersonal friction emerged between Blackmun and Burger in the early 1980s. Even with tempered moderation in his own conservatism after becoming chief justice, William Rehnquist did not buck this general trend of assigning to ideological allies. Rehnquist singled out for his highest assignments fellow conservatives Sandra Day O'Connor (with 195 assignments) and Antonin Scalia (with 178 assignments). In the Robert's Court, indications are that fellow conservatives Justices Scalia and Thomas are receiving the majority of opinion assignments. But as Court leaders, chiefs must be mindful of assigning opinions in an equitable ratio to avoid overburdening certain justices with too many assignments or alienating others with too few.

*Subject-Matter Specialization.* Justices possessing substantive specialization in a given area of law or policy, be it antitrust (Stephen Breyer), civil rights (Thurgood Marshall), business (Lewis Powell), land/real estate (Stephen J. Field), or obscenity (William Brennan),[80] can write quality opinions in their area of expertise much faster and more thoroughly than those lacking in expertise. Thus the main benefit for the Court of subject-matter specialization in opinion assignment is efficiency. Experts require less expenditure of time in research and writing. The expert justice understands the technical and legal nuances prevailing in the subject area and so can craft opinions more expeditiously and with greater clarity than would most nonexpert justices. Justice Harry Blackmun was assigned the politically salient case *Roe v. Wade* (1973) because of his expert knowledge of medical law. He served as general counsel for the nationally renowned Mayo Clinic in Minnesota before becoming a federal appeals court judge. It took Blackmun only five weeks to circulate an opinion draft.[81] Another benefit of opinion assignment based upon expertise is compliance. Expertise lends authority and weight to the opinion and makes compliance more likely.

*Anticipated Public Reactions.* How the opinion assigner expects the public to react to a Supreme Court decision can have an influence on who writes the majority opinion. In this sense, opinion assignment is geared toward calming potentially hostile *reactions* and ultimately enhancing *compliance* with Court decisions, especially in controversial cases. In 1944, following the Japanese attacks on Pearl Harbor, the Court decided the case *Korematsu v. United States*, upholding the federal relocation of approximately 112,000 individuals of Japanese ancestry (roughly 70,000 of them U.S. citizens) in the West Coast. At that defining moment in U.S. history, the most widely recognized civil libertarian on the Court based on voting record, Justice Hugo Black, was assigned to write the majority opinion in order to sooth public fears, communicate the necessity of the government's hostile actions against civil liberties, and possibly unite the nation behind the policy. The assumption was that if Justice Black wrote the opinion, the public would support the national security reasons "compelling" such an anticivil libertarian stance. But in *Korematsu*, the Court could not hide the fact that it rendered a manifestly racist and divisive opinion. Despite its civil libertarian author, the Korematsu opinion was vigorously criticized by various individuals and groups, including dissenting justices Robert Jackson and Frank Murphy, who accused the Court of placing a stamp of legitimacy upon the government's unscrupulous misdeed.

## DISUNITY VERSUS HARMONY ON THE SUPREME COURT

A definite historical pattern exists in the level of disunity and harmony within the Court. Disunity can be defined as disagreement among the justices over a point of law as manifested in the Court's dissenting opinions, while harmony is agreement among the justices. Unanimous decisions with no special concurring opinions represent the highest form of harmony, whereas judgments of the Court and 5 to 4 decisions with both special concurring opinions and dissenting opinions represent the greatest form of disunity on the Court. Both harmony and disunity might be grounded in fact or ideology.

Throughout much of the Court's history, the level of harmony among justices was quite high. Indeed, most decisions handed down during the Marshall and Taney Court eras were unanimous. This trend continued into the 20th century but not for long. Whereas between 80 and 90 percent of the Court's decisions were unanimous throughout much of the early part of the 20th century, institutional unity began to crumble during the Great Depression when President Franklin D. Roosevelt indirectly challenged the Court to support his controversial New Deal programs, causing a rift among the justices. Unanimity dropped sharply starting in 1935, reaching an absolute minimum of only 15 percent in 1953, the year Earl Warren took over as chief. Since then, unanimity has recovered slightly but has hovered around 40 percent, suggesting that disunity not harmony better characterizes the modern Supreme Court.

Contrary to the harmony described above, figure 6.2 shows the proportion of cases decided from 1800 to 2004 in which at least one dissenting opinion was issued. Whereas the proportion of dissents hovered around 10 percent from 1800 to 1940, it skyrocketed beyond the 90 percent mark

**Proportion of Supreme Court Decisions with at Least One Dissenting Opinion, 1800-2004**

**Figure 6.2** Proportion of Supreme Court Decisions with at Least One Dissenting Opinion, 1800–2004

temporally at mid-century but has settled around 60 percent ever since. This overall trend is important and meaningful for assessing Court's success as a policymaking force because disunity is a source of vulnerability, making its decisions more subject to challenge and willful noncompliance.

Scholars have pondered over the reasons for the rise in disunity in the Supreme Court. Definitive answers are hard to find. Some scholars blame the rise in disunity on an increase in very difficult economic and civil rights and liberties issues confronting the Court during the post–New Deal period, a period that coincided with the end of mandatory appellate review. More plausibly other scholars have emphasized hardened ideological attitudes among justices and differences in leadership styles among chief justices.[82]

Whereas earlier chiefs adopted leadership styles that encouraged justices to unite behind the majority opinion, later chief justices saw dissents as a necessary tool for maintaining judicial independence. The strongest and most eloquent endorsement of dissenting behavior is by Chief Justice Charles Evan Hughes: "A dissent in a court of last resort is an appeal to the brooding spirit of the law, to the intelligence of a future day when a later decision may possibly correct the error into which the dissenting judge believes the Court to have been betrayed."[83] Whatever the explanation, it is clear that ideological divisions within the Supreme Court reflect political divisions within the larger society from where justices are selected.

## CONCLUSION

At the end of the day, what really influences Supreme Court decisions? Perhaps we can draw a lesson or two from political scientist James Gibson who argued that "Judges' decisions are a function of what they prefer to do, tempered by what they think they ought to do, but constrained by what they feel is feasible."[84] Supreme Court justices hold different views about how the Constitution should be interpreted. They understand that they have the last word but remain humble enough to know theirs is not necessarily the best word. Their individual differences of opinion are encouraged by the principle of judicial independence, widely recognized to constitute a key strength of American Democracy. Despite these differences, it is heartening that justices do find common ground upon which to dispose of even the most politically and socially controversial cases. They compromise where necessary and accommodate the views of colleagues on the Court without sacrificing their own fundamental sense of justice.

Court decisions are influenced by a variety of factors (legal and extralegal), including the facts of the case, justices' ideological or policy preferences, the law itself in various forms, and external influences such as interest groups, views of the executive branch communicated through the solicitor general, public opinion, and strategic considerations. Every case is different and thus is imbued with unique facts. These explanatory factors influence justices in varying degrees. In cases tagged with strong ideological content (i.e., where a clear liberal or conservative dimension exists), the ideological preferences of the justices would typically exert the strongest influence on decisions. This is true especially when the case is highly politically salient. Similarly, in cases where the law is relatively clear and unambiguous, the facts and the law typically would have a significant impact on decisions, although such cases are relatively rare in the Supreme Court.

The Court simply cannot settle every important legal controversy in society. It lacks the capacity and resources. But the Court does have a constitutional duty to step in when monumental conflicts erupt and the political branches of government fail to take charge. Under those circumstances, the Court's role is merely to shock the "normal" political branches out of their complacency. After all, as political scientist Robert G. McCloskey suggested, "The great fundamental decisions that determine the course of society must ultimately be made by society itself."[85]

# The Impact of U.S. Supreme Court Decisions

John Marshall has made his decision, now let him enforce it.
President Andrew Jackson Responding to *Worcester v. Georgia* (1832)

Supreme Court justices hear and decide cases that have broad legal and political significance. For this reason opinions issued by the Court are most meaningful in terms of their substantive impact on society. For Court opinions to garner national impact the cooperation of citizens, organized groups, government officials and various key institutions, including churches, schools, police agencies, the media, and so on is required. These entities must embrace the change that Court decisions command. If public reaction to Supreme Court decisions is decidedly negative, the Court would have suffered an important repudiation. This can translate into a loss of public esteem and decreased legitimacy, the central source of its constitutional power.

The Supreme Court is the glue that binds the nation together. Recent census estimates peg the U.S. population at approximately 303 million, all from diverse ethnic, cultural, and religious backgrounds. Bringing unity and cohesion to a society with such profound internal diversity is a difficult task indeed. Yet the most important governing institution that commands sufficiently high public respect upon which the nation can rely to foster a cohesive society is the Supreme Court. What kind of impact does the Court have? Addressing this question is the centerpiece of this chapter. We focus on the impact of Supreme Court decisions on (1) litigants; (2) the development of legal policy; and (3) society. In doing so, we address these areas:

- Which social entity is usually first and most directly affected by Supreme Court decisions?
- What are the long-term social and political consequences of Court decisions?
- Why are some decisions embraced with faithful implementation and compliance while others are largely ignored?

## DEFINING AND LINKING KEY CONCEPTS

Irrespective of how powerful the Supreme Court is, it must be recognized that the institution cannot escape one important constraint: its decisions are not self-enforcing. The Court must rely on others to effectuate its decisions as President Jackson's retort to the Supreme Court in the aftermath of its *Worcester* decision rightly indicates.

We begin our discussion of impact by defining some key concepts: implementation, compliance, and impact. The three concepts are not mutually exclusive; rather they are systematically linked to enable an overall effect of a given Supreme Court decision.

Generally speaking, an action (e.g., a court decision) is said to have an *impact* on a particular target (high school education in North Carolina) when that action brings about change in the target (e.g., improved test scores in North Carolina). To be sure, the change could be positive or negative, planned or imagined. The target of the action could be any government policy (e.g., capital punishment), any event (e.g., a presidential election), or individual behavior (e.g., criminal trespassing).

We can define *implementation* as the process of putting into effect the policies or orders announced in Supreme Court decisions. It involves what happens after the Supreme Court speaks and, in particular, the set of activities and policy projects developed to ensure that the Court's decisions and orders achieve their desired effect. Many actors are involved in the process of implementation, including bureaucratic agencies, police departments, local school boards, prison officials. Because implementation is a complex governmental process, it is never fully complete either for lack of resources or for lack of political will.[1] Realistically, there will always be individuals or groups that stand to lose either directly or indirectly from a Court decision, and so might be motivated to sabotage the Court's policy objectives rather than to see them come to fruition.

Implementation and impact are, therefore, an important aspect of Supreme Court success because both concepts are closely linked. Implementation is a necessary precondition for impact. Without implementation, it is impossible for justices to achieve the goals they seek and the Court's policy impact will be severely limited or nonexistent.[2]

Finally, a necessary precursor to impact is *compliance*, which is the willingness of citizens, groups, and institutions to obey Court directives in order to achieve policy objectives. The relationship between the three concepts is depicted in figure 7.1, which shows a simple logical flow of activities in the impact process. Many actions must take place before impact. Specifically, Court decisions require implementation, which inevitably leads to compliance, which, in turn, leads to impact. The diagram contains a feedback loop to demonstrate that the policy impact of Supreme Court decisions typically invite further litigation, making impact the result of a truly dynamic process.

The Supreme Court decides on many issues each term that are intended to produce change in society. When such change occurs following the

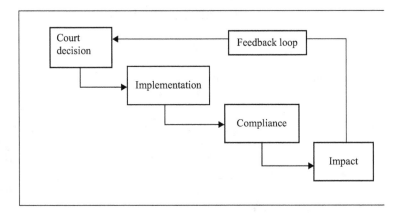

**Figure 7.1**   A Simple Model of Impact of Supreme Court Decisions

processes of implementation and compliance the Court is said to have produced an impact. After all, litigants pursue cases in the Supreme Court with the hope of obtaining a favorable outcome and possibly making a difference in society.

The Court's decision on the presidential election of 2000 is a case in point. That election hinged on the outcome of the vote in the battleground state of Florida. For several weeks after voters had gone to the polls and cast their votes, the election outcome remained in limbo. Florida state courts had to settle a disagreement over vote counting procedures (the question of whether voting recount should be continued) to determine if Vice President Al Gore or Texas Governor George W. Bush should receive Florida's 25 Electoral College votes. The disagreement over vote counting procedures was quickly appealed to the U.S. Supreme Court by George Bush after he suffered a setback in the Florida Supreme Court. Bush sought a favorable review from the Supreme Court in order to win the presidency and bring change to the nation. Since the U.S. Supreme Court exercises gate-keeping authority— meaning that the Court has the power to decide which cases to decide— justices had a choice. They could have concluded that the controversy was too much of a political matter and could have denied review. Instead, justices opted for the opportunity to stamp their own imprint on the election result. The justices ruled in the case *Bush v. Gore* that the vote recount must stop with immediate effect to begin the process of moving beyond the acrimony of the electoral battle and to unify what appeared to be a badly polarized citizenry.

The decision had a dramatic and immediate impact on the litigants and the nation. Because George W. Bush was ahead by a slim margin of about 550 popular votes in Florida when the stop order was issued, he garnered Florida's Electoral College votes and was declared the winner of the presidential election. Although Gore defeated Bush in the national popular vote tally by over 500,000 votes, he narrowly lost the election in the Electoral College where U.S. presidency is decided. Ultimately, Bush became president of the United States.

The decision to end the recount also demonstrates the Supreme Court's long-term political impact. Bush went on to win reelection four years later, aided in no small part by voter flashback to international events, particularly the terrorist attacks of September 11, 2001. But more importantly, from an implementation perspective, we can justifiably attribute the domestic and international failures and accomplishments of the Bush administration to the Court's decision in *Bush v. Gore* in 2000. The failures are many, including a slow and anemic response to the plight of hurricane Katrina victims in 2005, the administration's incoherent response to the 9/11 attacks, especially its ill-advised invasion of Iraq, the ensuing war and its drag on the U.S. economy and the administration's skepticism over the effects of global warming. Accomplishments include increased funding for research and development in science, education, and technology and improved economic relations with the People's Republic of China.

## IMPACT OF SUPREME COURT DECISIONS ON LITIGANTS

One way to understand the impact of the Supreme Court decisions is through a *litigant-focused* approach. Whether a Supreme Court opinion is narrow or broad in its pronouncement of the law, the impact of the Court's opinion usually befalls the direct litigants in the case first before reaching others. Thus a litigant-focused approach examines how direct litigants are affected by Court decisions. Whether the impact is immediate or gradual depends upon the nature of the case, the context of the decision (e.g., the resistance or support it engenders), and how it is framed.

For instance, on October 30, 2007, the Supreme Court granted a stay of execution request submitted by lawyers for a Mississippi death row inmate named Earl Wesley Berry who was scheduled for execution on October 31, 2007 for a 1987 murder. The Court stayed the execution in the context of growing public uneasiness over the death penalty and as justices considered whether the drug cocktail used for lethal injections caused unnecessary pain and suffering for inmates in violation of the cruel and unusual punishment clause of the Eighth Amendment. The decision had a direct and immediate impact on Berry because he was given a temporary reprieve from execution.[3] From examples such as this, we can understand the impact of Supreme Court decisions. In the next section, we look closely at two specific contemporary cases to discern impact on litigants. These cases are *Roe v. Wade* (1973) concerning abortion rights and *Quanta Corporation v. L.G. Electronics Corporation* concerning business practices.

### "Jane Roe" and Abortion Rights

Supreme Court decisions have varying impacts. Many litigants experience an immediate and dramatic change in their social position as a result of the decision. Others experience minimal impact, if at all. Sprinkled throughout Supreme Court history are landmark cases brought as part of an unstoppable social movement for change. But even here, the Court's decision can fail to change the status of one or more of the direct parties despite the larger socially transformative effects of the decision.

The landmark Supreme Court precedent *Roe v. Wade* (1973) is a case in point. *Roe* is a case of monumental social and political significance, but its effect on "Jane Roe" in the immediate aftermath of the decision is minimal at best. *Roe* both symbolizes and reaffirms the ongoing political struggle for women's equality, justice, and self-determination. "Jane Roe," the plaintiff who challenged the constitutionality of the Texas abortion statute was actually Norma McCorvey, a 21-year-old high school dropout and former traveling carnival worker already raising a 5-year-old daughter. After becoming pregnant the second time, she decided to have an abortion because she was unmarried and could not afford to raise a second child.

The challenged Texas abortion law was adopted in 1854. It was an antiquated law that state authorities still considered useful during the early 1970s. The law, along with laws in 28 other states, prohibited abortion unless to preserve a woman's life. Violators of the Texas law, including physicians who perform abortion and those who provide the means to procure an abortion, faced stiff penalties of up to five years in the state penitentiary. Ironically, the law imposed *no* punishment on women for self-administered abortions. As a consequence, women desperate for an abortion were compelled to submit to back-alley abortions, which were unregulated and dangerous. Most Texas women who obtained abortion in 1972 legally traveled to other states that allowed abortion. McCorvey considered traveling out of state to obtain a legal abortion but found the expense prohibitive. "No legitimate doctor in Texas would touch me" McCorvey would explain years later. "I found one doctor who offered to abort me for $500. Only he didn't have a license, and I was scared to turn my body over to him. So there I was—pregnant, unmarried, unemployed, alone and stuck."[4]

Empirical data from this period suggests that McCorvey had good reason to be fearful. In 1972, the year before the Supreme Court decided *Roe*, 65 women died in the United States from induced abortion. More than half of these fatalities resulted from illegal abortions.

McCorvey was caught in a predicament as she sought to avoid becoming yet another health statistic. To generate sympathy and possibly fulfill her wish for a legal abortion, she claimed the pregnancy was the result of rape, which she later recanted as a lie. She felt the Texas law was unreasonably punitive, and judging by the level of interest the case generated, we should conclude that many citizens and groups agreed with her, except most notably the state of Texas.

Oral arguments were held twice in *Roe*, an infrequent occurrence in the Court. During the first oral argument on December 13, 1971 only seven justices sat on the bench. Justices John Harlan and William O. Douglas had recently retired. The exchange was heated, centering on the beginning of life and the state's objectives. Justice Thurgood Marshall pressed Texas Assistant Attorney General Jay Floyd to explain the state's interest in the lawsuit. Floyd suggested that the state's overriding concern was to protect fetal life and to reduce promiscuity. Justices recognized the potentially transformative nature of the case. After the first argument session failed to yield a satisfied majority, enough justices agreed that with two new Nixon appointees awaiting confirmation, the case would benefit from having a full nine-person Court to decide it. Thus a second argument was scheduled for the following term. The opportunity for rearguments allowed the new justices William Rehnquist and Lewis Powell to participate in the case and enabled the lead attorneys (Sarah Weddington and Linda Coffee for *Roe* and Jay Floyd for Texas) to clarify their original arguments.

What then was the impact of *Roe v. Wade* on "Jane Roe"? When Justice Harry Blackmun announced the majority opinion in *Roe,* holding that a woman's right to obtain an abortion was protected under the due process clause of the Fourteenth Amendment, the status of "Jane Roe" as a pregnant woman remained materially unaffected. "Jane Roe" had carried her pregnancy to full term, apparently fearing the dangers of an illegal abortion. In June 1970, more than two years before the Supreme Court's opinion actually came down she delivered her baby and immediately gave the child up for adoption. Thus for all practical purposes, the case was moot and could have been dismissed outright, but was not. The Court proceeded to decide *Roe* because it was a class-action lawsuit brought on behalf of all pregnant women and those planning to become pregnant.

Although the *Roe* decision did not change McCorvey's pregnancy status, it did have an unprecedented impact on American women by empowering them, fuelling the feminist movement, and solidifying women's social standing. But in earnest, the decision *did little* in its immediate aftermath to change the status and personal life of Norma McCorvey.

## Product Safety and Intellectual Property Rights

Another area where Supreme Court decisions can have an immediate and powerful impact on direct parties is in business cases, especially those cases involving companies that are publicly traded on Wall Street. Much business litigation in the United States involves product safety and intellectual property rights, a generic term describing patent, trademark, and copyright claims.

Certainly, not all business enterprises that litigate in the Supreme Court are publicly traded. But for those that are, litigation is a zero-sum game, which usually creates an immediate redistribution of shareholder wealth. A win in the Supreme Court usually gives an immediate boost to the winner's stock price performance whereas a loss usually spells difficulties for the losing company's stock price because losing a court case creates uncertainty for future market prospects. For example, on August 19, 2005, a jury in Texas returned a verdict against pharmaceutical giant Merck Corporation in the case of *Ernst v. Merck,* which raised the claim that Merck's signature anti-inflammatory drug *Vioxx* was chiefly responsible for heart attacks in patients taking the drug. The case was brought by Carol Ernst whose husband Robert Ernst, a seemingly healthy 59-year-old marathon runner, died of heart complications apparently after taking the medication. The jury awarded Ernst's estate $229 million in punitive damages plus $24.4 million in compensatory damages. The reaction on Wall Street was predictable. On the day of the verdict, Merck's stock price plummeted 8 percent.[5] A few months later on November 3, 2005, another jury, this time in New Jersey, voted in Merck's favor in a separate lawsuit *Humeston v. Merck.* The market reacted predictably once again. Merck's shareholders were rewarded with an immediate stock price increase of 4 percent.

Although these verdicts came from state courts, numerous empirical studies have uncovered a similar relationship between litigation and stock price movements in reaction to Supreme Court decisions.[6] These examples along with ample empirical evidence suggest that Court decisions do have significant impact on corporate litigants. To be sure, there are many reasons why (e.g., the clarity and precision of the opinion, the type of remedy ordered). But in the aggregate, these effects are largely explained by rational expectations of the market place. In the minds of stockholders, a company's sales are likely to decrease upon a ruling that the company's product is defective or a ruling that the company fails to meet federal product safety guidelines.

*L.G. Electronics Corporation.* On June 10, 2008, the *Wall Street Journal* reported that the U.S. Supreme Court, in a patent infringement (or intellectual property rights) case *Quanta Corporation v. L.G. Electronics* (2008), ruled against L.G. Electronics (hereafter LGE), a Korean maker of computer chips. The case asks whether a patent owner (in this case, LGE) can write into its sale contract restrictions on the use of its patented technology after that technology has been licensed to another user. LGE alleged that the strict limits it placed on its licensing agreement with Intel Corporation about the transfer of LGE's patented technology were ignored in a deal between Intel and Quanta Corporation. Intel uses LGE's technology to make computer chips which it then sells to other companies including Quanta Corporation (a Taiwanese firm). Quanta installed the chips in computers it assembles for Dell Corporation. In the case, Quanta sued LGE alleging that it should not be required to negotiate a separate agreement with LGE before installing its chips in computers with non-Intel parts.

In an opinion written by Justice Clarence Thomas, the Court ruled unanimously that "LG Electronics overlooks important aspects of the structure of the Intel-LGE transaction. Nothing in the license agreement restricts Intel's right to sell its microprocessors and chip-sets to purchasers who intend to combine them with non-Intel parts."[7] Following the decision, LG electronics' stock price dropped sharply. The logic underlying a drop in stock price following bad news is that investing is a forward-looking activity in which uncertainty is disliked. Losing a case in the Supreme Court creates short-term uncertainty. For one thing, losing has the potential to affect the company's operations, revenue stream, and bottom line. Consequently, as pragmatists, investors react by transferring their wealth from the losing company by selling their stock in that company and investing it elsewhere.[8] Indeed, the mere act of filing a lawsuit can have a dramatic impact on stock price performance.

## IMPACT OF SUPREME COURT DECISIONS ON LEGAL POLICY

The impact of Supreme Court decisions can also be understood via a *legal-change* approach. The legal-change approach to judicial impact views legal policy as a "Court-created shift in (or a reversal of) a particular prevailing legal doctrine."[9] The approach emphasizes the importance of processes and constitutional doctrine in establishing the nature of public policy and in shaping how policy is understood by citizens. Under the legal-change approach, the impact of Court decisions is the extent to which existing law is transformed or improved to serve a social or political function. Understanding Court impact is not simply a matter of focusing on its human dimension but also on its normative ideal, on its contribution to the advancement of legal principles within the Court's special role as protector of rights in the democratic process. Political scientist Bradley C. Cannon maintains that the central significance of the Supreme Court for constitutional development is not the specific decisions the Court makes but the broad policies it fashions from a *series* of decisions on a particular topic.[10] In recent years, this important idea has been refined into what Mark Richards and Herbert Kritzer call the jurisprudential regime theory of judicial behavior.[11] This theory comes under the legal-change formulation and we examine it below.

## JURISPRUDENTIAL REGIMES THEORY

This theory states that decisional trends build cumulatively one case at a time on a standout landmark precedent and that this process represents an important way in which the Court establishes legal change by identifying which case facts jurists will consider important when deciding future cases. Examples of jurisprudential regimes include doctrines announced in *Roe v. Wade, Miranda v. Arizona, Chevron v. Environmental Defense Fund, Baker v. Carr.* Regimes provide a legal roadmap to structure the impact of Supreme Court decisions by establishing which factors in a given landmark decision are relevant to achieve a policy shift.

The importance of jurisprudential regimes can be understood both *vertically* (i.e., in terms of the hierarchical flow of the influence of legal doctrine from the top to the bottom rung of the judiciary) and *horizontally* (i.e., in terms of influence on future decisions of the Supreme Court itself).

Vertical perspective of the jurisprudential regimes means that once the Supreme Court has announced a particular legal doctrine, lower court judges are obligated to respect that doctrine and to issue their own decisions in a manner consistent with that doctrine. In this way, jurisprudential regimes structure the behavior of lower court judges. Empirical research testing the impact of the Supreme Court on the development of economic policy in the courts of appeals, for example, has found that when the Supreme Court shifts legal doctrine surrounding labor rights and antitrust policy in a liberal or conservative direction, courts of appeals judges quickly fall in line roughly one year later. This responsiveness suggests that lower court judges are fairly faithful agents of the Supreme Court.[12]

Decisional responsiveness or compliance of a lower court with a higher Court decision carries numerous advantages for the legal system. First, it reduces uncertainty in the law by making the adversarial world of courtroom drama more predictable. Imagine a world where lower court judges play fast and loose with legal policy by ignoring existing legal precedent whenever convenient without facing any repercussions. That would be a chaotic and unsettling world indeed! Fortunately, instances of egregious noncompliance are fairly rare in appellate courts and when they do occur, the probability is high that these recalcitrant decisions will be reversed on appeal. A second advantage for adhering to the High Court's doctrines is that it saves judicial resources by reducing the need to relitigate cases the Supreme Court has already decided.

When the impact of jurisprudential regime is viewed horizontally (or longitudinally), we consider how the legal doctrine influenced the development of future law in the Supreme Court itself. Influence here can be understood in terms of the Court's respect for its own landmark precedents or use of its own law to guide and shape the development of public policy in future decisions. This type of impact deserves a deeper look.

*Impact of Jurisprudential Regimes.* One of the most contested areas of litigation in the Bill of Rights is the establishment of religion clause of the First Amendment. It is an area awash in landmark opinions.

The First Amendment begins with these simple words: "Congress shall make no law respecting an Establishment of religion..." In 1802, Thomas Jefferson (one of the nation's Founding Fathers and vocal critic of the Constitution) wrote a letter to the Danbury Baptist Association of Virginia to explain his own understanding of the meaning of these words. In that letter, Jefferson conceived of the establishment clause as erecting "a wall of separation between Church and State." Jefferson's statement has long been accepted as an article of faith by fellow separatists, but not so by those who favor an accommodationist interpretation of the establishment clause. The statement is, therefore, a source of conflict in the Supreme Court and in public understanding of the First Amendment. The disagreement centers on how high and how thick the framers intended to make the wall of separation. Should the wall be high and impenetrable as to deny any form of government aid to religion? Should it be short, flimsy, and porous as to permit commingling of church and state so long as government does not discriminate among various religions? The Supreme Court needs a jurisprudential regime (a landmark case) that would set clear standards upon which future decisions will rest, which it eventually found in the case of *Lemon v. Kurtzman* in 1971.

*The Road to Lemon.* Starting with the very first Supreme Court case on the establishment clause, *Bradford v. Roberts* (1899), litigation over the issue has centered on the propriety of government assistance to religion. The Court ruled in *Bradford* that a federal appropriation of $30,000 for building a hospital to treat indigent patients in Washington DC was constitutional even though the facility will be administered by Roman Catholic nuns. In their decision, justices emphasized the clear secular (i.e., nonreligious) purpose of the aid as being paramount rather than the sectarian background of its intended Catholic administrators. By permitting this constitutional accommodation, the Supreme Court signaled for the first time that church and state can commingle.

The Court did not revisit the wall of separation debate in earnest until nearly 50 years later. Relying on the secular purpose standard announced in *Bradford,* justices ruled in *Everson v. Board of Education* (1947) that the community of Ewing, New Jersey, can reimburse parents for transportation costs they incurred for sending their children to private religious schools. The opinion was highly confusing. The Court "succeeded...in combining the strictest separationist rhetoric with an accommodationist outcome"[13] by announcing that the First Amendment established a wall of separation between church and state and that the "wall must be kept high and impregnable" even though justices accommodated religion by permitting the aid.

It was another 16 years before the Court would revise the secular purpose standard, this time in *Abington Township v. Schempp* (1963), a case involving the reading in public schools of the Lords prayer and a few verses from the Holy Bible.[14] The Court introduced a second prong to the secular purpose standard by emphasizing that the primary purpose of the law should neither advance nor inhibit religion (i.e., the law should be neutral). The Abington Township school district regulation failed to meet this two-pronged standard (secular purpose and neutrality) and the Court declared Bible reading and official prayer in public schools unconstitutional.

The onward march to secure the accommodation of church and state was thus halted in a significant way. It was a major setback for conservative interest groups that supported an accommodationist reading of the First Amendment. As legal doctrine on religious establishment clause was developed and refined, justices on both side of the ideological debate remained vigilant, with liberals often favoring separation and their conservative counterparts usually favoring accommodation. Of course, there is no guarantee about what outcome justices would come up with in any given case; jurisprudential regimes do not guarantee results in future cases, they simply provide guidance. But we know that justices were sharply divided over how to apply the two prongs of the Bradford-Abington standard to establishment clause questions, divisions that produced inconsistencies in case outcome.[15]

There was great optimism among both liberal and conservative groups for consistency as the Nixon administration came into power in 1969 with the expectation that President Nixon will remake the Court with justices poised to produce a more consistent set of rulings on religious establishment.[16] The new chief justice appointed by Nixon (an affable Minnesotan named Warren Burger) was determined to focus the Court's attention on religion issues. Early in his tenure, Chief Justice Warren Burger examined the law of establishment clause and agreed that the case law was rather schizophrenic. He worked tirelessly to convince fellow justices of the necessity of establishing consistent standards for establishment clause litigation. In 1971, the justices established the jurisprudential regime in *Lemon v. Kurtzman*.

*Lemon* has all the elements of a jurisprudential regime in that it laid down clearly the important conditions necessary to determine the constitutionality of laws challenged under the establishment clause. The case was brought by Alton Lemon against the Superintendent of Public Schools in Pennsylvania, David Kurtzman, to enjoin enforcement of a state statute that uses state funds from cigarette taxes to reimburse nonpublic schools for expenses incurred for teachers' salaries, textbooks, and instructional material. The Court announced the so-called *Lemon* test for judging the constitutionality of statutes granting government aid to parochial schools. *Lemon* stipulates that in order to pass constitutional muster under the establishment clause, the statute challenged in Court

- must have a secular legislative purpose;
- must have its principal or primary effect that neither advances nor inhibits religion (i.e. should have characteristics of neutrality);
- must not foster an excessive entanglement with religion.

The impact of this case on the development of law is that first it resulted in a unified and consistent standard for judging cases on religion without guaranteeing a particular outcome in future cases. Throughout the Burger Court, the *Lemon* standard was, indeed, employed and it remained good law well into the Rehnquist Court era. Second and perhaps the most lasting impact of *Lemon* is that it contributed to a shift in the focus of church-state ideals away from arguments over separation of church and state to arguments now over equal treatment of religions and religious views.

## IMPACT OF SUPREME COURT DECISIONS ON SOCIETY

Finally, at a much broader level is the *social-change approach* to understanding impact. This approach focuses on the capacity of Supreme Court decisions to fundamentally transform public understanding of an important social or political value of the nation. The social-change approach sets up a preexisting model against which current behavior can be measured. Current generation of Americans is able to reflect upon history and proudly proclaim: "Wow! How things have changed. We are not what we were!" No one would contest the idea that landmark decisions such as *Brown v. Board of Education,* *Roe v. Wade,* and *Miranda v. Arizona* challenged existing policies and started enduring conversations that produced fundamental shifts in civic values and public policy in American society. The policy impacts generated by these landmark precedents speak for themselves: integrating public education facilities; permitting women to terminate unwanted pregnancies and thus empowering them to take better control of their destinies; informing criminal suspects of their constitutional right to silence before active police interrogation. These are tremendous policy achievements, which are characterized by widespread public acceptance.

Whatever the theoretical approach one employs to assess the impact of Supreme Court decisions, two things are clear. First, Court decisions are not self-enforcing. Second, enforcement is a complex process that the Court is ill-equipped to handle. Underneath the powerful aura of the robe and the majesty of the law, the Court must contend with these institutional limitations and work to maintain good relations with those political institutions in and out of government that are best positioned to implement and thus advance the impact of Supreme Court decisions.

### *Miranda,* Police Interrogations, and the Right to Remain Silent

In this section, we examine the impact of *Miranda v. Arizona,* the most famous and perhaps most influential criminal law decision announced by the Supreme Court during the 20th century. In *Miranda,* the Warren Court in 1966 established the now familiar fourfold warnings to silence and appointed counsel before interrogation of crime suspects. Without these warnings being sounded by law enforcement officers at the start of a criminal inquiry, any admission or confession by a suspect is considered highly questionable and will invariably be excluded from a criminal trial. In the words of Justice Benjamin Cardozo, the constable has blundered and the criminal must go free.

The key legal holding in *Miranda* is now prophylactic, one that even a smart first grader is able to recite:

1. You have the right to remain silent;
2. Anything you say can and will be used against you in a court of law;
3. You have the right to an attorney;
4. If you cannot afford an attorney, one will be appointed for you at no cost to you.[17]

*Miranda* is a noteworthy decision for two primary reasons. First, it filled an important vacuum in the law by providing much needed procedural safeguards for crime suspects under the Constitution. Second, the decision brought a stunning reversal of the coercive interrogation policies that existed until the mid-1960s.

*Interrogations before the 1960s.* Before *Miranda,* law enforcement officers operated with impunity and used a variety of aggressive extralegal tactics to obtain incriminating evidence from suspects while in custody. Some examples include the use of physical force, psychological manipulation, deceit and other harsh techniques such as torture. These heavy-handed tactics were designed to wear down the suspect and overcome his or her rational decision-making capacity. Usually, evidence thus obtained was used to convict suspects.

Historically, police interrogation practices have been regulated by three key amendments to the Constitution: the Fifth Amendment protection against self-incrimination, the Sixth Amendment right to counsel, and the Fourteenth Amendment due process clause.[18] The Supreme Court started evaluating the admissibility of confessions in the mid-1880s under the due process clause of the Fourteenth Amendment. Justices established a rule that stood the test of time, namely that confessions will be admitted only if they have been given voluntarily by rationally capable citizens. Thus confessions were excluded when obtained as a result of undue police pressure and tactics. This "voluntariness" doctrine was reaffirmed in *Brown v. Mississippi* (1936),[19] which involves three black tenant farmers who were whipped and pummeled by sheriff deputies for a confession in the murder of a white planter. The Court ruled that the confessions were not produced out of rational will and were, therefore, excluded from Court proceedings.

The true precursor to *Miranda* was *Escobedo v. Illinois* (1964), in which the Supreme Court recognized custodial interrogation as the most critical stage of the criminal justice process for which suspects can most benefit from the protection of an attorney who can advice them before and during interrogation. The justices ordered law enforcement officers to provide access to a lawyer when a suspect requests one. Ironically, most criminal suspects then were ignorant of this constitutional guarantee. The question is: How can suspects become informed about this important constitutional requirement? The Supreme Court provided the answer on June 13, 1966, in *Miranda v. Arizona*. Justices reasoned that the most effective way for suspects to be apprised of their constitutional right to a lawyer was to have police officers inform suspects of that right.

*Post*-Miranda *Reactions.* In its immediate aftermath, *Miranda* generated enormous political controversy. The sharp dissenting opinion of Justice John Harlan predicting "harmful consequences for the country at large" helped fuel the fears of many.[20] The decision was assailed by police, prosecutors, politicians, and the media mostly for burdening law enforcement. Police officers complained bitterly that *Miranda* would effectively handcuff them and stymie their investigative flexibility. Politicians such as Richard Nixon linked *Miranda* to higher index crime rates[21] and denounced the decision as representing a victory of the "crime forces" over the "peace forces" in society. Members of Congress displeased with the decision called for the impeachment of Chief Justice Earl Warren. More importantly, legislators also attempted to invalidate the *Miranda* ruling through the Omnibus Crime Control Act of 1968.[22] That effort proved ineffective in the long run.

A careful review of the published evidence indicates that *Miranda* had immediate as well as long-term effects on law enforcement.[23] At the federal level, the Federal Bureau of Investigation (FBI) uses the clearance rate to measure effectiveness in fighting violent and property crimes. At the local level, police agencies are frequently evaluated on their effectiveness in solving crimes, especially murders and aggravated assaults via the clearance rate. The *clearance rate* is, therefore, widely recognized as an important barometer of good law enforcement. A crime is considered cleared when a suspect has been arrested, charged, and turned over to the Court system for prosecution.

An immediate effect of *Miranda* was that it dramatically reduced the clearance rates for a whole host of violent and property crimes. In one study of confessions conducted soon after the ruling was announced, *Miranda* was reportedly responsible for a 20 percent drop in the confession rate.[24] Long-term effects of *Miranda* on law enforcement have also been detected and recorded. According to a review by the National Center for Policy Analysis, "Without *Miranda*, the number of crimes police would have solved would have been 6.7 percentage points higher for violent crimes and 2.2 percentage points higher for property crimes."[25] Figure 7.2 depicts the long-term effects of *Miranda* on law enforcement in the area of violent crime. The data are from the FBI and are based on all reporting law enforcement agencies across the United States.[26] There is strong evidence of

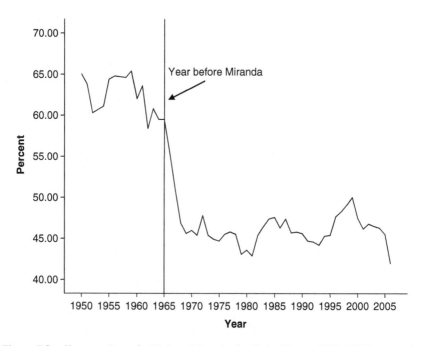

**Figure 7.2**   Clearance Rates for Violent Crimes in the United States, 1950–2006

a sharp drop in the clearance rate for violent crime from 59 percent in the last year before *Miranda* to 47 percent in 1968, two years after *Miranda*. Interestingly, this decline has been maintained in the ensuing 30 years, indicating that *Miranda* has had consistent and long-lasting effects on law enforcement.

Obviously, not all crimes cleared are due to arrest and prosecution. Law enforcement agencies may clear a crime by *exceptional means* when some element beyond law enforcement officers' control precludes the placing of formal charges against an offender. Examples of exceptional circumstances that can trigger a crime being cleared are the death of the offender via suicide or justifiable homicide, the victim's refusal to cooperate with prosecutors after offender has been identified, or the denial of extradition because the offender committed another crime in a different jurisdiction and is being prosecuted in that other jurisdiction. In all exceptional clearance cases, law enforcement must have identified the offender, must have enough evidence to support arrest, and know the offender's location.

*Miranda* also led to a dramatic drop in the clearance rates for property crimes. Compared to violent crimes, the clearance rates for property crimes are typically lower because law enforcement agencies tend to devote less

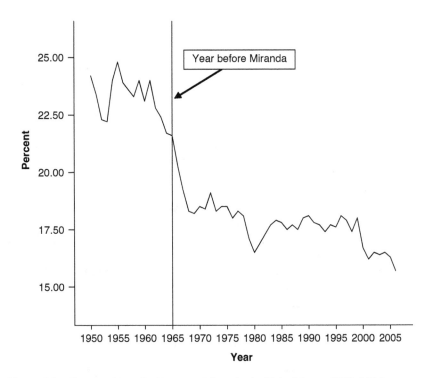

**Figure 7.3**   Clearance Rates for Property Crimes in the United States, 1950–2006

personnel and financial resources to solving them. Moreover, both officers and the communities they protect typically invest less emotional energy on fighting these crimes compared to violent offenses such as murder. Figure 7.3 shows the clearance rates for property crimes in the United States as reported by the FBI.

Ultimately, we are left with a lingering question: Has *Miranda* actually achieved its desired objective of compelling law enforcement agencies to honor the constitutional rights of suspects? The answer invariably is yes. There are two reasons for this.

First, the most vivid proof is in the long-term decline in the confession rate. Even when we consider the cyclical nature of the economy where crime fighting budgets tend to drop during recessionary periods (as in the 1970s) and to rise during the good times (as in the 1990s), the drop in clearance rates persisted. This would suggest that pre-*Miranda* confession rates were artificially inflated because many confessions were being obtained through illegal means in violation of constitutional principles.

Second, interrogation practices have been reformed. One of the most enduring impacts of *Miranda* has been to increase the level of professionalism during the investigative stage of the criminal justice process and to "transform the culture and discourse of modern detective work."[27] For instance, many police departments now make it a matter of policy to videotape their interrogation of suspects to discourage rogue officers from cheating the system and inviting bad publicity. In this way, the rights of suspects are preserved.

## FACTORS AFFECTING FAITHFUL IMPLEMENTATION AND IMPACT OF COURT DECISIONS

Implementation of Court decisions is a complex process that requires the involvement of multiple levels of government (federal, state, and local) and multiple actors (lower court judges, governors, police officers, and school boards) with diffuse and competing goals and expectations. As a result, there is no guarantee that Supreme Court decision will be faithfully implemented to achieve desired objectives. But a number of theoretical conditions are necessary (though not sufficient) for Supreme Court decisions to be reliably implemented. Theoretically speaking, these factors can be grouped into four dimensions: (1) institutional factors relating to the clarity with which the opinion itself was written; (2) community preferences over the opinion; (3) the set of selective incentives and disincentives offered by the government for implementing the policy; and (4) organizational norms and culture of the implementing populations.[28]

### Clarity of the Opinion

Among the most important conditions necessary for a Supreme Court opinion to be faithfully implemented is the clarity of the written opinion. Three important aspects of clarity are complexity, consensus, and ambiguity. Judicial and policy scholars have reported empirical findings that suggest that judicial opinions that lack clarity either because of subject-matter complexity, use of ambiguous or confusing language, or a lack of consensus among justices are more likely to be ignored or evaded by lower court judges and bureaucratic agencies that are in a position to be influenced directly by the Court.[29] A complex case on nuclear energy or patent and trademark regulation may be difficult for lower court judges to apply because they lack an understanding of the subject matter and the ruling. Yet complexity may be overcome if the opinion is written by a justice with special expertise in the subject matter of the case.

Cases decided by consensus are more likely to produce a clear opinion because justices are unified; they can speak with one voice and with clarity of purpose. But as the Supreme Court becomes more of a nonconsensual body, considerable concerns emerge about implementation of and compliance with its nonunanimous decisions. Imagine the Herculean task of deciphering with clarity and applying the legal rule announced in a decision such as *Church of the Lukumi Babalu Aye, Inc. v. City of Hialeah* (1993), which involves animal sacrifice for religious worship. The justices discerned a violation of the free exercise clause but the opinion was qualified by significant dissatisfaction on the part of many justices with the analytical standards. The stunning lack of consensus concerning the legal rule is indicated by the array of opinions:

> Kennedy, J., delivered the opinion of the Court with respect to Parts I, III, and IV, in which Rehnquist, C.J., and White, Stevens, Scalia, Souter, and Thomas, JJ., Joined, the opinion of the Court with respect to Part II-B, in which Rehnquist, C.J., and White, Stevens, Scalia and Thomas, JJ., joined, the opinion of the Court with respect to Parts II-A-1 and II-A-3, in which Rehnquist, C.J., and Stevens, Scalia, and Thomas, JJ., joined, and an opinion with respect to Part II-A-2, in which Stevens, J., joined, Scalia, J., filed an opinion concurring in part and concurring in the judgment, in which Rehnquist, C.J., joined. Souter, J. filed an opinion concurring in the judgment. Blackmun, J., filed an opinion concurring in the judgment in which O'Connor, J. joined.

Even the most patient lower court judge would likely experience a migraine when attempting to decipher and apply the legal holding in a case with these many divisions of opinion. For interpreters who are not predisposed to religious policy as an area of personal interest, it would be an even more arduous task to understand and apply this confusing configuration of views.

Ambiguity also hinders clarity and can lead to increased likelihood of noncompliance or evasion by those charged with interpreting and implementing Court decisions. Lower court judges, for example, are more likely to ignore a Supreme Court decision if they are unsure about what the High Court is communicating. Empirical research suggests that one reason why school desegregation orders of the Supreme Court were largely ignored by many Southern lower court judges was the ambiguity of the language used by the Court in its *Brown* majority opinion. In *Brown* justices called for integration to "proceed with all deliberate speed." To many lower court judges in the South, this is an equivocal requirement, which they interpreted to fit their own ideological opposition to integration. They viewed the statement as a call to proceed cautiously or slowly in integrating public education. While these judges were applauded by segregationist sympathizers, their interpretation effectively forestalled the Court's underlying objective of fostering optimal educational opportunity for children regardless of race. Only a few courageous and progressive judges, risking threats of physical violence against them, demanded a speedy end to school segregation in response to the Supreme Court's orders.[30]

What this analysis shows is that ultimately those in position to implement Supreme Court decisions face political pressure that is often different from the pressure faced by justices atop the judicial hierarchy. Consequently, what we find is significant variation in policy outcomes.

### Community Preferences

A second major factor conditioning effective implementation and impact is the nature and strength of community preferences over the particular policy announced by the Court. Preferences are important because they determine the breadth and scope of implementation, and whether implementation will be immediate or delayed. Community preferences are the desires of (1) local elites; (2) interest groups that have a stake in the policy announced; and (3) ordinary citizens. Combined, they are a strong positive force for implementation.

From a policy perspective, Supreme Court decisions can take either a restrictive or a permissive stance.[31] A *restrictive policy* stance imposes restraints on the actions of implementers as in *Miranda v. Arizona's* restriction on police activity before interrogation of suspects; *Brown v. Board of Education's* restriction on school boards over elementary school segregation; and *Engel v. Vitale's* restriction on state-mandated prayer in public schools. A *permissive policy*, on the other hand, is one that allows implementers to expand their services without requiring them to do so. For example, *Roe v. Wade* fashioned a permissive policy because it allowed hospitals and clinics to expand their abortion services without requiring it.

If preferences expressed by community elites, interest groups, and ordinary citizens are sufficiently strong and favorable toward a Supreme Court policy, whether it be restrictive or permissive, the policy is bound to benefit from such strong interest, ultimately enhancing compliance. On the other hand, if these groups are unfavorable toward the Court's policy, resistance to implementation would result, hindering compliance and impact.

The Supreme Court's audiences are not monolithic in their interests. Given the potential variation in community preferences, what happens when sharp splits in favorability among different community groups surface regarding Supreme Court policy? How might such splits affect implementation? Empirical studies focusing on the links between public opinion and agenda setting in government offer some guidance. The evidence is fairly strong that the preferences of elites (e.g., legislators, governors, police commissioners, mayors, members of the media, interest groups) help shape mass opinion, which is a proximate cause of public policy.[32] Therefore, for the sake of the Court's institutional legitimacy, it is imperative for elites to show support for the Court's policy pronouncements because elites can supply the fuel needed to achieve implementation without guaranteeing that it will be successful. Besides, it is often these same elites groups that had pushed successfully to bring the cases to Court in the first place. Their support for implementation, therefore, is a necessary ingredient for impact.

*Roe v. Wade* provides a clear example of a decision whose implementation was immediate because of strong elite support for the policy even before the decision was announced. Opposition to abortion that existed was dispersed and less well organized. Although abortion battles were fought largely at the state level in the pre-*Roe* years, there were important nationwide medical and legal professional organizations, including the American Law Institute and the American Medical Association, that helped to push proabortion legislative reforms.[33]

What impact did the decision have on the abortion rates? Figure 7.4 depicts the ratio of abortions per 1000 live births in the United States. The ratio of abortions to live births increased steadily after *Roe*, peaking in 1984 with 364 abortions for every 1000 live births. Interestingly, while *Roe* did increase the rate of abortions performed, the increase in abortion rates actually started before *Roe* was decided, suggesting that the decision reflected important social trends already in progress. The Court simply jumped aboard a train that had already left the station. But the decision's true impact is that it sustained the increase and availability of abortions deep into the future. Many factors helped to fuel this sustained increase. First, many hospitals, including church-affiliated ones, changed their abortion policies to permit elective abortions as opposed to only therapeutic abortions.[34] Second, market forces were introduced into the provision of abortion services.[35] Nothing motivates entrepreneurs more than profit. The establishment of for-profit abortion clinics in many jurisdictions across the nation for the sole purpose of providing pregnancy counseling, abortion, and other family planning services to women for a fee helped to increase the number of abortions. These private health clinics helped to fill the need that many hospitals failed to meet.[36]

But since 1984, the number of abortions performed in the United States has declined relative to live births as states have tightened abortion regulations along the lines approved in *Pennsylvania v. Casey* (including parental consent for minors, record keeping, and 24-hour waiting period). In addition, local governments and public service agencies have undertaken aggressive educational campaigns targeting young adults, including campaigns about abstinence and the difficulty of raising a child on a shoestring budget.

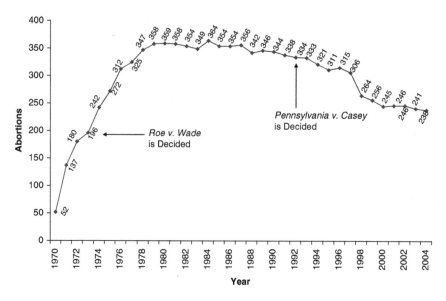

**Figure 7.4**    Abortion Ratio in the United States, 1970–2004.

These have helped to reduce the number of unplanned pregnancies nation-wide. Overall, *Roe v. Wade* can be a success insofar as it continues to provide American women with a personal choice. It has nevertheless been a qualified success because of the many regulations that now impinge upon a woman's right to have an abortion.

*Brown v. Board of Education* did not have immediate impact as did *Roe,* which had strong support from relevant elite community groups. The controversy the decision engendered was overwhelming. White Southern elites and masses strongly opposed integration and established a variety of ways to prevent or sabotage implementation of the Court's *Brown* decision. The techniques include punitive school closings, movement of children from public schools into private schools, and city councils' refusal to allocate budgets and assemble the infrastructure necessary for implementing *Brown.* Consequently, nine years after *Brown,* fewer than 2 percent of Southern elementary and primary schools were actually integrated. As Gerald Rosenberg described, "Despite *Brown,* public schools in the South remained pristinely white, with only one in a hundred black children in elementary and secondary school with whites by 1964, a decade after the ruling."[37]

But integration did eventually come to the South. This region occupies a large swath of the United States, an overwhelmingly metropolitan society, which is dominated by suburbs. The suburbs feature prominently as political battlegrounds in presidential elections and were historically regarded as the epicenter of white middle class. But increasingly suburbs are becoming racially and ethnically differentiated. The racial landscape of the South has been forever altered in the process. *Brown*'s attack on the structure of racially segregated schooling and of economic injustice has had its most profound impact in the South. Helped significantly by the Civil Rights Act of 1964, integration increased steadily in that region. Black students in majority white elementary and primary schools in the South reached a high of 43.5 percent in 1988.[38]

Since the early 1990s, however, the South has experienced growing resegregation, partly because of the repeal or nonenforcement of many segregation plans. As budgets become tight and the black middle class expands, political support for Court-ordered desegregation plans has suffered. And various administrations in Washington have cut funding for enforcement of desegregation plans. Moreover, the Supreme Court itself has become less vigilant. Indeed, in *Board of Education of Oklahoma City v. Dowell* (1991), the Court ordered that school districts that had sufficiently implemented their Court-mandated desegregation plans in the view of local federal district courts should be released from further implementation of the plans and to return to assigning students based on neighborhood schools that are segregated based on residential isolation.[39]

## Incentives and Disincentives for Implementation

Another important influence on implementation is incentives and disincentives associated with alternative responses to the Court's decision. Because Supreme Court decisions are not self-enforcing, those entrusted with implementation face a choice: to comply or not to comply. The Court, along with other branches of government, can take affirmative steps to make faithful implementation a reality by providing certain incentives or disincentives. Incentives and disincentives for compliance may be affected by legal conditions imposed by the government to force implementers to comply with Court orders. Incentives are efforts that reward or encourage implementers for working to achieve Court-directed goals. Disincentives are efforts that impose a sanction for noncompliance. Case studies of implementation of the desegregation order in 1954 tags the use of sanctions and rewards as an effective tactic by the government to aid implementation of *Brown v. Board of Education*.[40] It was only after Congress overcame strong Southern opposition and enacted the Civil Rights Act of 1964, empowering the Health, Education, and Welfare Department (now Health and Human Services) to withhold federal financial support to schools refusing to integrate that desegregation of public education effectively increased.[41]

## Organizational Norms and Procedures

Organizations charged with implementing Court decisions such as schools, police departments, local governments, and houses of worship all respond to internal norms and procedures within the organization. Because Supreme Court decisions and orders often have direct impact on these organizations, organizational perspectives and the values that characterize them can shape the actions taken to implement a policy. We can safely assume that leaders in these organizations have preferences over judicial policies they find salient to their organization. This along with attitudes of lower-level staff toward the Court's policy will affect how organizational leadership reacts to the Court's decisions. In the area of environmental protection, for example, research by political scientists indicates that the perspectives of lower-level staffers were instrumental in the policies and rules the Environmental Protection Agency promulgated during the Reagan administration.[42]

Attitudes of organizational leaders and those of rank-and-file employees, therefore, can be both a constraint and a boon on the choices that leaders make regarding implementation.[43] From an organizational standpoint, implementation is maximized when the policy goals expressed in Supreme Court decisions are consistent with the objectives of the implementing organization. Along these lines, early research suggested that the implementation of the Court's decision barring the reading of verses from the Holy Bible receives widespread noncompliance especially in the South because of skepticism of local school leaders and their staff.[44]

Is compliance more prevalent at the federal level compared to state and local levels? Analysis by James Spriggs focusing on federal bureaucratic agencies and their compliance tendencies toward Supreme Court decisions found that, for the most part, federal agencies do behave properly. They neither blatantly "defied nor evaded the Court's opinions."[45] Defiance and evasion are, of course, the strongest forms of noncompliance. So what about softer or narrower forms of noncompliance? Spriggs suggested that only in 6.8 percent of the cases examined did federal agencies narrowly comply with Supreme Court decisions. For the vast majority of Supreme Court opinions, the bulk of the evidence shows that federal agencies do faithfully comply with Supreme Court decisions.[46]

At state and local levels, however, the compliance picture is somewhat cloudy. Significant pockets of noncompliance exist in various jurisdictions depending upon the policy area investigated. As noted earlier, religion is one where noncompliance with Supreme Court decisions remains high. Bible reading in public schools was widespread throughout the United States prior to 1960. After separatist groups won in *Engel v. Vitale* (1962) in which the Supreme Court declared official prayer and Bible reading to be unconstitutional, many public schools in the South continued to defy the Court's edict. The incidence of Bible reading in public schools was approximately 77 percent in 1960 before the *Engel* decision. After *Engel*, nearly 50 percent of all public schools in the South continued to defy the Court and hold regular Bible reading and official prayer sessions in violation of the Court's decision.[47]

The Constitution does not permit official promotion or denigration of religious activities in public schools. Supreme Court decisions over the past 40 years have established principles that distinguish impermissible governmental religious speech from the constitutionally protected private religious speech of students. For example, teachers and other public school officials may not

**Table 7.1** Levels of Noncompliance with Select U.S. Supreme Court Decisions on Religion

| Activity (Decision) | South (%) | Non-South (%) |
| --- | --- | --- |
| Organized prayer (*Engel v. Vitale*, 1962) | 22.05 | 0.0 |
| Bible reading (*Abington Township v. Schempp*, 1963) | 0.79 | 5.56 |
| Posting the 10 Commandments (*Stone v. Graham*, 1980) | 3.94 | 5.56 |
| Private prayer (*Wallace v. Jaffree*, 1985) | 18.90 | 0.0 |
| Graduation prayer (*Lee v. Weisman*, 1992) | 55.12 | 27.78 |
| Prayer at sporting events (*Santa Fe v. Doe*, 2000) | 52.76 | 5.56 |

*Source*: Kevin T. McGuire. University of North Carolina at Chapel Hill.

lead their classes in prayer, devotional readings from the Holy Bible, or other religious activities. Nor may school officials attempt to persuade or compel students to participate in prayer or other religious activities. Such conduct constitutes state action and thus violates the establishment clause.

Devotional attitudes are faith-based, which makes them very difficult to disengage because they are attributed to God, a higher authority. As a result, noncompliance has continued unabated decades after *Engel* was decided. A survey conducted by political scientist Kevin McGuire in 2004 about non-compliance with religious decisions of the Supreme Court in public high schools indicates, for example, that "forty years after the fact, organized prayer is still reported in almost one quarter of [Southern] schools."[48] Table 7.1 indicates that the incidence of noncompliance with school prayer and other decisions concerning devotional activities remain generally higher in the South compared to the non-South, partly because of the high density of evangelical Christians in the South relative to other parts of the nation.

## CONCLUSION

In this chapter, we have sought to examine the nature and substance of implementation and impact of Supreme Court decisions. Implementation, compliance, and impact are all a matter of degree. When discussing these concepts, it is unreasonable to expect absolutes. Complete impact, complete compliance with Court decisions, and complete implementation are a myth even for the most admired Supreme Court decisions. But insofar as courts do have reasonable impact on their target audiences, how do we understand the nature of that impact and how might it be derived? We examined three theoretically plausible approaches for understanding impact: the *litigant-focused*, *legal-change*, and *social-change* approaches. We analyzed each approach with detailed examples of what the approach means and how it operates. Each approach contributes invaluably to our understanding of impact.

The approaches discussed in this chapter do not exist in a vacuum. A focus on a single approach is insufficient for realizing the full impact of Court decisions. Because impact is achieved only through a dynamic process that depends upon multiple actors and multiple institutional resources at different levels of government, it is beneficial to combine all three approaches in empirical inquiries in order to harvest the fruit of their cumulative strengths.

Finally, we examined the factors that contribute to faithful implementation and impact of Court decisions. The key factors noted are the clarity of the opinion, the incentives and disincentives associated with compliance, the strength of preferences of important community members such as elites and interest groups that often motivate the case's ascendance to the Court, and the organizational norms and cultures of leaders and lower-level staff of organizations that hold a stake in the Court's decisions. Perhaps the most important of these is the clarity of opinion. When the standards enunciated are clear, the ability of implementing authorities to shirk in their responsibilities is constrained. Because Court decisions are not self-enforcing, it is remarkably important for these various factors to converge in order for faithful implementation and impact of Court decisions to be realized.

# Appendix: List of Cases

*Gollust v. Mendel,* 501 U.S. 115 (1991)

*Green v. Biddle,* 21 U.S. 1 (1823)

*Griswold v. Connecticut,* 381 U.S. 479 (1965)

*Hazel-Atlas Glass Company v. Hartford Empire Corporation,* 322 U.S. 238 (1944)

*Hazelwood School District v. United States,* 433 U.S.299 (1977)

*Humeston v. Merck,* Docket No. ATL-L-2272–03

*INS v. Chadha,* 462 U.S. 919 (1983)

*Johnson v. Santa Clara County Department of Transportation,* 480 U.S. 616 (1987)

*Jones v. Clinton,* 990 F. Supp. 657 (E.D. Ark. 1998)

*Kelo v. City of New London,* 545 U.S. 469 (2005)

*Korematsu v. United States,* 323 U.S 214 (1944)

*Lemon v. Kurtzman,* 403 U.S. 602 (1971)

*Lewis v. United States,* 523 U.S. 155 (1998)

*Lochner v. New York,* 198 U.S. 45(1905)

*Mapp v. Ohio,* 367 U.S. 643 (1961)

*Marbury v. Madison,* 5 U.S. (Cranch 1) 137 (1803)

*Marsh v. Alabama,* 326 U.S.501 (1946)

*Martin v. Hunter's Lessee,* 14 U.S. 304 (1816)

*Maryland v. Wirtz,* 329 U.S.183 (1968)

*McConnell v. Federal Election Commission,* 540 U.S. 93 (2003)

*McCulloch v. Maryland,* 17 U.S. 316 (1819)

*Miller v. Texas,* 153 U.S. 535 (1894)

*Miller v. United States,* 307 U.S. 174 (1939)

*Miranda v. Arizona,* 384 U.S.436 (1966)

*Mississippi University for Women v. Hogan,* 458 U.S. 718 (1982)

*Mistretta v. United States,* 388 U.S. 361 (1989)

*Morrison v. Olson,* 487 U.S. 654, 677 (1988)

*National League of Cities v. Usery,* 426 U.S. 833 (1976)

*New Jersey v. New York,* 523 U.S. 767 (1998)

*New York Central Rail Co. v. Johnson,* 279 U.S. 310 (1929)

*Payne v. Tennessee,* 501 U.S. 808 (1991)

*Pennzoil v. Texaco,* 481 U.S. 1 (1987)

*Planned Parenthood of South Eastern Pennsylvania v. Casey,* 505 U.S. 833 (1992)

*Presser v. Illinois,* 116 U.S. 252 (1886)

*Printz v. United States,* 521 U.S. 898 (1997)

*Pryor v. United States,* 404 U.S. 1242 (1971)

*Quanta Computer, Inc. v. L.G. Electronics, Inc.* 553 U.S. _____(2008)

*Rasul v. Bush,* 542 U.S. 466 (2004)

*Regents of the University of California v. Bakke,* 438 U.S. 265 (1978)

*Roe v. Wade,* 410 U.S. 113 (1973)

*Schechter Poultry Corporation v. United States*

*Schenck v. United States,* 249 U.S. 47 (1919)

*Secretary of the Navy v. Avrech,* 418 U.S. 676 (1974)

*Shelly v. Kramer,* 334 U.S. 1 (1948)

*Sheppard v. Maxwell,* 384 U.S. 333 (1966)

*Sherbert v. Verner,* 374 U.S. 398 (1963)

*Spence v. Staras,* 507 F.2d 554 (1974)

*Swann v. Charlotte-Mechlenburg Board of Education,* 402 U.S. 1 (1971)

*Texas v. Johnson,* 491 U.S. 397(1989)

*TVA v. Hill,* 437 U.S. 153 (1978)

*United Mine Workers v. Red Jacket Consolidated Coal and Coke Company,* 275 U.S. 536 (1927)

*United States v. Burr* 159 U.S. 78 (1895)

*United States v. Carolene Products Company,* 304 U.S. 144 (1938)

*United States v. Cruikshank,* 92 U.S. 542 (1875)

*United States v. Ferreira,* 13 How. 40 (1852)

*United States v. Leon,* 468 U.S. 897 (1984)

*United States v. Nixon,* 418 U.S. 683 (1974)

*United States v. O'Brien,* 391 U.S. 367 (1968)

*Van Horne's Lessee v. Dorrance,* 2 U.S. (Dallas) 304 (1795)

*Weeks v. United States,* 232 U.S. 383 (1914)

*West Coast Hotel Company v. Parrish,* 300 U.S. 379 (1937)

*White v. Rochford* 592 F.2d 381 (1979)

*Wisconsin v. Yoder,* 406 U.S. 205 (1972)

*Wolf v. Colorado,* 338 U.S. 252 (1949)

*Worcester v. Georgia,* 31 U.S. 515 (1832)

*Youngberg v. Romeo,* 457 U.S. 307 (1982)

*Youngstown Steel and Tube Company v. Sawyer,* 343 U.S. 579 (1952)

# NOTES

## PREFACE

1. Alpheus T. Mason. 1962. "Myth and Reality in Supreme Court Decisions." *Virginia Law Review*, 68:1387–1406, at p. 1387.
2. Surveys indicate that Americans know little about the Supreme Court. For instance, a *Washington Post* opinion poll conducted in 1989 indicated that 71 percent of Americans could not name a single Supreme Court justice. Only 23 percent correctly named the first woman on the Court, Justice Sandra Day O'Connor, and only 9 percent could name William H. Rehnquist, chief justice at the time. Interestingly, a significantly higher proportion of Americans (54 percent) correctly named Judge Joseph Wapner, then host of the television show *The People's Court*. (See *Washington Post National Weekly Edition*, June 26–July 2, 1989, p. 37.)
3. Cullop, G. Floyd. 1969. *The Constitution of the United States: An Introduction*. New York: Signet Group, p. 5). Cullop once taught the Constitution to high school students in grades 8 through 12.
4. Footnote 4 established the Court as the protector of insular minorities, *United States v. Caroline Products Co.*, 304 U.S. 144 (1938). On the rights revolution, see Charles R. Epp. 1998. *The Rights Revolution: Lawyers, Activists, and Supreme Courts in Comparative Perspective*. Chicago: University of Chicago Press.

## CHAPTER 1: NATURE AND POWER OF THE U.S. SUPREME COURT IN AMERICAN POLITICS

1. Their original plan for the convention was simply to revise the Articles of Confederation, the nation's first governing charter. Delegates soon abandoned the Articles as unworkable since the charter authorized only a single legislature, no president, and no judiciary. The delegates began a fresh start on building a new Constitution in May and signed it in September. The last state required (Virginia) ratified the Constitution in June 1788 but only after amendments were added.
2. The first meeting was actually scheduled for February 1. However, only three justices showed up on that date. Chief Justice John Jay experienced transportation problems and so the opening session was postponed to February 2, 1790.
3. Sandra Day O'Connor. 2003. *The Majesty of the Law: Reflections of a Supreme Court Justice*. New York, Random House, p. 71
4. G.E. White. 1988. *The American Judicial Tradition*, expanded edition. New York: Oxford University Press, p. 9; also see Robert McCloskey. 1994. *The*

*American Supreme Court,* 2nd edition. Chicago: University of Chicago Press, p. 19

5.  Junius Davis. 1899. "Alfred Moore and James Iredell." An address to the North Carolina Society of the Sons of the Revolution. Raleigh NC: Edwards and Broughton Press, p. 24

6.  Warren Burger. 1992. *The Supreme Court of the United States: Its Beginnings and Its Justices 1790–1991.* Published by the Commission on the Bicentennial of the U.S. Constitution, p. 14

7.  David C. Frederick. 2005. "Supreme Court Advocacy in the Early Nineteenth Century." *Journal of Supreme Court History,* 30(1):1–16, at p. 4

8.  David N. Atkinson. 1999. *Leaving the Bench: Supreme Court Justices at the End.* Lawrence: University of Kansas Press, p. 13.

9.  For example, William H. Rehnquist was nominated twice, first by President Richard Nixon in 1971 as associate justice and then by Ronald Reagan in 1986 as chief justice.

10. These statistics were generated by author from Lee Epstein, Jeffrey A. Segal, Harold J. Spaeth, and Thomas G. Walker. 1994. *The Supreme Court Compendium: Data, Decisions and Developments.* Washington DC: CQ Press, pp. 265–273.

11. Id., p. 17

12. Indeed, the act permitted Supreme Court justices to sit as circuit judges but did not require it. Justices were happy to forego the practice of circuit riding entirely. Id., p. 18

13. R. Kent Newman. 1997. "Thomas Jefferson and the Rise of the Supreme Court." *Journal of Supreme Court History,* 31(2):126–140

14. This encouragement mixed with Jefferson's antagonism toward the Judiciary led him in 1804 to force the impeachment and later Senate conviction and removal of New Hampshire District Court Judge John Pickering for "picturesquely irrational behavior" manifested in senility, alcoholism, and utter failure to undertake his judicial duties, Id., p. 19; McCloskey. 1994, 28

15. See Burger. 1992, p. 19

16. McCloskey. 1994, p. 29.

17. O'Connor. 2003, p. 80.

18. Id., p. 80

19. The Sedition Act of 1798 was allowed to expire in 1801 without significant Court challenges to its validity and application (see Lee Epstein and Thomas G. Walker. 2001. *Constitutional Law for a Changing America: Rights, Liberties, and Justice,* 4th edition, Washington DC: CQ Press, p. 209).

20. The House has taken impeachment action against two other Supreme Court justices: Justice William O. Douglas in June 18, 1953, for temporarily staying the execution of Julius and Ethel Rosenberg, and Justice Abe Fortas in May 11, 1969, for "various ethical violations." Neither came to a House vote (see Epstein et al. 1994, p. 326).

21. This was a stunning role reversal, a real "macabre twist," to have an accused murderer actually preside over the trial of a judge for the crime of mere misconduct. See O'Connor. 2003, p. 82.

22. Cited in Bernard Schwartz. 1993. *A History of the Supreme Court.* New York: Oxford University Press, p. 58.

23. O'Connor. 2003, p. 83

24. McCloskey. 1994. p. 29

25. Burger. 1992. p. 20.

26. William H. Rehnquist. 1992. *Grand Inquest: The Historic Impeachments of Justice Samuel Chase and President Andrew Jackson.* New York: William and Morrow, p. 130

27. For early confirmation of this principle, see *United States v. Ferreira,* 13 How. 40 (1852). The Court also reaffirmed the principle in *Chicago & Southern Air Lines, Inc. v. Waterman S. S. Corp.,* 333 U.S. 103, p. 113 (1948): "This Court early and wisely determined that it would not give advisory opinions even when asked by the Chief Executive." More generally, the Court noted: "we have broadly stated that 'executive or administrative duties of a nonjudicial nature may not be imposed on judges holding office under Art. III of the Constitution.'" *Morrison v. Olson,* 487 U.S. 654, 677 (1988) (quoting *Buckley v. Valeo,* 424 U.S. 1, 123 [1976]). Finally in *Mistretta v. United States,* 388 U.S. 361 (1989), p. 385 they suggested that these restrictions on judicial activities "help ensure the independence of the Judicial Branch and to prevent the Judiciary from encroaching into areas reserved for the other branches."

28. For more on the Court's refusal to issue advisory opinion, see *U.S. v. Burr* (1807) as related in Archibald Cox. 1987. *The Court and the Constitution.* Boston: Houghton Mifflin, p. 6

29. McCloskey. 1994.

30. The unflattering term "inferior" is a sure sign that even a great wordsmith like James Madison can lose his way with the English language. The term refers to lower courts that serve as subsidiary to the Supreme Court.

31. Cited in Robert A. Carp and Ronald Stidham. 1998. *Judicial Process in American,* 4th edition. Washington DC: CQ Press, p. 24.

32. Felix Frankfurter and James M. Landis. 1927. *The Business of the Supreme Court: A Study in the Federal Judicial System.* New York: Macmillan, p. 4

33. For more on circuit courts, see Donald R. Songer, Reginald S. Sheehan, and Susan B. Haire. 2003. *Continuity and Change on the United States Courts of Appeals.* Ann Arbor: University of Michigan Press; Isaac Unah. 2001. "The Incidence and Structure of Conflict on the U.S. Court of Appeals for the Federal Circuit." *Law and Policy,* 23:69–93

34. McCloskey. 2004, p. 5.

35. The Electoral College is the body of electors responsible for choosing the president and vice president. In each presidential election, voters in each state must choose between slates of electors publicly pledge to one team of candidates or another. When the College meets the electors from each state (equal to the state's congressional delegation) then cast their votes for the team. The team with the highest Electoral College votes wins. In case of a tie, the House of Representatives chooses the president and vice president. The system was set up in the Constitution's Article 2, Section 1 and then altered by the Twelfth Amendment. Only Presidents Thomas Jefferson (1800) and John Quincy Adams (1824) have been elected by the House of Representatives. Given the Electoral College set-up, it is possible for a winner of the popular vote in a presidential contest to lose the election. Thus in 1888, Benjamin Harrison was elected even though Grover Cleveland received a greater share of the popular vote. In 2000, George W. Bush was elected after a Supreme Court decision in his favor (*Bush v. Gore,* 531 U.S. 98 [2000]) even though Al Gore won the popular vote.

36. Epstein and Walker. 2001, pp. 50–51.

37. George L. Haskins and Herbert Johnson. 1981. *Foundations of Power: John Marshall, 1801–1815.* New York: Macmillan, p. 184

38. See Robert Lowry Clinton. 1994. "Game Theory, Legal History, and the Origins of Judicial Review: A Revisionist Analysis of *Marbury v. Madison*." *American Journal of Political Science*, 38:285–302.

39. Burger. 1992, p. 18.

40. See McCloskey. 2004. Chapter 9

41. There are conflicting accounts about the number of days oral arguments were held in *McCulloch v. Maryland,* 17 U.S. 316 (1819). David C. Frederick noted that arguments were held for six days from February 22 to February 27 (1819). See David C. Frederick. 2005. "Supreme Court Advocacy in the Nineteenth Century." *Journal of Supreme Court History,* 30:1–16, at p. 10. Others including former solicitor general Archibald Cox claim arguments were held for nine days. See Cox. 1987, p. 75.

42. McCloskey. 1994, p. 43.

43. See Lawrence Baum. 1998. *The Supreme Court*, 6th edition. Washington DC: CQ Press, p. 200.

44. *United States v. Eichman,* 496 U.S. 310 (1990).

45. See, for example, Nathan Glazer. 1975. "Toward an Imperial Judiciary." *Public Interest,* 40:104–123; Donald Horowitz. 1977. *The Courts and Social Policy*. Washington DC: Brookings Institution; Raoul Berger. 1977. *Government by the Judiciary*. Boston MA: Harvard University Press. For arguments showing that courts are constrained and, therefore, cannot bring about fundamental social change, see Gerald Rosenberg. 1991. *The Hollow Hope: Can Courts Bring about Social Change?* Chicago: University of Chicago Press.

46. Quoted by Justice Robert H. Jackson in his concurring opinion in *Youngstown Steel and Tube Company v. Sawyer* [The Steel Seizure Case] 343 U.S. 579 (1952).

47. See Cox. 1987. p. 6

48. Andrew J. Dunbar. 1997. *The Truman Scandals and the Politics of Morality.* St Louis: University of Missouri Press

49. *Youngstown Sheet and Tube Co. v. Sawyer,* 343 U.S. 579 (1952); Maeva Marcus. 1977. *Truman and the Steel Seizure Case: The Limits of Presidential Power.* New York: Columbia University Press.

50. *United States v. Nixon,* 418 U.S. 683 (1974)

51. See Cox. 1987, p. 24

52. See *Clinton v. Jones,* 520 U.S. 681 (1997)

53. Id., p. 705

54. 990 F. Supp. 657 (E.D. Ark. 1998)

55. In the Lewinski affair, Clinton was compelled by a subpoena presented by Independent Counsel Kenneth Starr to testify before a federal grand jury. It would have been politically unwise to fight the subpoena all the way to the Supreme Court and lose there. Rather than fight, Clinton agreed to answer questions from members of the special prosecutor's office. The session was videotaped and presented to the grand jury on August 17, 1998.

56. The material on President Clinton's legal troubles was drawn largely from Craig R. Ducat. 2004. *Constitutional Interpretation*, 8th edition. Belmont CA: Thompson and West, pp. 241–242.

57. *Rasul v. Bush,* 542 U.S. 466 (2004)

58. The opinion was written by Chief Justice Charles Evans Hughes in *Aetna Life Insurance Co. v. Haworth,* 300 U.S. 227, 240–242 (1937).

59. Rosenberg. 1991.

60. *ExParte McCardle*, 7 *Wall*, (74 U.S. 506 (1869); for more, see Thomas G. Walker and Lee Epstein. 1995. "The Role of the Supreme Court in American Society: Playing the Reconstruction Game." In *Contemplating Courts*, ed. Lee Epstein. Washington DC: CQ Press, pp. 315–346.

## CHAPTER 3: APPOINTMENT OF JUSTICES TO THE U.S. SUPREME COURT

1. Thurgood Marshall Papers, Manuscript Division of the Library of Congress, Box 30, Folder #7.
2. Senator George Mitchell, speaking during the visit of British dignitaries to the Senate in 1992 stated that "The American Constitution does not assign different weights to the President's nominating power and the Senate's decision as to whether it shall 'advise and consent' to nominations. Instead, it establishes a process whereby the principal positions in our government can only be filled when the President and the Senate act jointly. Thus, the Senate has been a vital partner in the process of evaluating candidates for service in high government positions." See "Visit to the Senate by Members of the British House of Commons," remarks in Senate, *Congressional Record*, 138, February 4, 1992, p. 1346
3. Senator Robert Griffin. 1968. "Supreme Court of the United States," Senate remarks, *Congressional Record*, 114, part 22, October 1, p. 28929
4. Senator Mike Mansfield. 1968. "Supreme Court of the United States," Senate remarks, *Congressional Record*, 114, part 22, October 1, p. 28931
5. The Judiciary Act of 1789 placed the actual responsibility for judicial selection with the secretary of state. This responsibility remained there until 1853 when President Franklin Pierce decided to move it to the Department of Justice (See Goldman. 1997, 6).
6. Out of the 35 rejected nominees, 11 were not considered by the Senate because their nominations either died in committee without a vote or withdrawn. See Henry B. Hogue. 2005. "Supreme Court Nominations Not Confirmed, 1789–2004." *Congressional Research Service Report for Congress*, Order Code RL31171, p. 2. Data were updated by author to reflect withdrawal of Harriet Miers nomination in 2005.
7. Mark Silverstein. 1994. *Judicious Choices: The New Politics of Supreme Court Confirmations*. New York: W.W. Norton
8. *CBS Monthly Poll #1, July 2005 (Inter-University Consortium for Political and Social Research, 04396)*.
9. It was Warren's political skills and tenacity that led to the unanimous vote in *Brown v. Board of Education*, which eventually ended de jure racial segregation in public education.
10. Goldman. 1990, p. x.
11. See the insightful work of David A. Yalof. 1999. *Pursuit of Justices: Presidential Politics and the Selection of Supreme Court Nominees*. Chicago: University of Chicago Press
12. For further details about selection styles see Henry Abraham. 1999. *Justices, Presidents, and Senators: A History of the U.S. Supreme Court Appointments from Washington to Clinton*. New York: Rowman and Littlefield, Chapter 3.
13. Robert G. McCloskey. 1994. *The American Supreme Court*, 2nd edition. Chicago: University of Chicago Press, p. 60.

14. They were Chief Justice Charles Evans Hughes, Associate Justices Pierce Butler, Willis Van DeVanter, James McReynolds, Owen Roberts, and George Sutherland. All six except McReynolds were appointed by a Republican president.

15. Data are derived from Lee Epstein, Jeffrey A. Segal, Harold J. Spaeth, and Thomas G. Walker. 2003, *The Supreme Court Compendium:Data, Decisions, & Developments*, 3rd edition. Washington DC: CQ Press, Table 8.28, p. 736

16. David M. O'Brien. 1993. *Storm Center: The Supreme Court in American Politics*, 3rd edition. New York: W.W. Norton, p. 96

17. In the instance of Republican Senator Harold Burton of Ohio, the Senate confirmed him on the same day the nomination reached the Senate even though the appointing president was a Democrat and the Senate was Republican-controlled. Among the fastest confirmations was that of Senator George Sutherland of Utah. He was confirmed in open session of the Senate within 10 minutes after his name was received. See George H. Haynes. 1938. *The Senate of the United States: Its History and Practice*, vol. 2. Boston: Houghton Mifflin, p. 740.

18. The last *sitting* senator to be nominated and confirmed was Senator Harold H. Burton (R-OH) in 1945 by President Harry S. Truman. The last *former* senator to be nominated and confirmed was Sherman Minton (D-IN). He was appointed to the Court in 1949 also by Harry Truman. See, Denis Steven Rutkus. 2005. "Supreme Court Appointment Process: Roles of the President, Judiciary Committee, and the Senate." *Congressional Research Service Report for Congress*, Order Code RL31989, p. 18.

19. Abraham. 1999. p. 34.

20. In the 1970s, President Richard Nixon faced much pressure to appoint the first woman to the Court. He placed Mildred Lilly, a California state judge, on his short list of hopefuls. Nixon eventually bypassed Lilly and gave the nod to William H. Rehnquist. See Lee Epstein and Jeffrey Segal. 2005. *Advice and Consent: The Politics of Judicial Appointments*. New York: Oxford University Press, p. 55

21. Sandra Day O'Connor. 2004. *The Majesty of the Law: Reflections of a Supreme Court Justice*. New York: Random House

22. Thomas Marshall. 2008. *Public Opinion and the Rehnquist Court*. Albany: SUNY Press, Chapter 6.

23. Yalof. 1999, p. 39.

24. Thurgood Marshall Papers, Manuscript Division of the Library of Congress, Washington DC, Box 30, Folder #7.

25. American Bar Association, The ABA Standing Committee on Federal Judiciary, "Investigations of Supreme Court Nominees." http://www.abanet.org/scfedjud/SCpage.html last visited August 10, 2006

26. For a more detailed discussion on how the ABA rates judicial candidates, navigate to the primary source at www.abanet.org/scfedjud/home.html

27. Quoted from John Dean. 2001. *The Rehnquist Choice*. New York: Free Press, p. 21. Dean in turn quoted J. Myron Jacobstein and Roy M. Mersky. 1993. *The Rejected: Sketches of the 26 Men Nominated for the Supreme Court But Not Confirmed by the Senate*. Milipitas CA: Toucan Valley, p. 152

28. Richard Nixon is reputed to be perhaps the U.S. president who nominated the first homosexual to the Court in G. Harold Carswell. Nixon is well known for seeking notoriety through historical firsts. But this is the kind of notoriety the conservative Nixon might have actively avoided had his Justice Department and

the FBI conducted a more thorough investigation into the background of Judge G. Harold Carswell who was a homosexual. See Dean. 2001, pp. 19–20.

29. See the seminal work on the ABA by Joel B. Grossman, *Lawyers and Judges: The ABA and the Politics of Judicial Selection.* New York: Wiley, 1965.

30. At the time, 10 members of the committee rated Bork "well qualified," one voted "not opposed" and four rated him "not qualified." The mixed vote added to Bork's troubles as the Senate went on to reject his nomination by a vote of 42 to 58. See Epstein and Segal. 2006, p. 74 and p. 163.

31. With his two rejected nominations, Nixon became the first president since Grover Cleveland to have two Supreme Court nominees rejected in a row. President Cleveland was unable to have his two candidates William B. Hornblower and Wheeler H. Peckham confirmed by the Senate in 1893–1894 (Jacobstein and Mersky. 1993. 101–110).

32. Dean. 2001. p. 22.

33. Id., p. 22

34. Benjamin Wittes. 2006. *Confirmation Wars: Preserving Independent Courts in Angry Times.* New York: Rowman and Littlefield, p. 13.

35. Byron J. Moraski and Charles R. Shipan. 1999. "The Political of Supreme Court Nominations: A Theory of Institutional Constraints and Choices." *American Journal of Political Science,* 43:1069–1095; Sarah Binder and Forrest Maltzman. 2002. "Senatorial Delay in Confirming Federal Judges, 1947–1998." *American Journal of Political Science,* 46:190–199.

36. Charles R. Shipan and Megan L. Shannon. 2003. "Delaying Justice(s): A Duration Analysis of Supreme Court Confirmations." *American Journal of Political Science,* 47:654–668

37. Ibid., p. 655

38. George H. Haynes. 1937. *Senate of the United States, Its History and Precedent.* Boston: Houghton Mifflin, p. 737; Betsy Palmer. 2005. "Evolution of the Senate's Role in the Nomination and Confirmation Process: A Brief History." *Congressional Research Services Report for Congress,* Order Code RL31948, p. 6.

39. For more information on the Blue slip, see "The History of the Blue Slip in the Senate Committee on the Judiciary, 1917–Present." *Congressional Research Service Report for Congress,* Order code: RL32013

40. Hogue. 2005, pp. 1–6.

41. These statistics are cited in Epstein and Segal. 2006, p. 59; See also Robin M. Wolpert and James G. Gimpel. 1997. "Information, Recall and Accountability: The Electorate's Response to the Clarence Thomas Nomination." *Legislative Studies Quarterly,* 22:515–525.

42. Charles M. Cameron, Albert D. Cover, and Jeffrey A. Segal. 1990. "Senate Voting on Supreme Court Nominees: A Neoinstitutional Model." *American Political Science Review,* 84:525–534, at p. 530

43. Jeffrey A. Segal and Albert Cover. 1989. "Ideological Values and the Votes of Supreme Court Justices." *American Political Science Review,* 83:557–565.

44. The conversion is easy to perform. One simply adds 1 to each nominee's score, and divides the result by 2 to obtain a percentage. Robert Bork's ideology score was −0.81, Adding 1 and dividing by 2 converts his score to 0.095, which is pretty close to zero (i.e., very conservative). Since ADA scores range from 0 to 100, we simply divide by 100 to derive the percent ideology score for the senator. In 1987, when Bork was considered for the Court, Senator John Kerry received an ADA score of 58, converted to 0.58, which is moderately liberal.

45. For updated Segal and Cover scores, see Epstein et al. 2003. The ideology scores for John Roberts, Harriet Miers, and Samuel Alito are available at Jeffrey Segal's website: http://www.sunysb.edu/polsci/jsegal/

46. Robert Bork. 1971. "Neutral Principles and Some First Amendment Problems." *Indiana Law Review,* 47:1–35.

47. L. Marvin Overby, Beth M. Henschen, Michael H. Walsh, and Julie Strauss. 1992. "Courting Constituents? An Analysis of the Senate Confirmation Vote on Justice Clarence Thomas." *American Political Science Review,* 86:997–1006

48. James L. Gibson and Gregory A. Caldiera. 2009. "Confirmation Politics and the Legitimacy of the U.S. Supreme Court: Institutional Loyalty, Positivity Bias, and the Alito Nomination." *American Journal of Political Science,* 53:139–155.

49. Id.

50. Epstein et al. 2003.

51. See P.S. Ruckman, Jr. 1993. "The Supreme Court, Critical Nominations, and the Senate Confirmation Process." *Journal of Politics,* 55:793–805; Bruce A. Ackerman. 1988. "Transformative Appointments." *Harvard Law Review,* 101:1164–1184.

52. Id.

53. Jeffrey M. Berry. 1977. *Lobbying for the People.* Princeton: Princeton University Press, p. 5.

54. Alan Westin. 1951. "The Supreme Court, Populist Movement, and the Campaign of 1896." *Journal of Politics,* 15:3–41

55. Joseph P. Harris. 1951. *The Advice and Consent of the Senate.* Washington DC: Brookings Institution, p. 253–255

56. Gregory A. Caldiera and John R. Wright. 1995. "Lobbying for Justice: The Rise of Organized Conflict in the Politics of Federal Judgeships." In *Contemplating Courts,* ed. Lee Epstein. Washington DC: CQ Press, p. 48.

57. Thomas K. McGraw 1984. *Prophets of Regulation.* Cambridge MA: Harvard University Press, p. 82

58. *United Mine Workers v. Red Jacket Consolidated Coal and Coke Company* 118 Fd. 2nd 29 (1927)

59. Donald J. Lisio. 1985. *Hoover, Blacks, and Lilly-Whites: A Study of Southern Strategies.* Chapel Hill: University of North Carolina Press

60. http://www.brennancenter.org/programs/scnominations/robertsnomination.html, visited August 19, 2006.

61. See Gregg Caldiera and John Wright. 1995. "Lobbying for Justice: The Rise of Organized Conflict in the Politics of Federal Judgeships." In *Contemplating Court,* ed. Lee Epstein. Washington DC: CQ Press

62. See Caldiera, Gregory, and Wright. 1995, p. 58

63. John A. Maltese. 1994. *The Selling of Supreme Court Nominees.* Baltimore: Johns Hopkins University Press, p. 137–138

64. For further discussion of the importance of demographic and geographic factors see Henry J. Abraham. 2008. *Justices, Presidents and Senators: A History of U.S. Supreme Court Appointments from Washington to George W. Bush,* rev. edition. Lanham MD: Rowman and Littlefield.

## CHAPTER 4: AGENDA SETTING IN THE SUPREME COURT

1. See Robert McCloskey. 1994. The American Supreme Court, 2nd edition. Chicago: University of Chicago Press, p. 5.

2. Alexis de Tocqueville. 2004. *Democracy in America*. New York: Library of America, distributed by Penguin Putnam

3. John R. Schmidhauser. 1959. "The Justices of the Supreme Court: A Collective Portrait." *Midwest Journal of Political Science*, 3:1–57, at p. 4

4. 545 U.S. 469 (2005)

5. Craig R. Ducat. 2004. *Constitutional Interpretation*, 8th edition, Belmont CA: Wadsworth, p. 38

6. Donald R. Songer. 1987. "Concern for Policy Outputs as a Cue for Supreme Court Decisions on Certiorari." *Journal of Politics*, 41:1185–1194

7. Kevin McGuire and Barbara Palmer. 1996. "Issues, Agendas, and Decision Making on the Supreme Court." *American Political Science Review*, 90:853–865

8. Rebecca Stott. 2003. *Darwin and the Barnacle*. New York: W.W. Norton; Jan Sapp. 1994. *Evolution by Association: A History of Symbiosis*. New York: Oxford University Press

9. See Isaac Unah. 2008. "Federalism." In *World International Encyclopedia of the Social Sciences*, 2nd edition, ed. William Darity. New York: Macmillan

10. 295 U.S. 495 (1935)

11. 298 U.S. 238 (1936)

12. 300 U.S. 379 (1937)

13. Gerald Rosenberg. 1991. *The Hollow Hope: Can Courts Bring about Social Change*. Chicago: University of Chicago Press

14. See *Planned Parenthood of South Eastern Pennsylvania v. Casey*, 505 U.S. 833 (1992).

15. William H. Rehnquist. 2004. "2003 Year End Report on the Judiciary." U.S. Supreme Court. http://www.supremecourtus.gov/publicinfo/year-end/2003 year-endreport.html

16. Richard A. Posner. 1985. *The Federal Courts: Crisis and Reform*. Cambridge MA: Harvard University Press. The legislation was named after its chief advocate Chairman of the Senate Judiciary Committee William Evarts of New York. He guided the bill through his committee and reported it out of the committee for consideration by the full Senate.

17. Rehnquist. 2004.

18. Id.

19. Lynn Weisberg. 1988. "New Law Eliminates Supreme Court's Mandatory Jurisdiction." *Judicature*, 72: 138.

20. The data used in figures 4.1 through 4.3 are from Epstein, Segal, Spaeth, and Walker 2003. *The Supreme Court Compendium: Data, Decisions, and Developments*, 3rd edition. Washington DC: CQ Press. Caseload data were derived from Table 2.2 of the Compendium (p. 58). Data on petitions granted review were derived from Table 2.5 and Table 2.6 (pp. 68–71). Data on Supreme Court employees were derived from Table 1.16 (p. 49).

21. Marie Doris Provine. 1980. *Case Selection in the Supreme Court*. Chicago: University of Chicago Press

22. Cited by Justice Brennan in his dissent in *United States v. Leon*, 468 U.S. 897 (1984)

23. *Miranda v. Arizona*, 384 U.S. 436 (1966) as excerpted in Craig Ducat. 2004. *Constitutional Interpretation*, 8th edition. Belmont CA: Thomson/West, p. 519.

24. Id.

25. Id.
26. See Anthony Lewis. 1964. *Gideon's Trumpet.* New York: Vintage Books
27. Lawrence M. Friedman. 1969. "Legal Culture and Social Development." *Law and Society Review*, 4:29–44. See also Austin Sarat and Joel B. Grossman. 1975. "Courts and Conflict Resolution: Problems in the Mobilization of Adjudication." *American Political Science Review*, 69:1200–1217
28. Christine Harrington and Daniel S. Ward. 1990. "Patterns of Appellate Litigation, 1945–1990." In *Contemplating Courts*, ed. Lee Epstein. Washington DC: CQ Press
29. Data are from the U.S. Census Bureau and as of December 2006 can be found at http://www.census.gov/popest/archives/1990s/popclockest.txt
30. See *ACLU v. Reno*, 521 U.S. 844 (1997)
31. Epstein et al. 2007, pp. 74–75
32. Whereas most states call the highest courts Supreme Court, New York State calls its highest court the court of appeals.
33. *New Jersey v. New York*, 523 U.S. 767 (1998)
34. For further discussion of the routes of appeals to the Supreme Court, see Lee Epstein and Thomas Walker. 2004. *Constitutional Law for a Changing America: Rights, Liberties and Justice.* Washington DC: CQ Press, p. 12.
35. See rules 33 and 39 of the Rules of the Supreme Court of the United States. These rules can be found 515 U.S. (1197) or at the Court's official Web site at http://www.supremecourtus.gov/ctrules/rulesofthecourt.pdf.
36. Gregg A. Caldiera and John R. Wright. 1990. "The Discuss List: Agenda Building in the Supreme Court." *Law and Society Review*, 24:807–836, at p. 809
37. These papers are available at the Manuscript Division of the Library of Congress, Washington DC.
38. Charles Evans Hughes to Harlan F. Stone, September 30, 1931, Papers of Harlan F. Stone, Manuscript Division, Library of Congress, as cited by Caldiera and Wright. 1990, p. 810.
39. Papers of Justice Harry Blackmun, Manuscript Division, Library of Congress
40. The language of dead listing a case predates the discuss list. Indeed, the justices started using the language of dead listing in 1925. In 1950, there was a procedural change in which the justice started using the language of the discuss list (Provine [1980], p. 28).
41. Adam Liptak. 2008. "A Second Justice Opts Out of a Longtime Custom: The 'Cert. Pool.'" *New York Times*, September 28, p. A21
42. Id.
43. Justice Thurgood Marshall Papers, Manuscript Division, Library of Congress, Box 30, Folder #7.
44. Although this is not stated in the official rules of the Court, Justice William O. Douglas has made it clear in *Pryor v. United States*, 404 U.S. 1242, at p. 1243 that when the Court is not operating at full strength, three justices can vote to grant certiorari.
45. See Roy B. Flemming and Glen S. Krutz. 2002. "Selecting Appeals for Judicial Review in Canada: A Replication and Multivariate Test of American Hypotheses." *Journal of Politics*, 64:232–248, at p. 233. In Canada, would-be petitioners must first obtain permission from the Supreme Court of Canada to appeal a lower court decision. The decision to deny or grant leave to appeal is equivalent to the decision to deny or grant a writ of certiorari in the U.S. Supreme Court.

46. See, for example, Joseph Tanenhaus, Marvin Schick, Matthew Muraskin, and Daniel Rosen. 1963. "The Supreme Court's Certiorari Jurisdiction: Cue Theory." In *Judicial Decision Making*, ed. Glendon Schubert. Glencoe: Free Press, pp. 113–115; Donald R. Songer. 1979. "Concern for Policy Outputs as a Cue for Supreme Court Decisions on Certiorari." *Journal of Politics*, 41:1185–1194; H.W. Perry. 1991. *Deciding to Decide*. Cambridge MA: Harvard University Press

47. Perry. 1991, p. 1186.

48. Gerhard Casper and Richard A. Posner. 1967. *The Workload of the Supreme Court*. Chicago: American Bar Foundation, pp. 65–66.

49. Tanenhaus et al. 1963, pp. 113–115; Perry. 1991.

50. Robert L. Stern, Eugene Gressman, Stephen M. Shapiro, and Kenneth S. Geller. 1995. *Supreme Court Rules: The 1995 Revisions*. Washington DC: Bureau of National Affairs, p. 27.

51. Tanenhaus et al. 1963, pp. 111–132.

52. Lincoln Caplan. 1987. *The Tenth Justice: The Solicitor General and the Rule of Law*. New York: Knopf; Rebekah Mae Salokar. 1994. *The Solicitor General: The Politics of Law*. Philadelphia PA: Temple University Press.

53. Empirical evidence for policy concern as a variable in certiorari voting was initially documented and successfully empirically tested by Lawrence Baum. 1977. "Policy Goals in Judicial Gate-keeping: A Proximity Model of Discretionary Jurisdiction." *American Journal of Political Science*, 21:13–35.

54. See, for example, Robert L. Boucher, Jr. and Jeffrey A. Segal. 1995. "Supreme Court Justices as Strategic Decision Makers: Aggressive Grants and Defensive Denials on the Vinson Court." *Journal of Politics*, 57:824–837; Gregory A. Caldiera, John R. Wright, and Christopher J.W. Zorn. 1999. "Sophisticated Voting and Gate-keeping in the Supreme Court." *Journal of Law, Economics, and Organization*, 15:549–572; Perry. 1991.

55. Baum. 1977.

56. Caldiera and Wright. 1988. "Organized Interests and Agenda Setting in the U.S. Supreme Court." *American Political Science Review*, 82:1109–1128

57. Isaac Unah and Ange-Marie Hancock. 2006. "Supreme Court Decision Making, Case Salience, and the Attitudinal Model." *Law and Policy*, 28:295–320; Forrest Maltzman, James F. Spriggs, and Paul Wahlbeck. *Crafting Law in the Supreme Court*. New York: Cambridge University Press

58. James F. Spriggs and Paul Wahlbeck. 1997. "Amicus Curiae and the Role of Information at the Supreme Court." *Political Research Quarterly*, 50:365–386

## CHAPTER 5: ORAL ARGUMENTS IN THE U.S. SUPREME COURT

1. Carl Brent Swisher. 1960. "The Supreme Court and the 'Moment of Truth.'" *American Political Science Review*, 54:879–886, p. 885.

2. See, for example, Robert C. Carp, Ronald Stidham, and Kenneth L. Manning. 2004. *Judicial Process in America*, 6th edition. Washington DC: CQ Press, p. 32

3. Timothy R. Johnson. 2004. *Oral Arguments and Decision Making on the United States Supreme Court*. Albany: SUNY Press

4. John G. Roberts, Jr. 2005. "Oral Argument and the Re-emergence of a Supreme Court Bar." *Journal of Supreme Court History*, 30(1):68–81

5. David J. Danelski. 1989. "The Influence of the Chief Justice in the Decisional Process of the Supreme Court." In *American Court Systems,* ed. Sheldon Goldman and Austin Sarat. New York: Longman Press. See also Johnson. 2004.

6. 5 U.S. (1 Cranch) xvi (1803) (Rule VII, issued August 8, 1792; see also Maeva Marcus, ed. 1992. *The Documentary History of the Supreme Court of the United States, 1789–1800,* vol. 4, New York: Columbia University Press, at 181n and 595n.

7. David C. Frederick. 2005. "Supreme Court Advocacy in the Early Nineteenth Century." *Journal of Supreme Court History,* 30(1):1–16

8. Id., at p. 2. An example of such English books is *A Guide for Solicitors in All the Courts of Westminster,* published in 1702.

9. William H. Rehnquist. 1999. "From Webster to Word Processing: The Ascendance of the Appellate Brief." *Journal of Appellate Practice and Process,* 1:1

10. This number does not include briefs filed by amicus curiae participants. Rule 33 stipulates that amicus briefs have a limit of 30 pages for each participant. See http://www.supremecourtus.gov/ctrules/rulesofthecourt.pdf.

11. See Frederick. 2005.

12. Id., p. 3

13. Samuel Tyler. 1970 [c. 1872]. *Memoir of Roger Brooke Taney.* New York: Da Capo, at pp. 66–67

14. 14 U.S. (1 Wheat.) xviii (1816) Rule XXIII was issued in February 1812. For more information on this and other rules, see Stephen M. Shapiro. 1985. "Oral Argument in the Supreme Court: The Felt Necessities of the Time." *Supreme Court History Society Yearbook,* pp. 22–34

15. Frederick. 2005, p. 8

16. Id.

17. Letter of Louis D. Brandies to Alfred Brandies dated March 21, 1887. *Letters of Louis D. Brandies,* ed. Melvin I. Urofsky, and David W. Levy, 5 vols. Albany: SUNY Press, 1:6. Cited as footnote 5 in Melvin I. Urofsky. 2005. "Louis D. Brandies: Advocate Before and on the Bench." *Journal of Supreme Court History,* 30(1):31–46

18. For example, Luther Martin was attorney general of Maryland on and off for nearly 40 years; Walter Jones served as U.S attorney for the District of Columbia for nearly 20 years; Daniel Webster served several years as a congressman from New Hampshire and Massachusetts and then as a U.S. senator for 20 years. William Pinkney served in the Senate a year after he argued *McCulloch v. Maryland* (1819). See Frederick. 2005, p. 11

19. Robert H. Jackson. 1951. "Advocacy before the United States Supreme Court." *Cornell Law Quarterly,* 51:1–37, at p. 9.

20. Id., p. 7.

21. see Johnson. 2004, p. 2.

22. Elizabeth Brand Monroe. 2007. "The Influence of the Dartmouth College Case on the American Law of Educational Charities." *Journal of Supreme Court History,* 32:1–21, at p. 3

23. Id., p. 3.

24. Id., p. 2.

25. 42 U.S. (1 How.) at XXXV (Rule XL, issued 1833).

26. *Green v. Biddle,* 21 U.S. 1 (1823)

27. David Rohde and Harold J. Spaeth. 1976. *Supreme Court Decision Making*. San Francisco: W.H. Freeman Press, p. 153.
28. Jeffrey A. Segal and Harold J. Spaeth. 2002. *The Supreme Court and the Attitudinal Model Revisited*. New York: Cambridge University Press
29. Rehnquist. 1999, p. 2.
30. See Rehnquist. 1999.
31. 118 S.Ct. 1837 (1998)
32. 156 L. Ed. 2d (2003)
33. Segal and Spaeth. 2002, p. 280
34. Henry J. Abraham. 1998. *The Judicial Process*, 7th edition, New York: Oxford University Press, p. 209, citing seminar with Chief Justice Earl Warren, University of Virginia Legal Forum, April 25, 1973, p. 9.
35. Rehnquist. 1999.
36. Kenneth Turan. 1975. "Let Them Entertain You." *Washington Post*, "Potomac." February 2, 1975, quoting the *Philadelphia Inquirer*, April 9, 1963, "Oral argument," as Frankfurter once put it, "has a force beyond what the written word conveys."
37. For example, Johnson. 2004.
38. William Benoit. 1989. "Attorney Argumentation and Supreme Court Opinions." *Argumentation and Advocacy*, 26(Summer):22–38; Donald Cohen. 1978. "Judicial Predictability in United States Supreme Court Oral Advocacy: Analysis of the Oral Argument in *TVA v. Hill*." *University of Puget Sound Law Review*, 2(Fall):89–136; Linda Greenhouse. 2004. "Press Room Predictions." *Perspectives on Politics*, 2(December):781–784; Stephen L. Wasby, Anthony A. D'Amato, and Rosemary Metrailer. 1976. "The Functions of Oral Argument in the United States Supreme Court." *Quarterly Journal of Speech*, 62(December):410–422.
39. Roberts, Jr. 2005, p. 75. This article is the printed version of a lecture delivered by the Judge Roberts at the Supreme Court Historical Society annual meeting on June 7, 2004.
40. See James F. Spriggs, II and Paul Wahlbeck. 1997. "Amicus Curiae and the Role of Information at the Supreme Court." *Political Research Quarterly*, 50:365–386. These authors also reported that more than 73 percent of the information reported in amicus curiae briefs merely reiterate the information found in the party's briefs (p. 372).
41. Mary L. Clark. "Women as Supreme Court Advocates, 1879–1979." *Journal of Supreme Court History*, 30(1):47–67
42. Mark Sherman. 2007. "Black Lawyers Rare at Supreme Court." *USA Today*, October 28, 2007
43. Id.
44. Kevin T. McGuire. 1995. "Capital Investment in the U.S. Supreme Court: Winning with Washington Representation." In *Contemplating Courts*, ed. Lee Epstein. Washington DC: CQ Press, p. 77
45. Johnson. 2004; also see Timothy R. Johnson. 1991. "Information, Oral Argument, and Supreme Court Decision Making." *American Politics Research*, 29(July):331–351
46. Kevin T. McGuire. 1995. "Repeat Players in the Supreme Court: The Role of Experienced Lawyers in Litigation Success." *Journal of Politics*, 57:187–196
47. The use of Justice Blackmun's rating of attorneys' performance was first employed to assess the influence of oral argument by Timothy R. Johnson, Paul

J. Wahlbeck, and James F. Spriggs, II. 2006. "The Influence of Oral Arguments on the U.S. Supreme Court." *American Political Science Review,* 100(February):99–113, at p. 109.

48. Id., p. 110
49. David Austen-Smith. 1993. "Information and Influence: Lobbying for Agendas and Votes." *American Journal of Political Science,* 37(August):799–833.
50. 279 U.S. 310 (1929)
51. Chief Justice John Roberts made his comments on February 21, 2007. The speech was broadcast on C-Span television network on February 25, 2007. See also Robert Barnes. 2007. "Justice Counsels Humility." *Washington Post,* February 2, p. A15
52. For example, during oral argument in *Texas v. Johnson,* 491 U.S. 397 (1990), Justice Scalia injected himself into the argument to an extraordinary degree. He essentially took over from William Kunsler, the attorney for accused "hard core" flag burner Gregory Lee Johnson.
53. John G. Roberts, Jr. 2005. "Oral Advocacy and the Re-emergence of a Supreme Court Bar." *Journal of Supreme Court History,* 30(1):68–81, at p. 73.
54. Robert H. Jackson. 1951. "Advocacy before the United States Supreme Court." *Cornell Law Quarterly,* 37(Fall):1–16
55. Richard L. Abel. 1989. *American Lawyers.* New York: Oxford University Press, at p. 122
56. John P. Heinz and Edward O. Laumann. 1982. *Chicago Lawyers: The Social Structure of the Bar.* New York: Russell Sage Foundation; Kevin T. McGuire. 1990. *Lawyers in the Washington Community.* Charlottesville VA: University of Virginia Press
57. Roberts, Jr. 2005, p. 77.

## CHAPTER 6: DECISION MAKING ON THE MERITS

1. William H. Rehnquist. 1992. "Remarks on the Process of Judging." *Washington and Lee University Law Review,* 49:263–270, at p. 270
2. Robert G. McCloskey. 1994. *The American Supreme Court,* 2nd edition. Chicago: University of Chicago Press, p. 60.
3. For a detailed examination of this case, see Lynne Curry. 2007. *The DeShaney Case: Child Abuse, Family Rights, and the Dilemma of State Intervention.* Lawrence: University Press of Kansas.
4. Id.
5. *White v. Rochford,* 592 F.2d 381 (1979); *Benson v. Cady* 761 F.2d 335 (1985).
6. *Youngberg v. Romeo,* 457 U.S. 307 (1982)
7. *Spence v. Staras,* 507 F.2d 554 (1974)
8. *Benson v. Cady,* 761 F.2d 335 (1985).
9. James F. Spriggs and Paul Wahlbeck. 1997. "Amicus Curiae and the Role of Information at the Supreme Court." *Political Research Quarterly,* 50:365–386, at p. 374
10. Isaac Unah and Ange-Marie Hancock. 2006. "The Supreme Court, Case Salience, and the Attitudinal Model." *Law & Policy,* 28:295–320, at p. 309
11. Kevin T. McGuire. 1995. "Capital Investments in the United States Supreme Court: Winning with Washington Representation." In *Contemplating Courts,* ed. Lee Epstein. Washington DC: CQ Press
12. Lynne. 2007. p. 110.

13. Marc Galanter. 1974. "Why the Haves Come Out Ahead: Speculation on the Limits of Social Change." *Law and Society Review*, 9:95–160; Reginald S. Sheehan, William Mishler, and Donald R. Songer. 1992. "Ideology, Status, and Differential Success of Direct Parties before the Supreme Court." *American Political Science Review*, 86:464–471; Donald R. Songer, Reginald Sheehan, and Susan B. Haire. 2000. *Continuity and Change on the United States Courts of Appeals*. Ann Arbor: University of Michigan Press; Carol Seron. 1996. *The Business of Practicing Law*. Philadelphia: Temple University Press

14. Seron. 1996, p. 113

15. William O. Douglas. 1948. "The Dissent: A Safeguard of Democracy." *Judicature*, 32:104–107, at p. 106

16. Clare Cushman. 2007. "Rookie on the Bench: The Role of the Junior Justice." *Journal of Supreme Court History*, 32:282–296.

17. Bradley C. Canon and Charles A. Johnson. 1999. *Judicial Policies: Implementation and Impact*, 2nd edition. Washington DC: CQ Press, p. 19

18. During the 1970 term, 16 cases were decided by judgment, 1975 term 10 cases, 1979 term 12 cases, and 1988 term 10 cases. See Lee Epstein, Jeffrey A. Segal, Harold J. Spaeth, and Thomas G. Walker. 2007. *The Supreme Court Compendium: Data, Decisions & Developments*, 4th edition. Washington DC: CQ Press, p. 242

19. Randall T. Shepard. 2005. "Perspectives: Notable Dissents in State Constitutional Cases." *Albany Law Review*, 68:337–348; Douglas. 1948.

20. Thomas R. Marshall. 2008. *Public Opinion and the Rehnquist Court*. Albany: SUNY Press

21. Curry's 2007 account suggests that the justices did receive an outpouring of communication from citizens, some of it hate mail (pp. 132–133). My examination of Marshall's papers reveals several letters from citizens praising his decision in the case.

22. Id., p. 121

23. Mark J. Richards and Herbert M. Kritzer. 2002. "Jurisprudential Regimes in Supreme Court Decision Making." *American Political Science Review*, 96:305–320.

24. Segal, Jeffery A. and Harold J. Spaeth. 1992. *The Supreme Court and the Attitudinal Model*. New York: Cambridge University Press, p. 32.

25. Id., p. 53

26. Edward Levi. 1949. *An Introduction to Legal Reasoning*. Chicago: University of Chicago Press

27. Robert A. Carp and Ronald Stidham. 1998. *Judicial Process in America*, 4th edition, Washington DC: Congressional Quarterly Press, p.277

28. *California v. Federal Energy Regulatory Commission*, 109 L. Ed 2d 474 (1990), p. 486.

29. U.S. Supreme Court Judicial Database (Harold J. Spaeth). The figures were derived by specifying in the SPSS software: analu=0 and dec_type=1, 6 or 7 then alt_pres=1 and uncon=1 or 2.

30. 426 U.S. 833

31. 392 U.S. 183

32. 421 U.S. 542

33. Harold J. Spaeth and Stuart H. Teger. 1982. "Activism and Restraint: A Cloak for the Justices' Policy Preferences." In *Supreme Court Activism and Restraint*, ed. Stephen C. Halpern and Charles M. Lamb. Lexington MA: D.C. Heath.

34. Segal and Spaeth. 1992, p. 45

35. Linda Greenhouse. 1988. "Precedent for Lower Courts: Tyrant or Teacher." *New York Times*, January 29, p. 12

36. Jeffrey A. Segal and Harold J. Spaeth. 1996. "The Influence of Stare Decisis on the Votes of U.S. Supreme Court Justices." *American Journal of Political Science*, 40:971–1002

37. Joseph Story. 1833 [2008]. "Rules of Constitutional Interpretation." In *Documents of Constitutional and Legal History*, 3rd edition, ed. Melvin I. Urofsky and Paul Finkelman. New York: Oxford University Press.

38. *Gollust v. Mendel*, 501 U.S. 115 (1991), p. 118; "In deciding a question of statutory construction, we begin, of course, with the language of the statute" (*Demarest v. Manspeaker*, 498 U.S. 184 [1991]), p. 614.

39. Harold J. Spaeth. 1995. "The Attitudinal Model." In *Contemplating Courts*, ed. Lee Epstein. Washington DC: CQ Press, p. 298

40. The first case decided on the Second Amendment was *United States v. Cruikshank* (1876). This was followed 10 years later by *Presser v. Illinois* (1886). *Miller v. Texas* followed in (1894). The most important statement on the issue was made in *United States v. Miller* (1939) stating the purpose of the amendment as being to maintain effective state militias. In 1980, the Court decided *Lewis v. United States*. Finally in 1997, the Court decided *United States v. Printz*, striking down the Brady Handgun Violence Prevention Act of 1993. In 1997, *District of Columbia v. Heller* held that handgun ownership is an individual right.

41. Edwin Meese, III. 1989. "Toward a Jurisprudence of Original Intention." In *American Court Systems*, 2nd edition, ed. Sheldon Goldman and Austin Sarat. New York: Longman.

42. William J. Brennan, Jr. 1989. "The Constitution of the United States." In *American Court Systems*, 2nd edition, ed. Goldman and Sarat..

43. William Anderson. 1955. "The Intention of the Framers: A Note on Constitutional Interpretation." *American Political Science Review*, 49:340–352, at p. 345

44. Id., p. 344

45. Brennan, Jr. 1989, p. 590.

46. Kenneth A. Shepsle. 1992. "Congress Is a 'They,' Not an 'It': Legislative Intent as an Oxymoron." *International Review of Law and Economics*, 12:239–256; see also William Riker and Barry Weingast. 1988. "Constitutional Regulation of Legislative Choice: The Political Consequences of Judicial Deference to Legislatures." *Virginia Law Review*, 74:373–402

47. *Wisconsin v. Yoder*, 406 U.S. 205 (1972)

48. See Cynthia Cooper. 1995. *Mockery of Justice: The True Story of the Sheppard Murder Case*. Boston: Northeastern University Press; Also see Lee Epstein and Thomas G. Walker. 2004. *Constitutional Law for a Changing America: Rights, Liberties, and Justice*, 5th edition. Washington DC: CQ Press, pp. 603–604.

49. In spite of this victory, Sheppard's career as a doctor was destroyed because many people remained convinced that he murdered his wife. Sheppard became morbidly depressed, started drinking heavily, and died of liver disease in 1970 at the age of 46.

50. See *United States v. Leon*, 468 U.S. 897 (1984), Justice Brennan, joined by Justices Marshall and Stevens, dissenting.

51. This quote comes from C. Herman Pritchett. 1941. "Divisions of Opinion among Justices of the U.S. Supreme Court, 1939–1941." *American Political Science Review*, 35:890–898, at p. 890.

52. Most of the justices studied by for his book were appointed by President Roosevelt. See Pritchett. 1948. *The Roosevelt Court*. New York: Macmillan; C. Pritchett. 1941; Walter Murphy. 1964. *Elements of Judicial Strategy*. Chicago: University of Chicago Press; Glendon Schubert. 1962. "A Psychological Analysis of the Warren Court." *American Political Science Review*, 56:90–107.

53. David W. Rohde and Harold J. Spaeth. 1976. *Supreme Court Decision Making*. San Francisco: W.H. Freeman Press

54. Martin Shapiro. 1993. "Public Law and Judicial Politics." In *State of the Discipline II*, ed. Ada Finifter. Washington DC: American Political Science Association, p. 365

55. Id., p. 366

56. Pritchett. 1941. p. 891.

57. Id., p. 890.

58. Segal and Spaeth. 2002.

59. Tracy George and Lee Epstein. 1992. "On the Nature of Supreme Court Decision Making." *American Political Science Review*, 86:323–337; Unah and Hancock. 2006.

60. For greater details about the formulation of the contemporary attitudinal model, see Spaeth. 1995.

61. Hughes did not mean for his comment to convey cynicism over judging. See *The Autobiographical Notes of Charles Evans Hughes,* ed. David J. Danelski and Joseph S. Tulchin (Cambridge MA: Harvard University Press, 1973), 143.

62. David Klein and Robert J. Hume. 2003. "Fear of Reversal as a Determinant of Lower Court Compliance." *Law and Society Review*, 37:579–606; Wendy L. Hansen, Renee J. Johnson, and Isaac Unah. 1995. "Specialized Courts, Bureaucratic Agencies, and the Politics of U.S. Trade Policy." *American Journal of Political Science,* 39:529–557

63. This discussion of Newton's troubled relationship with some colleagues at England's elite scientific society comes from Michael Gullen. 1995. *Five Equations that Changed the World*. New York: Hyperion Press, pp. 40–43.

64. See Jeffrey A. Segal and Albert D. Cover. 1989. "Ideological Values and the Votes of Supreme Court Justices." *American Political Science Review*, 83:557–565; Jeffrey Segal, Lee Epstein, Harold J. Spaeth, and Charles Cameron. 1995. "Ideological Values and the Votes of U.S. Supreme Court Justices Revisited." *Journal of Politics*, 57:812–823

65. Walter F. Murphy. 1965. *Elements of Judicial Strategy*. Chicago: University of Chicago Press; Lee Epstein and Jack Knight, 2000. *The Choices Justices Make*, Washington DC: CQ Press; Forrest Maltzman, Paul J. Wahlbeck, and James Spriggs, II. 2000. *Crafting Law in the Supreme Court: The Collegial Game.* New York: Cambridge University Press.

66. Testimony of Justice Rehnquist during appropriations hearings for the Supreme Court. House Committee on Appropriations. Cited in Scott A. Camparato. 2003 *Amici Curiae and Strategic Behavior in State Supreme Courts*. Westport CT: Praeger, p. 28.

67. Greenhouse. 2005. *Becoming Justice Blackmun*. New York: Times Books, p. 129

68. Robert Clinton Lowry. 1994. "Game Theory, Legal History, and the Origins of Judicial Review: A Revisionist Analysis of *Marbury v. Madison*." *American*

*Journal of Political Science*, 38:285–302; Jack Knight and Lee Epstein. 1996. "On the Struggle for Judicial Supremacy." *Law and Society Review*, 30:87–120

69. James G. March and Johan P. Olsen. 1984. "The New Institutionalism: Organizational Factors in Political Life." *American Political Science Review*, 78:734–749, at p. 735; Thomas A. Koelble. "The New Institutionalism in Political Science and Sociology," *Comparative Politics* 1995.

70. Id. March and Olsen. 1984. p. 740

71. Douglas C. North. 1990. *Institutions, Institutional Change and Economic Performance*. Cambridge: Cambridge University Press

72. R. Kent Weaver and Bert A. Rockman. Eds. 1991. *Do Institutions Matter?: Government Capabilities in the United States and Abroad*. Washington DC. Brookings Institution Press

73. See *Planned Parenthood of Southeastern Pennsylvania v. Casey*, 505 U.S. 833 (1992); *Kelo v. City of New London*, 545 U.S. 469 (2005)

74. Howard Gillman and Cornell Clayton. 1999. "Introduction." In *The Supreme Court in American Politics: New Institutionalists Interpretations*. Lawrence: University of Kansas Press, p. 2

75. Id

76. Barry Weingast. 1996. Political Institutions: Rational Choice Perspectives. *A New Handbook of Political Science*. H.D.K.R.E. Gooding. Oxford: Oxford University Press, pp. 167–190

77. Theda Skocpol. 1995. "Why I am an Historical Institutionalist." *Polity*, 28:103–106

78. Unah and Hancock. 2006, p. 299.

79. Lee Epstein and Jeffrey A. Segal 2000. "Measuring Issue Salience," *American Journal of Political Science*, 44:66–83

80. Saul Brenner. 1984. "Issue Specialization as a Variable in Opinion Assignment on the U.S. Supreme Court." *Journal of Politics*, 46:1217–1225

81. Greenhouse. 2005. *Becoming Justice Blackmun*. New York: Times Books, p. 95

82. Thomas G. Walker, Lee Epstein, William Dixon. 1988. "On the Mysterious Demise of Consensual Norms in the United States Supreme Court." *Journal of Politics*, 50:361–89; David Danelski. 1978. "The Influence of the Chief Justice in the Decisional Process of the Supreme Court." In *American Court Systems: Readings in Judicial Process and Behavior*, ed. Sheldon Goldman and Austin Sarat. San Francisco: W.H. Freeman, pp. 506–519; Stacia Haynie. 1992. "Leadership and Consensus on the United States Supreme Court." *Journal of Politics*, 54:1158–1169.

83. Charles Evan Hughes. 1928. *The Supreme Court of the United States*. New York: Columbia University Press, p. 68.

84. James Gibson. 1983. "From Simplicity to Complexity: The Development of Theory in the Study of Judicial Behavior." *Political Behavior*, 5:7–49, at p. 32

85. Robert G. McCloskey. 1994. *The American Supreme Court*, 2nd edition. Chicago: University of Chicago Press, p. 60.

## Chapter 7: The Impact of U.S. Supreme Court Decisions

1. Randall B. Ripley and Grace A. Franklin. 1982. *Bureaucracy and Policy Implementation*. Homewood IL: Dorsey Press, p. 6.

2. An extensive literature exists on public policy implementation; see Bradley C. Canon and Charles A. Johnson. 1999. *Judicial Policies: Implementation and Impact*, 2nd edition. Washington DC: CQ Press

3. Robert Barnes. 2007. "Stay of Execution Is Granted for Mississippi Murderer." *Washington Post*, October 31, p. A03.

4. Barbara Hinkson Craig and David M. O'Brien. 1993. *Abortion and American Politics*. Chatham NJ: Chatham House, p. 5. Quoting Lloyd Shearer. 1983. "Intelligence Report." *Parade*, January 12.

5. This verdict was later reversed by the Fourteenth Court of Appeals in Texas in an opinion filed May 28, 2008, in the case of *Merck v. Ernst*.

6. Michael G. Hertzel and Janet Kiholm Smith. 1993. "Industry Effects of Interfirm Lawsuits: Evidence from *Pennzoil v. Texaco*." *Journal of Law, Economics, and Organization*, 9:425–444; Kathleen Englemann and Bradford Cornell. 1988. "Measuring the Cost of Corporate Litigation: Five Case Studies." *Journal of Legal Studies*, 17:377–399; George L. Priest and Benjamin Klein. 1984. "The Selection of Cases for Litigation." *Journal of Legal Studies*, 13:1–56

7. *Wall Street Journal*, June 10, 2008, p. A4

8. Isaac Unah. 2003. "Explaining Corporate Litigation Activity in an Integrated Framework of Interest Mobilization." *Business and Politics*, 5:65–94, at p. 68

9. Lee Epstein and Joseph F. Kobylka. 1992. *The Supreme Court and Legal Change: Abortion and the Death Penalty*. Chapel Hill: University of North Carolina Press, p. 5.

10. Bradley C. Canon. 1973. "Reactions of State Supreme Courts to a U.S. Supreme Court Civil Liberties Decision." *Law and Society Review*, 8:109–134; see also Mark J. Richards and Herbert M. Kritzer. 2002. "Jurisprudential Regimes in Supreme Court Decision Making." *American Political Science Review*, 96:305–320

11. Richards and Kritzer. 2002.

12. Donald R. Songer. 1987. "The Impact of the Supreme Court on Trends in Economic Policy Making in the United States Courts of Appeals." *Journal of Politics*, 49:830–841

13. Frank Sorauf. 1976. *The Wall of Separation*. Princeton: Princeton University Press, p. 20

14. This case came at the heels of *Engel v. Vitale* (1962) involving a state-written prayer to be recited by teachers and students every day in the morning in school. The Court ruled that government has no business composing official prayers for any group of Americans to recite as a part of a religious program implemented by the government. The Court did not announce a new legal standard in *Engel*.

15. Joseph Kobylka. 1995. "The Mysterious Case of Establishment Clause Litigation: How Organized Litigants Foiled Legal Change." In *Contemplating Courts*, ed. Lee Epstein. Washington DC: CQ Press

16. Examples of liberal interest groups on Establishment clause litigation include the American Civil Liberties Union (ACLU) and the American Jewish Congress. Examples of conservative groups include the Christian Legal Society and the National Jewish Commission on Law and Public Affairs (COLPA).

17. See *Miranda v. Arizona*, 384 U.S. 436 (1966)

18. For a detailed review of the history of criminal law procedures and their evolution as they relate to police interrogations see Yale Kamisar, Wayne R. LaFave,

and Jerold H. Isreal. 1994. *Modern Criminal Procedure: Cases, comments and Questions.* 8th edition. St. Paul MN: West.

19. *Brown v. Mississippi,* 297 U.S. 278 (1936)

20. *Miranda v. Arizona,* 384 U.S. 436, at p. 504, Justice John Harlan dissenting.

21. Index crime offenses are murder and nonnegligent manslaughter, forcible rape, robbery, aggravated assault, burglary, theft, motor vehicle theft, and arson. Attempted murder is usually classified as an aggravated assault.

22. See *Omnibus Crime Control and Safe Street Act of 1968,* Pub. Law No. 90–351

23. Id. See also Paul G. Cassell and Richard Fowles. 1998. "Handcuffing the Cops? A Thirty-Year Perspective on Miranda's Harmful Effects on Law Enforcement." *Stanford Law Review,* 50:1055–1145

24. Richard Seeburger and R. Stanton Wettick, Jr. 1967. "*Miranda* in Pittsburgh—A Statistical Study." *University of Pittsburgh Law Review,* 29:1–26

25. National Center for Policy Analysis, study # 218(1998), p. 2

26. Clearance rates for 1950–1974 are derived from James Alan Fox. 1978. *Forecasting Crime Data.* Lexington KY: Lexington Books, Table A-1, p. 86. Post-1974 data are from the Federal Bureau of Investigation.

27. Richard A. Leo. 1996. "The Impact of Miranda Revisited." *Journal of Criminal Law and Criminology,* 86:621–692, at p. 652.

28. Jon Bond and Charles A. Johnson. 1982. "Implementing a Permissive Policy: Hospital Abortion Services after *Roe v. Wade.*" *American Journal of Political Science,* 26:1–24

29. Johnson and Canon. 1984, p. 49; Steven Wasby. 1970. *The Impact of the United States Supreme Court: Some Perspectives.* Homewood IL: Dorsey Press, p. 250; Samuel Krislov. 1972. "The Perimeters of Power: The Concept of Compliance as an Approach to the Study of Legal and Political Processes." In *Compliance and the Law: A Multidisciplinary Perspective,* ed. Samuel Krislov, Keith O. Boyum, Jerry N. Clark, Roger E. Shaefer, and Susan O. White. Beverly Hills CA: Sage, pp. 343–344; James F. Spriggs, II. 1997. "Explaining Federal Bureaucratic Compliance with Supreme Court Opinions." *Political Research Quarterly,* 50:567–593, at p. 582

30. Jack Peltason. 1961. *Fifty- Eight Lonely Men: Southern Federal Judges and School Desegregation.* New York: Harcourt, Brace Press.

31. Bond and Johnson. 1982.

32. Benjamin I. Page and Robert Y. Shapiro. 1983. "Effects of Public Opinion on Policy." *American Political Science Review,* 77:175–190

33. Gerald N. Rosenberg. 1991. *The Hollow Hope: Can Courts Bring about Social Change?* Chicago: University of Chicago Press, p. 184

34. Bond and Johnson. 1982.

35. Gerald N. Rosenberg. 1995. "The Real World of Constitutional Rights: The Supreme Court and the Implementation of the Abortion Decisions." In *Contemplating Courts,* ed. Lee Epstein. Washington DC: CQ Press.

36. Kathleen A. Kemp, Robert A. Carp, and David W. Brady. 1978. "The Supreme Court and Social Change: The Case of Abortion." *Western Political Quarterly,* 31:19–31

37. Rosenberg. 1991. p. 74

38. These data show the level of cross-racial exposure are from Gary Orfield. 2001. "Schools More Separate: Consequences of a Decade of Resegregation." http://www.civilrightsproject.ucla.edu/research/deseg/Schools_More_Separate.pdf

39. *Board of Education of Oklahoma City v. Dowell,* 498 U.S. 237 (1991).

40. Charles S. Bullock. 1980. "The Office of Civil Rights and Implementation of Desegregation Programs in the Public Schools." *Policy Studies Journal,* 8:597–616; Robert V. Strover and Don W. Brown. 1975. "Understanding Compliance and Noncompliance with Law: The Contributions of Utility Theory." *Social Science Quarterly,* 56:363–375

41. Rosenberg. 1991.

42. Rosemary O'Leary. 1993. *Environmental Change: Federal Courts and the EPA.* Philadelphia: Temple University Press; Shep R. Melnick. 1983. *Regulation and the Courts: The Case of the Clean Air Act.* Washington DC: CQ Press.

43. Charles A. Johnson. 1979. "Judicial Decisions and Organizational Change: Some Theoretical and Empirical Notes on State Court Decisions and State Administrative Agencies." *Law and Society Review,* 14:27–56; Michael Giles and Thomas G. Walker. 1975. "Judicial Policy Making and Southern School Desegregation." *Journal of Politics,* 37:917–936

44. Kenneth M. Dolbeare and Phillip E. Hammond. 1971. *The School Prayer Decision: From Court Policy to Local Practice.* Chicago: University of Chicago Press.

45. Spriggs, II. 1997, p. 582

46. Lawrence Baum. 1976. "Implementation of Judicial Decisions." *American Politics Quarterly,* 4:86–114; Johnson. 1979; Giles and Walker. 1975; James F. Spriggs, II. 1996. "The Supreme Court and Federal Administrative Agencies: A Resource-Based Theory and Analysis of Judicial Impact." *American Journal of Political Science,* 40:1122–1151; Spriggs, II. 1997.

47. Frank F. Sorauf. 1976. *The Wall of Separation.* Princeton: Princeton University Press, p. 297.

48. Kevin T. McGuire. 2008. "Schools, Religious Establishment, and the Supreme Court: An Examination of Policy Compliance." *American Politics Quarterly,* 37:50–74.

# INDEX

CPSIA information can be obtained
at www.ICGtesting.com
Printed in the USA
LVHW020747050921
696998LV00016B/2084